UNIMAGINABLE STORMS

UNIMAGINABLE STORMS

UNIMAGINABLE STORMS

A Search for
Meaning in Psychosis

Murray Jackson
Paul Williams

Foreword by
John Steiner

London
KARNAC BOOKS

First published in 1994 by
H. Karnac (Books) Ltd.
58 Gloucester Road
London SW7 4QY

British Library Cataloguing in Publication Data.

Jackson, M.
    Unimaginable Storms: A Search for Meaning
    in Psychosis
    I. Title   II. Williams, P.
    616.89
    ISBN: 1 85575 075 9

Printed in Great Britain by BPC Wheatons Ltd, Exeter

DECTORA: Does wandering in these desolate seas
   And listening to the cry of wind and wave
   Bring madness?

FORGAEL: Queen, I am not mad.

DECTORA: Yet say
   That unimaginable storms of wind and wave
   Would rise against me.

FORGAEL: No, I am not mad —
   If it be not that hearing messages
   From lasting watchers, that outlive the moon,
   At the most quiet midnight is to be stricken.

DECTORA: And did those watchers bid you take me
   captive?

FORGAEL: Both you and I are taken in the net.

W. B. Yeats, "The Shadowy Waters", 1906

ABOUT THE AUTHORS

MURRAY JACKSON is a psychiatrist and psychoanalyst, formerly a consultant at King's College Hospital and the Maudsley and Bethlem Royal Hospitals in London. Born in Australia, he came to England 45 years ago to train at the Maudsley. His interest in psychotherapy led him to undertake training in analytical psychology, where he learned of Jung's early work with psychotic patients. Further experience in child and adult psychiatry led to an interest in the significance of the work of Melanie Klein in the understanding of psychotic conditions. He trained as a psychoanalyst and pursued a part-time psycho-analytic practice in conjunction with work in the National Health Service. He was appointed to the Maudsley Hospital as consultant to a unit created to develop the application of psychoanalytic principles to the treatment of severely dis-turbed Health Service in-patients. His unit shared a general psychiatric ward with a general psychiatry unit directed by Robert Cawley, Professor of Psychological Medicine. This partnership lasted for 13 years and led to the development of a psychodynamically oriented ward milieu, and an approach to psychotic states that sought to integrate neurobiological and

viii ABOUT THE AUTHORS

psychoanalytic knowledge. The enterprise continued until the
closure of the ward at the time of Murray Jackson's retirement
from the Health Service in 1987. He lives in France and teaches
regularly in Scandinavia. He is a Member of the British Psycho-
analytical Society and a Fellow of the Royal College of Physi-
cians and of the Royal College of Psychiatrists.

PAUL WILLIAMS is a psychoanalyst. After obtaining a First in
Anthropology from University College London, he undertook
two years' fieldwork research, as part of a PhD degree, on the
Cawley–Jackson ward (Ward 6) at the Maudsley Hospital. His
study concerned the place of "talking treatments" on a general
psychiatric ward within a biologically oriented institution. At
the time, he also worked as a psychoanalytical psychotherapist. In the mid-1980s he was instrumental in setting up the
charity S.A.N.E. (Schizophrenia—a National Emergency). He
has an interest in borderline and psychotic thinking processes
and, from an anthropological perspective, their relationship
to methods of social organization. Paul Williams is in private
analytic practice in London and teaches at University College
Hospital, London.

CONTENTS

FOREWORD

John Steiner

The suffering of patients tormented by psychotic illness emerges so vividly from these pages that the reader finds himself immersed in the events as they are described and comes to share the experiences of both patients and staff. It soon becomes apparent that an important difference exists between patients and staff in relation to the search for meaning that appropriately constitutes the subtitle of the book. Meaning is so often dreaded by the psychotic patient whose priority is to gain relief from mental pain and persecution, and it is the author and his staff who can be seen to struggle to understand. It is the willingness to persevere in this search that makes this book so impressive and enables the reader to emerge with the capacity to render the unimaginable storms a little more imaginable.

Murray Jackson is very aware of his patients' intolerance of meaning and offers them an environment in which relief of suffering takes priority in his treatment approach. He recognizes that his patients need to feel understood but may not themselves wish to understand, and as a result he does not force meaning onto his patients but is ready to offer a broad spectrum of treatments in which drugs and social support play a significant role. Nevertheless, understanding the patient and his illness is the central preoccupation, and it is this that the reader will learn from and admire.

As we read the accounts of his patients, we can follow the struggle to understand and the battle to preserve meaning. The staff find themselves suffering with their patients, and as they develop relationships with them they have to face their own hopes and disappointments. This is especially painful when hard-won understanding cannot be maintained, especially after the patient leaves the unit. At other times the hatred of reality that is characteristic of many psychotic patients comes to be directed at the staff, who are seen, despite their evident humanity, as the purveyors of unwelcome meaning. It is a striking feature of the transcripts of the interviews that the staff are very conscious of their own involvement, and they are always afraid that they may unwittingly hurt their patients. Even the recording of the sessions is recognized to be potentially persecuting, and great care is taken to use tact and to ensure that the patients recognize that they may veto the recording if they wish.

Murray Jackson brings a wide experience to this particular task. He trained first as a Jungian analyst and subsequently as a Freudian Psychoanalyst, where he was particularly influenced by the work of Melanie Klein and her followers, among whom Herbert Rosenfeld and Henri Rey were perhaps the most important. With Segal and Bion, Rosenfeld was one of the first British analysts to treat psychotic patients, and it was Henri Rey who introduced some of the basic ideas developed by these pioneers to work with psychotic and borderline patients in the ordinary and often trying conditions of the National Health Service.

It is not uncommon for psychotic patients to frighten both relatives and professional staff, who are bewildered and upset by the intensity of the feelings they produce in others. Psychiatrists have responsibility for these patients thrust upon them and have struggled to find humane ways of coping and of relieving suffering. Unfortunately, they have often shared the patient's fear of making sense of psychotic thoughts and feelings, and they have, as a result, shied away from intimate contact with their patient's illness. The search for meaning has sometimes been replaced by attempts to classify the form and to categorize the emotional experiences of the patients. In itself this is an important and valuable contribution, but it is of little comfort to the patient who finds that his experiences remain incomprehensible and frightening and he can only rarely find anyone willing to listen to him and to take him seriously.

The case reports in this book both help us to understand why the search for meaning can be such a disturbing task and at the same time persuade us that it is not only possible to understand psychotic patients, but that such understanding can help them recover their sanity.

It is the author's training in clinical psychoanalysis which enables him both to recognize primitive mental mechanisms, particularly splitting and projection, and to understand the intense and yet fragile transferences that the psychotic patient develops in all his relationships. Freud himself has argued that the schizophrenic believes his world has been destroyed, and he showed in his comments on Schreber's autobiographical account (Freud, 1911c [1910]) of his illness that it was his attempts to reconstruct this destroyed world that gave rise to many of the active symptoms of psychosis.

Klein described these mechanisms in detail and saw many of the defensive struggles of the patient as attempts to deal with unbearable fragmentation produced by pathological splitting. Bion extended her work and added the important idea of containing an object into which the fragments are projected. Many of the patients Murray Jackson—ably assisted by Paul Williams—describes have entered hospital confused and dis- oriented, with extensive fragmentation of their thinking and with extreme anxiety, often leading to de-personalization and even catatonia. If the staff can cope with the anxiety generated in them and can convey their willingness to understand the patients, a sense of containment develops and the anxiety is gradually relieved. Containment is not, however, a passive phenomenon, and the patient has to feel understood in order to feel contained. He may then come to believe that someone can enter into his experience and share some of his suffering without themselves collapsing.

This function of the staff is amply demonstrated in virtually all of the clinical accounts in this book. What is perhaps more controversial is the question of the long-term change that can result from the kind of intervention described. Here the book, with an impressive honesty, presents a mixed picture, some patients clearly benefiting from their stay on the ward and from their therapy, while others remain largely unchanged or relapse when they are discharged. This raises important theoretical as well as practical questions. How does containment lead to a lasting change? Bion suggests that the experience of containment itself can lead to the internalizing of a containing object, and with it the gradual development of the capacity to contain. It has always seemed to me that Bion condenses his theoretical account of the stages that have to follow containment if permanent change is to result. In my view, containment is necessary but not sufficient, and while the immediate result is a lowering of anxiety, it is accompanied by a reliance on the containing object which is necessary for the relief. This is one of the reasons for the intensely dependent transference that develops between the psychotic patient and those who have to cope with the disturbing and often unbearable mental contents that the patient has projected into them. Separations are then poorly tolerated and often lead to a recurrence of the anxiety and to a relapse to a dependence on omnipotent psychotic mechanisms.

The problem that follows containment has then to do with the task of relinquishing the object and of forging a separate identity, and this requires that the patient is able to negotiate the task of re-possessing the painful and frightening mental contents. Our understanding of these processes is yet far from complete, but I believe that the regaining and integration of parts of the self is related to a capacity to face the pain of loss, and this requires the capacity to mourn. The work of Rosenfeld and others on narcissistic object relations, which can so effectively interfere with the mourning process, has advanced our knowledge of the obstacles in important ways. An investigation of these difficult questions is beyond the aims of this volume; the book does, however, amply demonstrate how a containing environment can lead to a clinically meaningful improvement.

The unit at the Maudsley Hospital where Murray Jackson inspired such devotion and perseverance in this difficult task was certainly unique in this country. It is a credit to the Maudsley that it was able to establish such a unit, and it is sad that, on the author's retirement, under the pressure of conflicting ideologies, the hospital decided to close it down.

Murray Jackson shares some of the optimism of the pioneers whose belief in meaning is inspired by those who have gone before and sustained by the support of the team who devotedly followed his teachings. Those who come after him will have to build on this understanding, and this book will give them a taste of the unimaginable storms they will have to contend with.

PREFACE

Forty years in the National Health Service as a psychiatrist and psychotherapist, combined with 25 years' private practice in psychoanalysis, provided me with a personal experience of psychotic patients which was in some respects unusual, at least in the United Kingdom. This experience was acquired principally at the Maudsley Hospital within the British National Health Service, which offered a work environment free from many of the stresses imposed on psychiatric staff in traditional mental hospitals. This freedom perhaps limited my experience of the wide variety of chronic psychotic patients encountered in traditional mental hospitals, but it offered the opportunity for long-term, intensive psychodynamic study and treatment of a significant number of first-episode and relapsing psychotic conditions. This type of work was not accorded any special privileges, and the hospital unit we describe was run on very limited resources, like most psychiatric wards in the public service. The private practice of psychoanalysis afforded an opportunity to study a small number of psychotic patients in depth, with the help of psychoanalyst teachers eminent in the field. Experiences in these two careers led to a conviction that psychoanalysis offers an indispensable source of knowledge for the understanding and treatment of psychotic disorders. We hope to demonstrate in this book that all psychotic patients can benefit from a psychodynamic approach, and some, but by no means all, from long-term individual psychotherapy.

In the early post-war period the theories of psychoanalysis were accorded importance in the teaching of psychiatry. Sir Aubrey Lewis, Professor of Psychiatry at the Institute of Psychiatry and the Maudsley Hospital, was of the opinion that psychoanalysis should have a place in all psychiatrists' training (Lewis, 1967). His successor, Sir Denis Hill, was even more active (Hill, 1970, 1978), setting up a unit in the Maudsley for the application of psychoanalytic ideas to the treatment of psychiatric in-patients on a general ward. When John Steiner, the first consultant appointed to this unit, eventually moved from the Maudsley to the Tavistock Clinic in 1975, I was appointed his successor, and for 13 years I directed the unit in cooperation with Robert Cawley.

The ideas that follow reflect the way that I personally have understood the knowledge bequeathed by Freud and Klein and others, in an effort to understand the clinical material that has confronted me. I have tended to treat explanation principally as a means to the end of making clinical decisions and therapeutic interventions. Concepts have been valued more for their clinical usefulness than for their pedigree, precision, or tidiness.

Assessment and treatment of the psychotic patient using psychoanalytic concepts in this way, and in collaboration with other forms of treatment, should ideally be undertaken within a hospital setting or special institution, where sufficient, skilled nursing care and observation are available—key requisites in the treatment of psychosis. The work reported in this book was done in a psychiatric ward of the Maudsley Hospital. Although psychodynamic work with psychotic patients was done in other centres in the United Kingdom, it was one of very few wards—if not the only one—dedicated to the application of a psychoanalytic perspective to the treatment of severely disturbed patients within a general psychiatric context. The unit closed in 1987 and has not been replaced.

* * *

The inspiration for this book comes from Paul Wiliams. In the early 1980s, Paul Williams was appointed to the ward and became closely involved in the life of the ward as a participant observer. For two years he attended almost all the events in which I interviewed patients—an experience that contributed to his undertaking training to become a psychoanalyst. He made close relationships with the patients, several of whom confided their in-patient experiences in detail in order to help him with his study. This concerned the elucidation of the value systems, structural conflicts, and processes of legitimization arising from the implementation of the unit's philosophy within the institutional setting. With the consent of patients, he made many video- and audiotape recordings of these encounters, which included ward-round interviews, and some years later he suggested that these recordings might be helpful to those who were trying to understand and provide assistance to psychotic patients. He also considered that they might exemplify a way of thinking about, and talking with, psychotic patients, which workers in the field, including those of limited experience, might find interesting. He outlined to me the form of a book, specified relevant passages from extensive transcripts, and launched a dialogue in which he criticized and sharpened my ideas and added many of his own. He also edited the manuscript. Having earlier conceived the acronym *S.A.N.E.* for a mental health charity he had helped to found (Schizophrenia— a National Emergency), he proposed "Unimaginable Storms" as an appropriate title for a work that deals with the cataclysmic events that so often underlie psychotic suffering. I am immensely indebted to him for his creative contributions and his prodigious energy. Without his efforts, this book would never have seen the light of day.

We should like to express our gratitude to the following for their assistance in the preparation of this book: to Drs Henri Rey, Nina Coltart, and Michael Feldman for their enthusiasm and help in reading and commenting upon the manuscript; to

Dr Leslie Sohn for his valuable clinical insights; to Dr Clare Adams, Dr John Alderdice, Dr Susan Davison, Dr Michael Farrell, and Mr David Morgan for important clinical information; to Cynthia Jackson and Lucinda Williams for their patience and constructive comments at every stage; to Scandinavian colleagues who gave access to centres where high-quality psychodynamic work has long been pursued with psychotic patients; and to our publisher, Mr Cesare Sacerdoti, who gave us sympathetic, unwavering support from the beginning. Finally, special thanks are due to Professor Robert Cawley, Mrs Beatrice Stevens, and the staff and patients of the former Ward 6 of the Maudsley Hospital.

Murray Jackson
London 1994

UNIMAGINABLE STORMS

UNIMAGINABLE STORMS

INTRODUCTION

Psychotic disorders bring immense suffering to victims and relatives and constitute the heaviest burden on mental health services throughout the Western world. Although a great deal is known about the nature of these devastating disorders, many conjectures are still to be confirmed or refuted, and much remains to be understood. The precise mode of action of biological methods of treatment has yet to be elucidated, and claims for psychoanalysis and its offspring, psychoanalytic psychotherapy, as an effective treatment for psychotic disorders have not been substantiated at the level of formal scientific proof.

Whilst the definition of psychosis is generally agreed upon, the same cannot be said for schizophrenia, and these two orders of classification bear examination. Psychosis encompasses a wide group of mental disorders that have in common a serious impairment of the individual's capacity to remain in contact with reality. They are often accompanied by confusion and disorders of thought and perception, which can find expression as delusional thinking and hallucinatory experiences. The causes of an individual psychotic episode or of long-term

1

vulnerability are to be sought in biological, social, or psychological factors. Each of the related disciplines has its own language and method of investigation. Bridges, conceptual and operational, between these disciplines may be difficult, sometimes impossible, to construct. Yet each is relevant, individually or in combination, to the acquisition of a deeper understanding of the nature and treatment of psychosis. The cooperation of different specialists is also required if the needs of the psychotic individual are to be met fully. It would seem reasonable, under these circumstances, to expect practitioners skilled in particular specialities or sub-specialities to acquire a level of general understanding of, or contact with, other disciplines to permit constructive debate to take place. In practice, however, cooperation appears to be the exception rather than the rule. This book will argue for a change in this position.

The term "schizophrenia" remains the subject of some continuing controversy. Schizophrenia is regarded as a disorder, or group of disorders, within the broader category of psychotic conditions. It is characterized by the prominence of negative and positive symptoms with associated tendencies towards passivity and withdrawal, and activity. Disorders of thought and perception also prevail. The illness seems to arise on a basis of a predisposition, manifested as a vulnerability of biological or psychological origin, or both. It tends towards a chronic course, although recent studies have shown that the long-term outcome is better than has been believed. The presence of structural brain abnormality in a large proportion of cases has been amply demonstrated by modern neurophysiological research using non-invasive methods that permit direct observation of brain function (see, for example, McNeil, Cantor-Grace, Nordstrom, & Rosenlund, 1993; Rubin, Karle, Moller-Madsen, et al., 1993). Abnormality of biochemistry has been demonstrated in many cases, and although the nature and origin of this is not fully clear, the dramatic suppression of positive symptoms such as hallucinations by anti-psychotic drugs during an acute attack is open to no other explanation. Recent advances in the theory and technique of family therapy have brought benefits to many schizophrenic patients and their families. In addition, research and clinical practice in the early detection of patients at risk of breakdown (see Falloon, Boyd, & McGill, 1984), of the education of patients and families in methods of stress management—a field opened up by the work on expressed emotion (E.E.) of Leff and colleagues (see Leff, Kuipers, Berkowitz, et al. 1982)—and of psychological treatments embodying cognitive and behavioural techniques represent major, permanent improvements in the care of schizophrenic patients. The anti-therapeutic aspects of traditional mental hospitals are now recognized (Pylkkanen, 1989), and the therapeutic possibilities of care in the community have been accepted. Improving after-care programmes and more professional case-management methods have brought the hope that the isolation and abandonment that faces most schizophrenic patients after discharge from hospital may one day end. Notwithstanding these impressive developments, deficiencies in community care provision and an overall neglect of the severely mentally ill, notably in the United Kingdom, continue to be reported in the national and medical press as a disgraceful state of affairs.

Research into the development of more effective and less potentially dangerous psychotropic and anti-psychotic drugs is being pursued zealously by major Western pharmaceutical firms. Despite the over-optimism that frequently accompanies the arrival of these new products, and the well-known toxic consequences of over-prescribing, psycho-pharmacology has made an inestimable contribution to patient welfare. In the process, public awareness and expectations of more rapid treatment have increased. Inadequate government funding for the provision of treatment and aftercare for psychotic patients, especially in Britain, has generated financial support for charitable organizations operating in the sphere of mental health. These private charities tend to pursue specific ideological and scientific goals, and one has recently initiated the foundation of a research centre to investigate neurobiological and psychosocial aspects of schizophrenia (SANETALK, Winter 1993). This kind of research and the growth of public concern for the plight of the schizophrenic are widely believed to justify an optimism that the next decade will bring a breakthrough in the understanding and treatment of psychotic disorders in general and of schizophrenia in particular, a hope that tends to be couched in terms of biological and psychosocial advances. It is often associated with a devaluation of psychoanalytic concepts and of the relevance of psychoanalysis and its derivative, psychoanalytic psychotherapy. Such views have found increasing expression in the popular media and in psychiatric publications. Since psychoanalysis and psychotherapy have long been applied to psychotic conditions in the United States, criticism there is more vocal than in the United Kingdom, where psychotherapy has rarely been regarded as of relevance to psychotic illness. Studies on the outcome of psychotherapy with schizophrenia patients have at times been used to conclude that psychoanalytic psychotherapy is of little or no value in the case of psychotic patients. Although often inaccurate and even misleading, these inferences can succeed in damaging opportunities for collaboration between potentially complementary disciplines (see, for example, Mueser and Barenbaum, 1990). The 1990s, hailed as the "Decade of the Brain" (Gabbard, 1992), have given rise to such headlines in the United States as "Pills for the Mind", "The Eclipse of Freud", and "Is Freud Dead?" (TIME International, 6 July 1992; 29 November 1993). In our present intellectual climate which tends too readily towards polarization and, worse, reductionism, the rise of polemicism seems more calculated to stimulate circulation figures than informed debate.

The view that schizophrenia is a neuro-developmental disorder of organic origin is based on research findings that are sound and impressive. However, the application of these findings as general truths about the nature and treatment requirements of schizophrenia can be quite misleading. Studies of brain pathology reveal statistical significance only, and the common structural disorders detected in the "schizophrenic brain" are by no means confined to schizophrenia. It is not yet known how frequently such structural disorders occur, or how often they have pathological consequences for personality development and psychological functioning. Genetic studies of schizophrenia have proved to be more complex than many had imagined. The essential fact that genes represent tendencies, and thus may be modifiable by favourable early environmental conditions, has been demonstrated by studies that show that where a genetically predisposed infant is born into a secure and mature family, the genetic effects may be neutralized (Tienari, 1992a, 1992b). Lewontin, speaking of the "doctrine" of DNA, criticizes the current tendency to overemphasize the role of genetics in human development. He points out that "genes affect how sensitive one is to environment, and environment affects how relevant one's genetic differences may be" (Lewontin, 1993, p. 30).

Psychoanalytic concepts help those working with psychotic patients in three ways:

1. They help give meaning to confusing or bizarre communications, and this can be a relief to all concerned (by furthering understanding of the patient's preoccupations and problems, they also help to reduce the risk of inappropriate behaviour by professional staff towards the patient).

2. They can act as a foundation for the formulation and implementation of comprehensive treatment plans. A psychoanalytically informed perspective enables a variety of treatment modalities to be employed in a truly complementary manner. Individual psychotherapy, behavioural, cognitive, family, or group-analytic therapy, and psychopharmacological procedures may be appropriately used according to the patient's needs and capacities at a given point in treatment.[1]

3. They permit the selection of psychotic patients who are likely to benefit from long-term individual psychoanalytic psychotherapy or from formal psychoanalysis.

Psychoanalysis and its derivative method, psychoanalytic psychotherapy, have proved themselves to be, when applied under the right conditions with the right patients, powerful and effective treatment methods. Whatever form of treatment, psychodynamic or otherwise, is proposed for severely disturbed patients, experience has taught that treatment should be planned on a long-term basis. There are no short-cuts to reliable and lasting change where psychotic patients are concerned. Many of the concepts used in this book derive from the work of Melanie Klein, who is widely acknowledged as having opened up a deeper understanding of the psychotic mind. This should not be taken as an undervaluation of other trends in psychoanalytic thought, which may not always be compatible with the views of Klein or later Kleinian theorists. Valuable work has been published in the United States and in Europe, such as that of Benedetti (1987) in Switzerland (psychoanalytic work informed by Jungian and existential concepts) and that of Freeman (1981, 1985, 1988, 1989) and Yorke and colleagues (Yorke, Wiseberg, & Freeman, 1989) in the United Kingdom (in the context of classical Freudian theory). Many international workers have also contributed since 1956 to the Triennial International Symposium for the Psychotherapy of Schizophrenia (see also Hansen, 1993). These and others have provided inspiration for many workers, including ourselves.

Psychoanalysis is, above all, a *psychodynamic* psychology. What distinguishes this theoretical system from others is its developmental perspective and its fundamental concepts. Instinctual mental life, conscious and unconscious, developmental phases, conflicts and defences, internal (psychic) reality, the tendency to repeat the past in the present, the phenomena of transference, countertransference, and the dynamic working-through of pathogenic concepts during the course of treatment—these concepts constitute a psychoanalytic or psychodynamic theory and *perspective*. This perspective permits a search for the intra-psychic and subjective *meaning* of mental events to take place. It also provides a sufficiently comprehensive theoretical framework to allow other treatment methods to make their individual contribution in undiluted form.

The psychodynamic work on which this book is based was carried out in a psychiatric ward of the Maudsley Hospital.[2] The patients we describe were selected from a larger group, in which recordings of evaluation interviews were made. These were accompanied by detailed written records and subsequent monitoring of progress. Such procedures reduced the possibility of retrospective distortion of facts. All the patients cited had been ill, chronically or recurrently, for at least five years prior to assessment. All received some individual psychotherapy within the context of general psychiatric care whilst on the unit. One of us [MJ] supervised most of the work and personally treated one case (Nicola). Although we have not presented first-attack or chronic, deteriorating "nuclear" schizophrenic patients, we believe that the mental mechanisms involved were essentially the same. Our experience on the ward included a number of such cases, but recordings were not made, and so they could not be included in this book.

The interval of several years (four to twelve) after the completion or termination of treatment has allowed a longer follow-up of patients than is usually available and has made the task of protecting their identities less difficult. Although follow-up information was in some cases not always detailed, we believe that it carries conviction in a psychodynamic sense and gives a sufficient impression of degrees of success or failure of treatment and of subsequent adaptation to life circumstances to remain valid. Where there has been success we try to show why, and we discuss where and why there has been failure. Psychiatric follow-up studies assess vocational and psycho-social adjustment, residual symptoms, medication levels, and re-admissions. Our criteria took these into account but added a psychodynamic evaluation. The therapeutic, anti-therapeutic, and non-therapeutic aspects of the patient's stay in hospital were also considered. In addition, less measurable influences, such as beneficient relationships, clarification of conflictual issues, and education in coping methods could also be seen to be important. In retrospect, we consider that some of the cases referred to the unit with a diagnosis of schizophrenia might be more appropriately considered as schizo-affective or reactive psychoses, but because of the often unsatisfactory nature of diagnostic classification and the instability of these conditions over time we have not pursued this issue.

We have given careful attention to the matter of confidentiality and exposure of intimate material. The patients' formal consent for recording and using the material for educational purposes was obtained at a time when they were in a sufficiently stable state of mind to be capable of giving informed consent. We have followed the normal practice of disguising key elements in the accounts to minimize the risk that any patient might be identified. It is, of course, just possible that a patient quoted may be able to identify himself or be identified by a member of the staff who cared for him. If this occurs, we hope that an understanding of the purpose of this book—to use past experiences for the benefit of future patients—will make such an intrusion acceptable. In contrast to presentations of a purely theoretical nature, these detailed accounts of clinical work allow the reader to form his own opinions about what is being put forward and to consider what the patient means, why the interviewer says what he does, and what seems to be going on. What follows is verbatim clinical material, presented in the knowledge that it may generate agreement or disagreement with specific ways of proceeding, with the conclusions reached, and with speculations that may be made. Constructive criticism is necessary and welcome, since wider discussion of the subject of the psychotherapy of psychosis is long overdue. What follows, therefore, is not a demonstration of psychoanalysis *in vivo*, but, rather, a way of using psychoanalytic ideas and knowledge clinically, within a hospital setting, in order to deepen the understanding of psychotic disturbance and hence offer patients more effective psychiatric help.

The "diagnostic–therapeutic" interview

Many years ago, when teaching medical students the principles of clinical psychiatry and psychosomatic disorders, I [MJ] began to conduct exploratory interviews with selected psychotic patients in the company of small groups of students. I gradually found that it was possible to gain a reasonable understanding of what was troubling the patient, and to illustrate psychoanalytic concepts of mental defence mechanisms in ways that students found interesting and convincing. I was surprised to find that it was not uncommon for severely confused patients to become markedly more coherent during the course of a 45-minute interview, and occasionally to make it clear that they even felt they were being understood. However, when the conversation[3] drew to a close, they tended to withdraw or return to their original, confused state. Such experiences spurred my interest in trying to understand, through these interviews, when and how these patients came to feel more, or less, sane. I recall being deeply impressed by an experience with a chronically schizophrenic man, whom I had been asked to see. He had been visited by several colleagues during previous weeks, but there had been little contact made with him. He sat tensely in his chair as I entered the room. Suddenly, he turned and stared out onto the courtyard outside. A moment later he turned back to face me, and with some vehemence he enquired whether I had seen the aircraft that had flashed past the window. I thought that this was a visual hallucinatory experience, the meaning of which concerned what was happening between us. I told him that I thought he was afraid that I was too busy, or insufficiently interested, to give him much of my time. He smiled and relaxed visibly. His complaint that I, like the colleagues who had preceded me, would flash into his field of vision and disappear without trace confirmed for me Rosenfeld's view that the statements of a psychotic patient should always first be considered as a communication, however disguised, to the clinician.[4] I do not know whether the interview was of any ultimate benefit to him, but by trying to grasp the symbolic nature of his communication and its personal reference it at least proved possible to talk with him. From that time onwards, as my "diagnostic–therapeutic interview" technique gradually began to take shape, so the theoretical extensions of Freud's work by Melanie Klein assumed critical importance in my attempts to make sense of an abundance of confusing material and diversity of conceptual models.

It also became clear that if a reasonable level of contact was reached during such interviews with patients, an ongoing supportive interest from some member of the psychiatric team was essential if the benefits of the psychotherapeutic perspective were to survive. Also, exploration of this type in cases of very severe disturbance required the availability of skilled nurses to cope with unforeseen reactions. At that time there were few psychotherapists working in general psychiatry, and psychotherapy was rarely considered a treatment option for psychosis. Selected patients had long been treated in the United States and Britain by a small number of pioneering psychoanalysts with impressive results, but promoting a psychotherapeutic attitude towards psychotic patients was difficult, and finding suitable psychotherapists prepared to undertake long-term individual psychotherapy with psychotic patients in the hospital service was almost impossible. The prevailing psychiatric view that exploratory psychotherapy was contraindicated for psychotic patients added to the difficulties. The view that exploratory psychotherapy is dangerous for the psychotic patient is justified if it is undertaken by an inadequately trained therapist, with a badly selected patient in an inappropriate setting. Under proper conditions it is not. Fortunately there were always some individuals amongst the psychiatric and nursing staff in the hospital who wanted to learn this approach, despite being overloaded with work and operating in poor conditions.

The milieu

The emotional forces involved or released in the course of psychotic illness can at times be of such magnitude, and find expression in such inappropriate and damaging action, that they are often beyond the capacity of the individual psychotherapist to withstand and utilize therapeutically. For this reason alone, individual psychotherapy of such seriously disturbed patients is best approached as the undertaking of a team[5] comprising complementary skills. The combined abilities of such a team can create a milieu in which the patient discovers a container for his disturbed self and from which, in the best cases, he may progress towards an autonomous existence. At the very least, he will retain a base in the event of crisis. The sooner the patient receives and responds to constructive assistance, the better will be his outlook. In a clear-cut, first-onset case of psychotic disturbance, it is usually not difficult to discern the major psychotic preoccupations, prodromal processes, and precipitating events. Tentative reconstruction of the developmental difficulties that have contributed to the patient's predisposition to a psychotic reaction can be undertaken. The longer the patient is denied this perspective, the more difficult it is likely to be for him to recover from the attack, integrate its place in his life history, and make use of its meaning. In cases that follow a remitting or chronic course, psychotic processes are likely to assume growing control over his mental life and make recovery increasingly difficult.

* * *

In the first clinical chapter, we report on a ward round that includes both the interview with the patient and the staff discussion. This has been done to convey something of the attitude of the unit team (which is elsewhere in the book taken for granted), its level of intellectual and emotional participation, and its ways of expressing concern—in this case, for a paranoid schizophrenic woman. Concern, as we try to demonstrate, did not imply idealization of the task or sentimentalizing the activities of listening and caring. Meaningful aggressiveness, for example, felt by the patient to be in the interests of survival, must be distinguished from destructiveness deriving from various forms of hatred, including of pathological envy, and genuinely reparative wishes must be recognized and respected for what they are. By including the ward-round discussion, we hope to provide a glimpse of the unit's attitude towards patients and their suffering. In each chapter, a longitudinal perspective of the patient's life is given in the form of a brief outline of his psychological development from childhood to the time of his admission to the unit. Progress on the unit is reported, and a follow-up report on life adjustments during the ensuing years is given. Much more could have been written about each patient at every stage, but to do this would have made the book unwieldy. Following the series of clinical presentations, we provide a description of the ward's setting and its therapeutic philosophy. Finally, we point to some of the lessons learned in the course of the work and to some implications for the present and future practice of psychiatry and psychoanalysis in respect of psychotic conditions. A glossary of certain fundamental psychoanalytic concepts is included at the end.

The individual interviews presented below are not intended to be a model to follow. Although, no doubt, some practitioners do employ a comparable procedure, the complexity of the psychodynamic processes involved in such interviews dictates caution, considerable experience, a well-functioning ward milieu, and, ultimately, on-going scrutiny and refinement of one's own technique in order to develop a reliable and personal approach to such difficult material. If these requirements are met, then this way of proceeding can offer a valuable treatment input and learning experience for all concerned. What we do not present in this book is an account of the work of the unit staff. Nevertheless, we hope it will be clear to the reader how much the work owes to the sustained commitment of the ward staff and the psychodynamic framework they maintained, in the face of many and varied difficulties.

The interviews have been edited to delete extended pauses and repetitions, without altering the sense or sequence of the content. Brief pauses are not specified, and where the word "Pause" appears, it refers to a delay of several minutes. Although unsatisfactory, to avoid confusion regarding gender we have adopted "him" and "his" in the text, unless otherwise indicated. This should be understood to refer equally to women as well as men. We should point out that many of the digressions, reflective silences, uncertainties, misunderstandings, and the myriad of nuances that emerge when two people meet to talk seriously, especially in a therapeutic setting, are omitted in the text for the sake of clarity and brevity. A certain cost to authenticity is paid. For example, the pace of the interviews can at times seem quicker than it was, the interviewer perhaps overly prompt or apposite in his reply, or appearing to be too talkative with quieter patients. This may, of course, sometimes be the expression of a failure of technique, but it is also the outcome of transcription and editing processes that compress, intensify, and over-unify language and communication. We suggest that the reader keep in mind that each interview lasted for at least an hour, sometimes longer, and that the passages quoted are abbreviated, central sections from extended and by no means straightforward encounters in which both interviewer and interviewee were often uncertain as to what was taking place. With regard to the justification of making video-recordings of psychotic or other patients, there exists a well-known view that it is an indefensible and intrusive procedure, which also distorts the authenticity of the proceedings. In the case of individual psychoanalysis and psychotherapy where absolute privacy is a pre-requisite, this view is justified. In the context of psychodynamic research with the informed consent and cooperation of the patient, things are different. Artefactual distortion is detectable and can be allowed for, and intrusiveness is largely contingent upon the sensitivity and humanity of those engaged in the enterprise. Our view is that, provided the patient's interests remain at the forefront of any procedure, wherever possible endorsed by the patient himself, then the risks of abuse are minimized.

CHAPTER ONE

Paranoid schizophrenia: "the radio loves me"

SALLY

Sally, a very disturbed 30-year-old woman, is the second child and eldest daughter of a large Catholic family of eight children. The family lived in a council house in a small town in the Midlands. The parents' marriage was unhappy, and the father left to live in another country when the patient was 12. Sally's relationship with her mother seems to have been highly ambivalent: however, she made close relationships with several siblings. She survived well until adolescence, at which point her schoolwork disintegrated and paranoid ideation began to colonize her mind. By 21 she was convinced that when she masturbated, the whole of the town was watching her; subsequently, she believed she was being filmed. She suffered extreme persecutory guilt feelings, which seemed to be linked to her past sexual activity. After careful investigation, it became apparent (beyond reasonable doubt) that she had had an incestuous relationship with her father from the age of 11, before his departure. It seemed likely that several of the children had been sexually interfered with in one

way or another. Sally felt that her mother had abandoned her
and had handed her over to her father, and she hated her
mother for it. These feelings may also have had their origin
earlier in her life, when she was displaced by six siblings at
close intervals. She felt her mother had forced her into the role
of being a mother to her younger siblings, which had prompted
her to turn to father for affection. She viewed him in many ways
as a mother. At the same time, it seems that Sally's father also
viewed Sally to some extent as a maternal figure, thus adding
to the confusion. Her longing for intimacy with her mother drew
her into relationships with women, not overtly sexual but sufficient to make her feel sometimes that she was homosexual. At
other times, she was afraid that she was masculine in her
orientation. This was expressed concretely in moments of psychotic dread that she was turning into a man—a fear that may
have partly been the expression of a wish to be in her father's
place in order to have possession of the mother for whom she
longed. It was interesting to observe that, when the theme of
her longing and despair in relation to her mother emerged
openly during treatment, she became quite sane and coherent
for the duration of the conversation about that theme.

Between the ages of 21 and 30, she was admitted to several
different mental hospitals, but her condition deteriorated, and
on arrival at the unit she was chronically psychotic, unkempt,
thought-disordered, and exhibiting somatic and olfactory hallucinations. She had been referred from a ward of the Maudsley
where the consultant was of the opinion that the unit's psychodynamic orientation might better support the elements of
healthy functioning he had found in her. When she arrived, she
was clutching a photograph of two church spires, which, she
said, reminded her of needles that had been put up her bottom
by doctors in the hospital. She complained of a sensation in her
abdomen as if she were being inflated. Whilst on the unit, she
broke crockery and used the pieces to cut her wrists. She said
that she wanted to die, and she cried a great deal, saying her
life was a complete waste. She was occasionally violent, hitting,
kicking, and scratching the nurses. She complained that there
was a smell of gas everywhere and accused the nurses of trying
to turn her into a paraffin addict; she insisted that Chlorpromazine was paraffin and that her food tasted of petrol. It

gradually became clear that her delusional states had developed as an attempt to survive the psychic consequences of incest, but they also served as a defensive retreat from the pain of severe depression resulting from a long-held sense of abandonment by her mother.

The following interview is taken from her second attendance at a ward round three weeks after her arrival. We have included a full recording of the proceedings before and after the interview with this, the first patient, in order to give a sense of the kind of staff debate generated by these extended, multi-disciplinary meetings. Over the next few months, Sally's functioning improved considerably, but when she experienced loss—as when any staff member to whom she had begun to make an attachment departed—she quickly slipped back. It became quite clear that she had very little capacity to hold on to significant relationships in the face of separation.

Pre-interview discussion

Present in the ward round are MJ and team members Dr A, Dr B, Nurse C, Nurse D (Sally's Primary Nurse), the Social Worker, and the Clinical Nurse Specialist. In addition, there is the Anthropologist [PW] and two overseas visitors, Dr E and Professor F. The meeting takes place in a room adjacent to which, behind a one-way mirror, is a small observation room. Chairs in the interview room are arranged in a circle, and key staff members remain during the interview, whilst others retire to the observation room. A video camera and recorder is available if the staff wish to record the interview, which, in this case, they eventually decide to do.

MJ: If she believes that everyone is watching her masturbate, she seems to be talking about guilt, maybe about the incest. Perhaps there is meaningful content there that we might be able to help her with. Have we got her primary nurse's report?

Nurse D [*reads from her report*]:   Yes. Over the past two weeks Sally has been a safety risk. Her destructive impulses have been mainly directed at herself. She broke crockery and used the pieces to make grazes to her wrists. Subsequently she hit me and another nurse, and these incidents were felt to contain a spiteful kind of childish defiance. They occurred when it was a helping kind of intervention we were involved in: in one case care plans and in the other when a nurse was trying to help her make a telephone call. When I asked Sally why she was so angry with me, she said it was because she hated me. She's also been a fire risk, smoking cigarettes in the dormitory, and we had to take her cigarettes and her matches away from her.

MJ: With this lady one would be thinking in terms of a psychotic transference. She says she hates you, and we know that she has some quite violent feelings towards her mother, but you had nothing to go on to think that there was anything that had happened to make her say to you, "I hate you"? It could just as well have been delusional as anything else?

Nurse D: Yes.

MJ: Yes, thank you.

Nurse D [resumes]:   Her self-care is poor, and she's resistant to the idea of having showers or baths. Soon after arriving on the unit she refused to go to the canteen, because, she said, the last time she went there, somebody broke a plate, and whenever somebody broke anything it reminded her of a male nurse from the hospital in her home town, and that upset her. Food was brought up to the ward for her at mealtimes, but she'd rarely eat it: she said that everything tasted of paraffin. She'd occasionally take a yoghurt back to the dormitory and eat it there.

MJ: She spoke of a memory of the male nurse from her home town? Why was that an upsetting memory?

Nurse D: It was someone she had formed an attachment to who left. I think she was talking about it in the group today—that she missed someone, a nurse from her home town.

MJ: Okay . . . a relationship that was lost.

Nurse D [continues]:   She started going to the canteen this week, but she's lost a lot of weight, about 5.5 kilos. During her first week on the unit her sleep was very disturbed. She was awake for most of the nights talking to the night nurses in a disturbed way.

MJ: She was on medication at that time?

Nurse D: No, she started medication on the second week.

MJ: I see. So she came in on a smallish dose of Pimozide, and then, at this stage that you're telling us, she was not on Chlorpromazine. Okay, carry on.

Nurse D: Prior to and over the weekend, she was expressing paranoid-sounding ideas. She accused the nurses of trying to make her into a paraffin addict and that the Chlorpromazine we wanted to give her was paraffin. She was complaining of smells in the kitchen—gas—and she was having peculiar sensations in the bottom of her stomach. She expressed feelings related to her mother and said if she didn't love her mother, then her mother would go away. She'd never see her mother again, her mother would go away, to get more money.

MJ: She had sensations in the bottom of her stomach? Let's think about pregnancy fantasies for a moment: I wonder if she was able to say what the bottom of her stomach was? The pit of the stomach? The pelvis? She didn't specify?

Nurse D: It was just her lower stomach, I think.

Nurse C: In the community groups, she talked about wanting to have a baby.

Dr A: She said she would never have a baby. She knew she would never have a baby.

MJ: I see. She wants a baby but she knows she'll never have one. Nurse D,[1] you were saying, when I interrupted you, something about her mother?

Nurse D: Yes: if she didn't love her mother, she would go away for more money.

MJ: For more money?

Nurse D: Yes. I don't know what that means. When she was disturbed and walking about the ward, she kept saying my name, and I asked her, "What do you want, Sally?" And she just kept saying: "I want my Mummy." She was kicking the table. At other times, she says she's destroying, killing her nurses. She's been quite hostile towards them, but she still approaches us to speak and appears to know us by name. Her relationships with other patients were initially hostile and rejecting, particularly in the small group.

Nurse C: In the first small group she was very distressed and saying she didn't want to be here, she wanted to go back to her previous ward. Nobody here liked her.

Nurse D: I think the patients are wary of her. She was quite aggressive and hostile. She spends her days on the unit cut-off, listening to her Walkman and lying on her bed for long periods of time. She's self-absorbed and preoccupied. She sleeps a lot of the time. Generally she's quite isolated. That's it.

MJ: Well, thank you very much.

Social Worker: Can I say something about the family? I see she's got four brothers and three sisters, but it doesn't say where they come.

Dr B: There's an elder brother of 31, then Sally, brother, 29, another brother, 27, then another brother, 25, sister, 23, and another sister, 21, and another sister, 20. They all, apart from the two eldest brothers, live in her home town.

MJ: Eight.

Dr A: And the youngest must have been born just before father left.

Dr B: They were divorced when Sally was 13.

Social Worker: Was this the result of the incest being discovered?

Dr B: If I remember, it was definitely part of it.

Dr A: There's also the aunt who would qualify as a super "high-expressed-emotion"-relative. She's not, in fact, a relative, but within three minutes of visiting Sally, she was saying, "You are my wonderful little darling", and then she swore at her and told her she was a naughty little girl, how could she do such things. This aunt's view is that she, a sort of adoptive mother-cum-aunt, is the only person who cares for Sally, and that "that lot"—i.e. her family—don't care at all. I think that she considers herself Sally's mother by affinity.

MJ: So there are two mothers—the real mother and the self-styled mother—and eight children, a boy of 31, then Sally, then a displacement at 1 year, 3 years, 5 years, 7 years, 9 years, and 10 years. Three new brothers appear within the space of 5 years and three new sisters, and then we have the incest and father's off and mother is said to have breakdowns in her past life. Not a happy, stable background, to put it mildly. So what happened—you put her on some Chlorpromazine, and she's calmed down?

Nurse C: Yes she has, and she can tolerate the groups more now, is vocal and comes out with a lot of psychotic talk, but at the same time she talks fleetingly about feeling things and then not wanting to feel and that she's all muddled about coming here and being in the groups. She takes on a lot of what the groups are about: at one stage last week she said that she was Elizabeth. She picks up readily any emotion in the group and takes it on board.

PW: Often in a concrete way; when there's any talk of leaving, she has to leave the group.

MJ: I see. When she or someone else speaks of leaving, she tries to walk out?

Nurse C: Yes, and has walked out. In the previous registrar's last group, when they were talking about him and about missing him when he leaves, she stood up and roared at me, but it was really meant for him.

Nurse D: I don't know if this is helpful, but I tried to talk to her about what she remembered about the last time she talked to you (MJ). Initially, she said that she didn't remember anything, saying "I'm certain I never talked to him", but then a couple of hours later she came up to me and said, "What was it you were talking about me talking to Dr Jackson?" and she did remember it. She then came out with psychotic things like "My mother didn't abandon me" and "I can taste petrol in my mouth. I've got this funny taste in my mouth".

Nurse C: In yesterday's small group, she was saying whilst sitting close to a nurse that she could smell paraffin on her breath.

MJ: Okay, let's just think about her for a moment. She seems to have an extensive loss of her ego functions, and she's confused in her identity. She functions partly by identifications, which, presumably, replace object relations, and in terms of what troubles her it seems to be that attachments are dangerous because you get abandoned, even though she says she doesn't. She then regresses to very concrete perceptual experiences, which have to do with fantasies about her body and its functions. Her "mouth" is something into which petrol goes, there's gas all round the place, and her anus is something two church spires get stuck up. So she does seem to feel herself being persecuted in that everybody's trying to push things into her—bad paraffin, bad petrol, bad church spires. One theory would be that she's functioning in a psychotic fashion, using massive projective identification to rid herself of all disturbing feelings and objects. She's pushing them out so much that she then feels everything's being pushed back inside her: two church spires—and presumably father's penis, too—and the content of her delusions included people spying on her while she's masturbating. There seems to be a triangle: herself, her masturbating, and somebody looking on making a record, which may possibly be a reflection of her early wishes to pry on parents who produce babies one after the other. She may also have deep feelings of being pushed out; rage, abandonment, and a primitive feeling of possessiveness. All that might be one way of understanding her, but what can we do to help? We have to make contact with her, but how? If I've got it right, she wants to leave the unit but isn't insisting and is no longer cutting herself. Was this cutting to establish some sense of boundary or identity in a strange place, or is it more a deflected attack on the object—namely, her mother? She said, "I've got to love mother, or she'll go away for more money". There's an awful lot of magical and omnipotent thinking going on, isn't there? The problem is going to be making contact with her. When I last saw her, there seemed to be a little more contact possible than there appears to have been since.

Dr A: We speculated on why she has withdrawn more recently. We wondered about the reduction in medication, about the fact that she arrived a week before her registrar then left, and we wondered about the ward—whether the pressures of the ward were just too great for her.

MJ: That puts it succinctly. Ward pressures would be important, because she already feels that the nurses are trying to poison her, put paraffin into her. The ward pressures might be not just the stresses of being on the ward, but also the introspective climate where you are asked to think about what's going on. That can be a real pressure, and sometimes people might break down under an insensitive approach. Then, of course, at the level of fantasy, ward pressure may be that she feels she's being invaded from all sides, including by food, so she stops eating and gets a psychotic anorexia. There are several aspects to it: if it's the reduction of medication before she came in, then that we can do something about; if it's the loss of her former registrar and now the loss of the next one, then we can help her to work through it; but you may be saying that ward pressures might in the end mean that she hasn't got enough ego strength for us to feel that it is realistic for us to do anything with her.

Nurse C: I had the thought in the group yesterday that it was cruel to put her through all of this, because she is clearly in a lot of pain. She was in floods of tears, saying she found it all too much.

MJ: Floods of tears. The thing is whether these tears are tears of persecution or tears of somebody who is depressed and might be able to think about why she is feeling depressed. However, it is extremely important whenever staff feel that things are too much for the patient. We had a similar situation with a chronic schizophrenic boy, who cried all day—you remember—and it was felt that it wasn't helping him to generate the sheer amount of pain he and the staff were required to bear. Should we expect her to be exposed to such an intensity of feelings? Perhaps we can no more stand her feelings than her parents or anyone else could, and we should try to stand them. We need to decide. Your feeling is, at the moment there is not much contact, just upset at seeing her so miserable and paranoid. You're concerned that she hasn't got enough ego strength for us to feel that it is realistic to do anything for her?

Nurse C: There's contact, but I don't think she's able to use it. She's way too fragile. The understanding is all on our side, or a lot of it, and anytime she grasps something, she quickly loses it.

Nurse D: I agree, it's very fleeting.

MJ: She doesn't hold onto it for long. Do we want to add to her troubles by videoing her? It might not add to them at all, but what are our motives for the video, apart from the fact that it would be very interesting?

Dr A: I think we might video her, and if we do, I think her registrar who's just left ought to be able to see it.

Nurse C: I'd like to see the whole assessment through, including the video. I think it would be good if she could at least stay with us for the full six weeks before we decide what to do.

Dr B: I remember when she was on the other ward, she was disturbed there many times too and was never free of persecutory ideas. They are always to the fore, so I'm not sure whether the video would exacerbate these or hardly affect her.

MJ: Okay, I think we'll set up the video, and I'll simply ask her about it.

* * *

Interview

Nurse D, Sally's primary nurse, leaves the meeting to go to the ward and collect Sally. They return and enter the room. Sally and MJ greet each other, and they take their respective seats.

MJ: I thought first I'd like to tell you that we have a couple of people attached to the unit, and we put them behind that mirror there, so there aren't too many people in the room. There's a room behind there.

Sally: Is there someone behind, looking in?

MJ: That's correct. There's a small room on the other side of that mirror.

Sally: I'd rather see them.

MJ: Certainly. Would you like me to introduce you to them, or would you want them to come and sit in the room with us?

Sally: I think I'd rather they stayed in that room.

MJ: I see. The other thing is that we take a video recording of our interview, which is so that we can discuss our interview afterwards. This can enable us to see more clearly what we can do to help you, but you don't have to have this recording happen if you don't want to. [*Pause.*] Can you tell me what you're thinking about?

Sally: I'm thinking about . . . I've already been recorded, so it's alright . . . I've been on television. I don't mind. It's a while since it happened.

MJ: You speak as though my making a recording would be a relief in some way.

Sally: Yes it would. It means that you have got . . . you want to protect the privacy of this interview, and you've got a copy of it, so it means that it belongs to you.

MJ: I would have a copy, and I would make sure no one would see it who wasn't authorized by me. [*Pause.*] In any event, I'll ask you again about it later, because you may change your mind. I wonder whether the slight relief might also be because in the past you've felt that you were being spied upon. This camera is watching you and we both know it is, but sometimes you feel uncertain as to what is going on.

Sally: It comes and goes. I haven't been thinking about it for a while. I think about, more about . . . the way . . . the way I'm cut off in that ward. I'm on a lot of drugs, and I feel dizzy, and . . . I think you're playing around with my head.

MJ: Playing around with your head.

Sally: Putting me in front of mirrors and . . . videos and stuff like that . . . I just find quite frightening.

MJ: Although in one way it might be a relief, it feels frightening, because you feel something is being done to your head. You feel that you are being influenced in ways that will harm you.

Sally: Things of mine . . . I just . . . I don't care about space any more . . . I want to be with somebody who loves me, and I feel as if people don't care. And the radio doesn't work, and that frightens me a lot, and every time I phone people up . . . that frightens me . . . because they answer, or they don't answer and the phone seems to be phoning.

MJ: The phone is phoning. In what way is the phone phoning?

Sally: Well, you phone up, and they answer, and then . . . you . . . they ask you if you're going to put any more money in . . . and then it goes . . . it cuts off and then . . . I think they come back again as well.

MJ: Yes. [Pause.] You feel that nobody loves you. [Pause.] Do you think that's a feeling you had before you came into hospital?

Sally: I felt looked after a little bit on the other ward . . . and I felt my privacy was respected.

MJ: I understand that one of the doctors who you felt did care about you and who you trusted was about to go away.

Sally: Yes, he did go away. Dr L went away as well. I saw him quite a lot, and then I got into a state. Then I got used to Dr R.

MJ: You get close to someone and they then go away and you lose them . . . [Pause.] . . . Do you think you've had the feeling that anybody loved you really?

Sally: I thought that the radio loved me . . . [begins to cry].

MJ: You thought the radio loved you, but it's not working. [*Pause.*] It must feel like a great loss to you.

Sally: It does . . . [*crying*].

MJ: What it was like when you felt the radio did love you?

Sally: It was just . . . it was like being . . . nursed. It was like having sweet music coming out of the headphones and nice voices. I trusted them.

MJ: You trusted them. And they are there all the time when the radio's working.

Sally: I didn't think I was listening to the programmes on my own . . . a lot of people were listening to the programmes as well as me, and . . . it was if you knew a broadcast . . . for example . . . a DJ who had his own particular type of humour, and . . . he used to get people to phone him up . . . I could never do the competitions . . . but his listeners could . . . and you just felt part of a gang then.

MJ: You felt you belonged?

Sally: Yes.

MJ: And then the radio ceased to work?

Sally: It sort of works, but the records are out of tune, and I can't hear the interviews properly. There's buzzing . . . and . . . the news . . . just seems . . . all I know, is my reception . . . is badly . . . is in a bad way.

MJ: Have you ever felt that you belonged to a gang, felt loved? Apart from the radio experience?

Sally: Yes, I have. I felt loved by my boyfriends, but it's a long time since I saw them. They didn't want me. Except the last boyfriend, who was called Helmuth . . . [*Yawns.*] . . . I was unfaithful. In England. And he . . . he . . . and myself decided I wasn't going to go back to Germany with him. So we split up that way, and he . . . and he found another girl-friend quickly.

MJ: The feeling that nobody cares about you sounds as if that's a problem you had before you came into hospital. You feel that you're not really loved, except by boyfriends and the radio. [*Pause.*] I wonder, do you think your mother loves you?

. . . *Pause* . . .

Sally: I think she must have done, but not any more . . . not very much . . . But it doesn't mean to say that I don't love her . . . [*Becomes distressed, cries.*] . . . I'm scared my mum's going to have to go to prison.

MJ: Then you would lose her.

Sally: [*crying*]: Yes I would. I don't want her to go to prison.

MJ: What would she have done to go to prison?

Sally: I'm being filmed . . . these are the things that . . . get sort of . . . that go round and round in my brain . . . I thought my brothers and sisters were going to go to prison, my mother, I thought that Jane was in trouble, that Erica was in trouble, Helmuth, . . . something to do with blood, and then I thought it had to do with sex, and I thought a radio DJ who I used to go and see when I was little, when I was 16, well . . . I . . . I mean the thing I felt most secretive and brokenhearted, wasn't a secret any more. The fact that I got this dog to lick me sexually. It was in front of one of his programmes, I thought that because it was illegal . . . everybody was saying I had done it as an exhibitionist thing, and that . . . and that he'd been split up from his family because I wrote to him and told him that I loved him, but it was before I realized about the dog . . .

MJ: You got the dog to lick you sexually in front of the programme, you thought. And that was illegal?

Sally [*distressed, crying*]: It was horrible, because I didn't want anyone to know about it. I thought that I was being filmed. I didn't at the time. Afterwards I thought that somehow ever since I've been little everything I've done has been done with cameras, and . . . there's also something else that talks about being alive and being dead, which I refused to . . . to . . . you know. You can say if you punch yourself you feel dead because you can't feel the punch . . . but not that . . . you're dead . . . oh, I don't know . . .

MJ: You can't feel the punch, and you remain feeling dead?

Sally: Yes.

MJ: But if you could do something that you could feel, then you might feel more alive.

Sally [calmer]: Yes. [Pause.] Something wicked happened to do with blood . . . because I get periods, and I slept with men with my period . . . they were being penalized for it, and I thought because my mother kept asking me what drugs I'd been taking—I've taken LSD and cocaine and . . . marijuana —I thought that my mother was penalizing my friends who had taken those drugs with me, and I just thought it was terribly unjust, because . . . because it had been done in private.

MJ: This seems to be what you are most concerned about: private things secretly done that shouldn't come out in the open but do. It upsets you so much that things come out in the open, and then people will get sent to jail or penalized for it. The dog licking you sexually should have been kept private. Nobody should ever have found out about that.

Sally: No.

MJ: Can you tell me, who do you think is the most important person in your life, including since you were little?

Sally: I always used to love my father [cries].

MJ: That hurts too . . .

. . . Long pause . . .

Sally: He lives in Spain [crying].

MJ: In Spain, and has nothing to do with you. Might as well be dead.

Sally: He's not dead. He's alive; it's different from being dead, if somebody's dead it's . . . I felt guilty about that because I went to hospital [distressed] and I told them all about my family. I'm not even sure how much of it I was making up . . . then I thought it had been done on film. I kept remembering that I'd been on television when I was in hospital, and one of the things I remembered was I thought the new baby John had been named after my father, because I'd been saying all these horrible things about my father, I thought he was named after my father.

MJ: It sounds as though you felt you were killing your father with your accusations. Deadening his good name. So John was new life which put these bad things right.

Sally: Yes. I feel as if I've been killing a lot of people, actually. What happened between my father and me never affected me until I was 25, when I split up with Helmuth and came back to England, and I started reliving the experiences . . . on my bed . . . I'd just be reliving having to have sexual contact with him, having to suck his penis, having to play with his penis, things like that . . . and also I . . . [*very distressed, sobbing*] . . . I got stuck in these things with my mother hitting me because my mother used to hit me when I was younger, and just used to be half awake and half asleep, just keeping rolling around, just being hit. [*Shouts*] I don't like being hit [*loud sobbing*].

Bleep sounds. Male registrar leaves ward round; Sally looks upset and extremely concerned.

MJ: He had to go. You heard his bleep?

Sally: Yes.

MJ: Why did you think he had to go?

Sally: Because of his bleep.

MJ: Why do you think your father had to go?

Sally: My father fell in love with another woman. [*Pause.*] Why did the registrar have to leave? Was it because of something I said?

MJ: It was because of his bleep, but you became confused because you thought it was something you'd said which drove him away. Can you tell me the thought that you thought sent him away? You perhaps felt he couldn't stand hearing what he was hearing about you. Telling us about your father, the dog . . .

Sally [*cries, long pause*]:   I am afraid that he can't stand me . . .

. . . Long pause as Sally reflects on this . . .

MJ: I think you must feel that I can't stand you either.

Sally: No I don't feel that . . . are you going to tell me that you can't stand me as well?

MJ: I think you can't believe that anybody wouldn't disapprove of you. You're afraid that anybody who hears your story would get to the point where they would feel, "I can't stand this girl".

Sally cries, then sobs violently.

MJ: Can you tell me, why are you feeling so unhappy?

Sally: Because . . . something funny's going on . . . a bad smell . . . it seems to do with the radio, and it seems to do with . . . everything else. And that's why people can't stand me. I've spoilt it for them.

MJ: I think that you're afraid that anybody who learns about you thinks you're a bad smell. Someone they shouldn't have anything to do with.

Sally: Do you think I should go to prison?

MJ: You think you should go to prison because you feel so very guilty. If you think you should go to prison because you're so wicked, you think that I will think that you ought to go to prison, which I don't happen to think.

Sally: Don't you?

MJ: Not in the slightest.

Sally sobs violently for several minutes, then gradually becomes calmer.

Sally: There's something I want to tell you. I went to my brother's house, and I did consider the police and these . . . perceptions of reality, and I started writing down how I was going to sue all these people. I felt enraged, because I'd done things in front of my mirror and I haven't always been clean, I thought that I'd been sort of raped, so I started writing all these things, and police cars used to go up and down the street whenever I wrote people's names down. I wrote the names of my family and I was trying to burn it up, but it left little holes in the carpet in the room, so I stopped doing it. I had it in this broken carrier bag, and I went back to hospital with it in the bag and . . . I . . . [crying] I took it to bed with me and I kept my clothes on. I wouldn't take my clothes off in front of anybody. I just kept this bag in bed with me, and I ran away from hospital. I thought Jimmy Young [a popular disc jockey] was going to lose his job on Radio 2 and that . . . I think a film was going to be made because I went off with this man and I felt very guilty and I felt very guilty for having gone bonkers in my brother's house, because . . . [crying] . . . they think I'm nasty.

MJ: You think you're terribly nasty and terribly dirty, and nobody could love you because you think you've done such nasty, dirty things. You can't believe anybody could wish to help you and not blame you.

. . . Pause . . .

Sally [crying]:   I turned from being an attractive girl into being unattractive. I cut off my hair because I thought friends were being forced to cut off their hair. I picked my spots in front of the mirror. I was just squeezing, squeezing, to get it out of me.

MJ: Get the nasty stuff out of you?

Sally: Yes.

MJ: And then you felt it would all get pushed back into you.

Sally: My mother was coughing. She was telling me not to masturbate. I just thought you have no right to intrude on my privacy like that. It was anger. It wasn't love, it was anger.

MJ: Angry masturbation?

Sally: Yes. I thought the social work department was trying to make me into a spy. I once said when I was . . . when I was . . . drunk . . . that I'd make a good spy, because I never gave contacts away.

MJ: Don't you think that when you were a little girl, that girls perhaps wish to spy . . . want to spy on their parents and what they do to make all those babies?

Sally: No, I just remember things like blood and how I used to hide my . . . I couldn't cope with menstrual blood when I was a child, and how I used to hide these sanitary towels in the wardrobe, and . . . how my mother found one one day and just called me a filthy slut . . . and knickers, you know that you had to wash the blood out of. She just found them one day and called me a filthy slut. Oh I don't want everybody to know this, because it's bad enough knowing that you've done all these things without other people knowing about it.

MJ: Know, and make you feel that they think you're filthy.

Sally: Yes, I do think they'll think I'm filthy.

* * *

The interview continues for several minutes more, following which there is a pause for Sally to compose herself and to say good-bye. She has shown no direct sign of concern about the video camera and does not ask to meet the observers in the adjoining room. She leaves with Nurse D for the ward, and the camera is switched off. There is a break. Staff leave their seats, those behind the screen come into the room, and an informal discussion takes place. After ten minutes staff re-take their seats. The audio recorder is switched on. The discussion turns to a more formal review.

Discussion

MJ: Could you recapitulate on what you just said?

PW: What was going through my mind was the way we were talking earlier about how difficult it was to make lasting contact with her. I was struck by how accessible she was today, and how her confused sexual identity and terrible guilt seemed to unfold in a clear-cut way, and I did think that she seemed eminently treatable.

MJ: I agree. She's eminently understandable, provided one knows about primitive mechanisms of splitting, projection, introjection, concrete thinking, and the confusion between past and present. Also, simply listening to the delusional experiences of a psychotic and taking them seriously is helpful. This lady is treatable, but she requires skill and a great deal of time and care. I would have thought we ought to keep her for a while—I know we weren't planning to discharge her—before considering psychotherapy. But I think your feeling, Nurse C, is that it is cruel to expose her to this level of pain, isn't it?

Nurse C: She comes out with this kind of painful material a great deal, but because of our lack of experience it's a question of what we can do with it.

PW: Isn't the grief the key, or at least one of them, to dealing with her problems?

MJ: So long as it's the grief about feeling bad and the memories of feeling treated as though she's filth, which we don't yet know enough about. We don't know how real it is, but it is her psychic reality. Mother says you are shit; you are menstrual blood; you are paraffin; you are gas; you stink. She has transformed these thoughts into concrete perceptions, olfactory hallucinations. They are pre-verbal presentations of thought—mother thinks I am shit—but it's degenerated into a percept; it's perceptual thinking. Ah, here's Nurse D. Any feedback?

Nurse D: She didn't say anything, but she did heave a great sigh when we got outside. Then she said "I'm still sectioned [compulsorily detained in hospital under the provisions of a section of the Mental Health Act], I'm still on drugs, and the radio doesn't work."

MJ: You see how she is on the edge of metaphorical thinking, but has a variable loss of the capacity for symbolic thinking and is literal and concrete on certain issues, for instance, "the radio loves me". She's partly lost her capacity for metaphor—a theoretically fascinating issue as well as being a human tragedy. Yes, I think that in her grief, you might say, lies her humanity, but not if it were persecutory grief. What she feels is good about the radio is that it makes her belong to the human race. Perhaps it might be her siblings, and maybe mother, but I think it's probably more that she feels totally unacceptable to anybody or anything other than a radio, the Disc Jockey, and the fans.

PW: Bereft.

MJ: Bereft of anybody who could understand her. She's thinking omnipotently, partly functioning like a 2-year-old in an "anal", magical world. She is regressed and replacing object relations by identifications. Ideally, we should have the facility for an experienced psychotherapist to take this girl on straight away and try to deal with the conflicts it would cause in the ward, where she would be the only one receiving such intense attention. Any further comments?

Dr E: She talked about feeling dead, and I wondered whether this was an expression of mourning to do with her entire past or, rather, not mourning, because she can't talk about it.

MJ: I'm sure that's right. As much as this girl needs to mourn what she has lost she can't mourn. [*Pause.*] Professor F, do you want to say anything about this patient? You don't have to, of course.

Prof. F: It's a new field for me! I'm just so surprised at the way in which it is possible to establish this degree of understanding. It's so different from what one would view as conventional psychotherapy.

MJ: Well, this *is* a different approach, I agree, and tailored to the psychotic patient's ways of functioning, and it is to my mind a most rewarding field in psychotherapy, but unfortunately the psychotherapists and psychiatric staff who have the potentials rarely get the opportunity to practice it.

Dr A: I agree that the grief is palpable, but I think the key to our management of her is to recognize how she deals with grief, which is quite transitory. She disposes of it in various ways, including by a lot of projective identification and splitting. I think we are going to be left with a great deal of her grief. If we empathize with her, we immediately have it projected into us. We then have to hold it and bear it and piece it together ourselves. I think that this task is extremely painful. Some of those moments were so hard to take on board . . .

MJ: To tolerate . . .

Dr A: . . . I'd like to forget them myself within two minutes. The thought of the private hell of this girl, the wardrobe, being in the wardrobe with her tampons and in the bed half-asleep with fantasies or reality of mother beating her and father's abuse. On top of that is the overriding counter-transference she creates in us—that she's being abused. She's being abused by the screen, by the claustrophobic ward, by the lack of privacy, by giving her drugs, by putting her on a section. We're going to go on finding ourselves in the role of abuser, and I thought of it again during this video. The average reaction to seeing this video would be that this is an abuse of the patient. Whether we ourselves can tolerate the guilt of feeling we are abusing her, I don't know.

MJ: This is really very important. You are quite right. This girl is understandable, she's eminently workable with, but she can hold on to pain for only so long and then gets rid of it. She would be difficult even if we had all the nurses necessary and a very skilled psychotherapist. One other thing about getting rid of things and feeling persecuted, I think, is the projective symbolism of the two spires. This sounds very primitive. The symbolism of the church and spire suggests to me an idea of a mother and a father joined together, a "combined parent" image, which many psycho-analysts regard as an important mental representation encountered in many different forms, from the delusion of the psychotic to the dreams of the relatively normal person. Some patients have nightmares that present this union in a violent or damaging way, as, for instance, when a pylon topples and smashes onto a church or other building. I think this expresses thoughts and feelings aroused by the fact of the parents' union, sexual and otherwise. Even good-enough parents can become distorted by jealous and other feelings in a child's mind and hence represented as "bad" or dangerous. The evidence suggests that Sally's mind is profoundly confused in its view of her parents, presenting them as bi-sexual symbolic objects that are going to stick up her anus. There seem to be two maternal objects in conjunction with a phallic object and an abusing father, and the whole thing is highly dangerous. Instead of being good like two breasts or parents, what goes into her mouth is paraffin, dangerous shit, and what intrudes into her bottom are two spires. Whether or not she has in the past been given injections in her buttocks, it is the internal reality, the fantasy that we are hearing about. [*Pause.*] Nurse C, what are you thinking?

Nurse C: Well, I agree with a lot of what Dr A said, and I was thinking back to the discussion on Friday regarding the decision to section her. What we have done already is to stop her from bringing all this out by sectioning her and medicating her, because it's so painful for us to take on. We don't have the nursing staff to hold on to her. That's what I would have preferred to have done. To have a nurse with her all the time.

MJ: Yes: some psychotherapists believe, and frankly I think they're wrong, that the moment you give psychotic patients drugs, they immediately feel that you can't stand their feelings any better than they can stand them themselves . . .

Nurse C: I think there's an element of that in it.

MJ: I think they're usually wrong if they think that's the whole story. Given our present state of knowledge, you can't do what is needed without the option of using drugs. If we had enough staff and enough other methods, we might just be able to get through without the drugs.

PW: I remember thinking that while on the one hand she was treatable, the amount of containment needed to hold her might be enormous. All the blood and death . . . it is quite explosive.

MJ: Blood . . . death . . . punching herself. That's what she said. "My registrar doesn't like me any more. My registrar was interested in me as a person, and then he had to put me on drugs for that very reason." The drugs are sometimes given for the staff, sometimes for the situation. This is very interesting. Patients know that sometimes drugs are for their own disorder, but they can also feel that they're necessary because of doubts about the staff's capacity to bear the emotional burden they have to face, and sometimes they're right. So "my registrar doesn't like me any more, he can't stand me, because he has to give me drugs. He can't stand my feelings any more than I can."

Clinical Nurse Specialist: This may be a simple remark, but I was surprised that she was so coherent by the end. I

thought she would be as confused as she was at the beginning, and she wasn't. I was impressed by this and I thought
to myself "this girl's got something!"

PW: Yes, I was thinking when we were saying that she was
confused, how correct is it to use the term, confused?

MJ: There is so much one could say about this patient that I
myself am beginning to feel confused . . .

Laughter . . .

*The discussion continues for a further 15 minutes, at which
point the audiotape is switched off and the ward round draws
to a close.*

* * *

The interview with Sally took place after the first three weeks of
her six-week assessment period on the ward. The nurses had
made detailed observations of her behaviour and speech and
had achieved some understanding of her way of thinking and
of the many things that disturbed her. Her dread of abandonment, aggression towards staff, paranoid preoccupations,
guilty feelings, and the longings of a little girl-self within her, all
emerged clearly. Her disturbed reality sense and confusion of
identity were repeatedly noted, and although rational and emotional contacts with her were quite good, they were of variable
quality. Issues concerning medication and the reasons for her
legal detention were Sally's ostensible concerns during this
period, and they received a great deal of attention.

In interviews such as this, the staff's observations and
views served as a basis for the discussion prior to the interview.
This phase of the proceedings usually occupied 30 to 40
minutes of the ward round. The interview itself, which could
last up to an hour or more depending upon the level of contact
achieved, was usually an event of considerable psychodynamic
complexity—a fact that raises many questions concerning what
is and is not being said, what is being understood, by the
interviewer, the patient, and the staff, what is being not understood or misunderstood, and what are the merits and demerits
of the interview procedure itself.

The aims of the interview are: (1) to make emotional and
intellectual contact with the patient; (2) to render the patient

more available to, and more understandable by the staff; (3) to elucidate the psychopathology and the patient's strengths and weaknesses; and, finally (4) to provide the staff with a learning experience. The interview is not a psychotherapy session, although it is hoped that it will have a psychotherapeutic effect. It also differs from a conventional assessment interview in that the lack of privacy—not least the presence of audio or video equipment—needs to be taken into account. Transferences, potential or already operating in relation to the interviewer (and the staff), and their consequences—positive, negative, or both— may remain unexamined or unclear, yet are complex factors influencing the course of the encounter. The interviewer tries to listen to the patient and to his own subjective responses with a psychoanalytic ear in order to understand the more essential meanings of communications concerning immediate experience, perceptions of reality and of fantasy. He tries to provide the patient with the experience of being listened to with particular attention and, under ideal circumstances, of being understood, in the knowledge that this will bring the patient relief and a realistic hope for improvement.

In this particular interview, it was necessary to let Sally know from the outset about the setting and to seek consent for the fact that she was being recorded. It seemed that the presence of the video camera might not disturb her if she could manage to distinguish its reality in the actual world from the fantasized camera of her long-standing delusional system. Nevertheless, videotaping the interview inevitably aroused persecutory anxiety.

After an interesting comment about space, she showed the nature of her distress and her confusion between fantasy, wishful delusions, and reality. There is a good, loving, ever-present, and highly desirable object always available via the radio, as well as a bad, highly undesirable object preoccupied with the task of keeping her under constant scrutiny. This invisible spectator has been her unwelcome companion for a long time, as has her faithful, loving ally, the radio. It is unclear how long these delusional objects have existed for her. She dates them to her childhood. It seems possible that the loving figures also served to protect her from the loss of her lover, Helmuth. These defensive constructions have begun to fail, and she is exposed to a dreadful sense of loss, abandonment, and isolation and to partial and terrifying recognition of her psychosis. Her choice of language indicates that she can, to some extent, talk sanely about her madness: the phone "seems" to be phoning; she "used to think" that the radio loved her; her "reception" is in a bad way; she "went bonkers" in her brother's house. Perhaps the radio, with its sweet music, loving voice, and group companionship, is a delusional creation analogous to the illusional creation of a soft toy "transitional object" in early life. Her absorption in radio programmes places her in vicarious contact with others, and this may represent a partial effort to reconstitute members of her family who are, intrapsychically, lost.

As she relates her past sexual activities, with their associated guilt, shame, and confusion, she becomes increasingly distressed. She refers to incestuous activity and to reporting her family to the police, but she does not know how much of this she has made up and how much actually happened. The theme of fellatio, a universal fantasy and a common practice, has the quality of a memory of an actual traumatic event and may help explain the meaning of her olfactory hallucinations and associated delusional thinking. Her self-neglect may be a statement about maternal neglect (herself being identified with the neglected child; perhaps also with the neglecting mother), or a literal-minded expression of feelings of dirtiness and badness, or a struggle to maintain a grasp on reality in the face of constant inner condemnation and confusion about who is bad and who deserves to go to jail. Striving to maintain some sense of certainty over even minor aspects of external reality can bring great relief to the confusion of a psychotic individual. This is reflected in the way small but genuine improvements in intrapsychic coherence yield impressive results in the functioning of many psychotic patients.

Characteristics of Sally's ways of thinking begin to emerge. It is magical, omnipotent, and self-centred. She has merely to write a condemnatory list of names, and the police appear. Although she hears and understands the registrar's bleep, she believes that his departure refers to her own nastiness. Her sense of identity is diffused, unstable, and constantly shifting.

She becomes depersonalized, bereft of feelings; she experiences herself as dead, and she punches and perhaps cuts herself to recover a sense of being an alive self. She detects some quality of her own in another patient (Elizabeth) and briefly believes she is that person. This type of experience, called "transitivism", is variously attributed to weakened ego boundaries within a constitutionally vulnerable mental structure, or to the defensive or offensive use of projective identification. In this instance, the invasion of the mental representation of another person provided a helpful explanation for the staff of Sally's bitter and indignant complaints of being the victim of constant intrusions. The violent projective expulsion of unwanted elements from the mind can lead to a "boomerang" effect, or "projectile re-entry" of these elements, no longer recognizable as such, but sometimes taking the form of "bizarre objects" (Bion), such as the church spires. Invasion of an object to avoid separation and separateness may also result in a feeling of being invaded. Impairment of Sally's ego functions is evident in her faulty reality testing and the loss of the capacity to differentiate reliably between fantasy and reality, past and present, and memory and immediate perception. Memories of sexual abuse had led to excited re-enactments in masturbatory fantasies as a way of coping with the loss of her departed lover, a loss that appears to have its roots in a sense of abandonment by the "Mummy" of her early childhood. Her thinking is often literal and concrete, and at such times she is deprived of the emotional distance afforded by a capacity for symbolic representation. For example, she gives the impression, in a phobic and spatial manner, that the memory of a broken plate must be avoided at all costs due to the intensity of what appears to be a grief reaction. She must literally stay away from the canteen because to be there might present her not simply with a reminder of a painful past loss, but with some kind of deluge of unmanageable, heart-broken, depressive feelings.

The theoretical concept of a psychotic part of the personality leading an autonomous existence and working against the development of rational thinking, which might give rise to mental pain (Bion, 1959; Steiner, 1982, 1987, 1993), has led many psychoanalysts to the belief that such an "organization" is formed during the infancy and early childhood of the future psychotic individual and is responsible for the vulnerability of perceptions of the self, of personal identity, of body image, and of the capacity to test reality. The presence of all these symptoms in Sally determined the fact that her mental disturbance was a psychotic and not a neurotic one.

As the interview proceeds, her disturbance and poor functioning become more apparent. The incest seems to have exerted a particularly traumatic effect in view of the prior underlying crisis in her relationship to her mother. The central paranoid delusion of being spied upon is likely to have a complex psychodynamic structure and would probably prove difficult to influence therapeutically. This is a typical characteristic of chronic paranoid delusions, and it is interesting to consider why it should be so. The patient did not seem to be interested in the suggestion that the source of her preoccupation might lie in any of her own wishes, which she locates outside herself. This explanation was not necessarily true, but even if it had been, an intellectual recognition of it by Sally might have made little difference.

If a part of the self is being projected, for the purposes of expulsion, containment, or communication, into the external world, then an attempt to suppress, silence, or return the projected material is likely to prove ineffective (cf. Searles, 1965). This is especially so if the part that is projected, because originally felt to be bad and unacceptable to the ego, contains something valuable that might, under more favourable circumstances, be transformed into, say, useful assertiveness or curiosity. The deluded patient may be very reluctant to give up the delusional state for fear of losing a precious asset, which could in such a case be regarded as containing a lost part of the self. A further explanation for Sally's unresponsiveness may lie in an underlying dread of being abandoned. Extreme splitting of good and bad selves—loveable and utterly unacceptable— and their associated phantasy figures (in Sally's case, the disc jockey and the invisible spectator) has the effect of producing a situation in which the patient is *never alone*. Perhaps it is felt to be better to be constantly attended to, even by a persecutor—however much the creation of a part of the self—than to feel oneself the subject of indifference (see Auchincloss &

Weiss, 1992). A further factor in the problem of intractability concerns the psychodynamic consequences of chronicity. The longer a patient remains in a psychotic state, often characterized by unconscious identifications, the more difficult it becomes to emerge into sanity. Psychosis originated as the best possible solution to intolerable psychological conditions, and as such, however distressing, it had a protective effect for the subject. In other words, the pains human relationships can bring seem to be worse than psychotic dread. A patient who recovered from a schizophrenic illness expressed the dilemma succinctly:

> . . . sanity came through a minute-by-minute choice of outer reality, which was often without meaning, over inside reality, which was full of meaning. Sanity meant choosing reality that was not real and having faith that some day the choice would be worth the fear involved and that some day it would hold meaning. [Anonymous, 1992]

The staff discussion

The interview with Sally was moving, perhaps more so for the staff listening than for the interviewer, and it is tempting to think of Sally's outbursts—of despair over her isolation, of her longings and of guilt—as a therapeutic breakthrough, thanks to the interviewer's skill. This would probably be a mistake. Breakthroughs can occur during such interviews, but in this case the staff made it clear that they had coped with the same extreme levels of distress on a daily basis, as had Sally's previous consultant. Despite the difficulties of this situation, concern, respect, and sympathy for Sally had been maintained, as had a capacity to empathize with the catastrophe of her psychosis.

The concern of the staff can be of great value to the patient if communicated appropriately. Above all, listening with respectful interest to the patient's delusional ideas without colluding with them can break the isolation often inflicted by psychosis. Feelings of aloneness and helplessness in the patient may not be obvious, but they almost invariably exist, and the restoration of human contact is an essential step on the road to recovery. When, however, it comes to assisting the patient with psychotherapy, love is not enough, and a knowledge of mental mechanisms is essential. The staff's feeling was that to work psychotherapeutically with Sally might expose her, and the staff, to emotions that could be too much to bear. They used their own distressed reactions, provoked by the interview, in a countertransference sense to learn about Sally's inner world and their own therapeutic limitations. The chief nurse observed that the staff knew about being on the receiving end of confusing material, but they did not have enough experience to allow them to use it. Neither did they have sufficient trained staff to give Sally the attention she needed. Others considered that Sally might eventually become more capable of normal, healthy mourning for what she had lost, psychologically and in the real world. The consensus was that she was sufficiently responsive to justify cautious optimism about the chances of the unit being able to help her, but that the full six-week assessment period would be needed to confirm this. Caution was necessary, not only because of the patient's limited psychological resources, but also because of the limited number of staff available to enable a useful milieu therapy to proceed.

The effect of staff changes also needed to be taken into account. A degree of staff turnover is inevitable on any ward; some might even argue it is desirable, but, when a patient's difficulties concern attachment and loss, the departure of key staff in whom the patient has begun to trust can be damaging.

Perhaps the most serious resource problem lay in the difficulty in finding an experienced psychotherapist to give Sally (and other patients like her) the time they required. This lack— a central concern of this book—has deep philosophical, political, and economic roots. It proved to be crucial in Sally's case, because she did not get the psychotherapy she needed after discharge, and this gave rise to unfortunate consequences. Although experienced psychotherapists are insufficiently available to help such patients in public hospital practice in Britain, it is interesting to note that, in Finland, nurses with only a little training in psychodynamics can undertake good supportive psychotherapy with psychotic patients if they are offered skilled supervisory help (Alanen et al., 1986).

Progress

When the six-week assessment was over, a full treatment plan was drawn up, comprising individual supportive psycho-therapy alongside the ward's milieu activities. Her treatment would centre around the relationship with her primary nurse, strengthened by the psychosocial resources of the unit.

The aim was to improve her weak ego functions and to foster her self-esteem. On this programme she made significant improvements. She mixed with patients in a constructive manner, and her paranoid ideation decreased. However, her fundamental anxieties remained unresolved, as evidenced by regressive responses to staff departures and her inability to tolerate group discussions that referred to separation and loss. Her individual supportive psychotherapy was regularly inter-rupted by staff changes, to the point where it was decided that brief periods of therapy risked doing her more harm than good. It was decided to seek a more experienced psychotherapist, who could offer Sally treatment on a longer-term basis—an opportunity she welcomed. The search proved unsuccessful. Despite much effort, no psychotherapist could be found—either within the N.H.S. or from the private sector—to take her on, even though she herself had begun to feel acceptable to others and had acquired an awareness of her sensitivities to attach-ment and loss. Her isolation had lessened, and she had also become able to recognize that her delusional world was insane. Psychodynamically speaking, her persecutory guilt had dim-inished, and the non-psychotic part of her personality had strengthened. A lessening of her projective defences had given rise to more confusional states, but it seemed quite possible that she could work through these in psychotherapy. These gains were probably lost as a result of not being able to provide her with the treatment she needed.

Follow-up

Sally stayed on the unit for over a year and was discharged to out-patient care with a moderate dose of neuroleptic medica-tion and social work help. It was clear that she needed long-term support, since it had been repeatedly observed that when individual care was threatened she deteriorated quickly. She would then become increasingly preoccupied with delusional beliefs and took time to recover. She went to live in a hostel; soon afterwards the ward was closed and responsibility for its patients re-distributed. The social-work help Sally received proved inadequate for her needs, and she eventually failed to comply with her medication. She relapsed and had four subsequent admissions over the next few years. She then became sexually involved with, and pregnant by, another psychiatric patient. Supported by the social services, she decided against termination and gave birth. This event revived the worst of her paranoid anxieties. The baby was immediately included in her delusional system, being constantly watched by the invisible spectator. She felt that the baby's eyes were unsynchronized and that the watcher was also appearing in the form of alien creatures in the sky. When last heard of, she had broken off from the father and was caring for the baby alone, with the support of social workers.

* * *

It has often been noted that supportive psychotherapy with psychotic patients can bring about lasting improvements. However, if the fundamental experience of separation, with all its associated feelings of loss and negativity, is not worked through in the therapeutic relationship, any gains made are likely to be vitiated when the relationship is terminated. It is likely that Sally's severest vulnerabilities lay in this area, which the unit was ultimately unable to help her overcome. However, we are left with the conviction that a promising start to the treatment of this intelligent, tragic young woman was annulled by the failure to provide her with the long-term psychodynamic understanding and support she badly needed. Although the outcome of her case was deeply disappointing and her future is uncertain, much was learned that has been of help to other patients. It is to be hoped that Sally herself may have retained something of value from her time on the unit.

CHAPTER TWO

Schizophrenic self-burning: which self?

S elf-destructiveness, a common feature of mental illness, may afflict the psychological self, the bodily self, or both. In psychological self-destructiveness, motivations of varying psychodynamic complexity are discernible, often involving guilt regarding internal objects and deriving from destructive and reparative desires. Bodily self-destructiveness takes various forms, of which the most common is self-poisoning with prescribed or other drugs. Of all forms of self-harm, burning by fire is the most dramatic and rare, and it is one of the most difficult to understand. An investigation undertaken with colleagues at the Maudsley Hospital approached the subject in the following way:

> Acts of self-poisoning, cutting, jumping and hanging are often explicable in terms of depressive or destructive motivations, the choice of methods being determined by what is available, occasionally with imative or symbolic significance. Minor self-mutilation, which includes self-cutting and less often small burns with cigarettes is encountered frequently, particularly in female adolescents

and young adults with personality disorders or in association with anorexia nervosa. It is usually repetitive, causes
little harm and is not a suicidal act. Although studies of
self-cutting are highly informative regarding clinical and
motivational correlates, they do not explain the psychopathology or clinical features of major self-mutilation (ampu-
tation, castration, blinding, tooth avulsion) which appears
to be both a rare and more psychotic act. Fatal or potentially fatal self-burning is an extreme form of self-mutilation and needs to be distinguished in its clinical and
psychosocial aspects from minor self-burning and from
other violent self-harm. Although death may ensue, suicide
may not necessarily be the conscious intent. [Jacobson,
Jackson, & Berelowitz, 1986]

Further studies have lent support to the view that the
motives underlying any episode of dramatic, violent self-harm
may be more complex than a wish solely to die by suicide.
Although "existential" suicide (e.g. the escape from a life of pain
or futility or from severe organized violence) may not be uncommon, an unambiguous desire for death in preference to life
appears to be relatively rare. If the self-destructive action alone
is studied, it may reveal only conscious intentions. Psychoanalytic scrutiny may be necessary to expose the often hidden
motivations of aggressiveness towards others (Hale &
Campbell, 1991), which is then turned against the self. Freud's
discovery that the psychodynamics of melancholia (psychotic
depression) depends on aggressive wishes originally directed
against a frustrating "bad" object but turned onto the self,
permits us to ask: "who is this 'self' unconsciously involved
in an act of self-criticism or self-destruction?" Contemporary
object-relations theory offers further help in understanding
self-destructiveness from the perspective of the subject's
internal object relationships and patterns of identification.

The following case reveals the complexity of motivation in an
act of repeated psychotic self-burning. Each burning was a
response to a hallucinatory command to pursue a course of
total self-immolation.

ANTHONY

Anthony, a highly intelligent, articulate young man, was 28 when admitted to the unit, having suffered from a schizophrenic illness for ten years. He had no overt psychiatric symptoms until the age of 17, when he withdrew from reality following the death in a car accident of Keith, his brother, who was one year older. He became preoccupied with quasi-philosophical ruminations of a humanistic–ecological nature, and he dropped out of the further education course he had begun. He then undertook a laborious ascent of a high mountain, where he had an intense, mystical experience—the delusional belief that God was leaving the earth because He could no longer tolerate the greedy destructiveness of mankind. An alien hallucinatory voice commanded Anthony to burn himself to death, telling him that his sacrifice was the only way in which the catastrophe could be avoided. By dying, he would enable God to forgive and tolerate mankind. He proceeded to obey the command, seeking out various places—a hut, his mother's car, and a dance hall—within which he performed the self-immolation. Sometimes he was too terrified to carry it through, but on two occasions he did so, burning the structures to the ground and escaping unharmed at the last moment when he realized what he was doing.

As Anthony's disturbance intensified, so his speech became saturated with mystical talk. When admitted to a local mental hospital, he was diagnosed as suffering from schizophrenia of a hebephrenic type and treated with neuroleptic medication and supervision. For five years he continued this régime, struggling with self-burning impulses and preoccupied with an unrequited love for a girlfriend. When one day this young woman invited him to tea, he felt blissfully happy, but later, as he left her, his self-burning impulses became irresistible. He dreamt that an old man told him that he must consummate his sacrifice, and soon afterwards he poured petrol over a hut and set light to it, with himself inside. His screams attracted attention, and he was rescued, having sustained serious burns, which fortunately spared his face and genitals. Several months later, when he had sufficiently recovered, he was admitted to the unit for assessment.

In the first few weeks, the nursing staff found it difficult to make meaningful contact with him. They were flooded by his apparently empty philosophizing and found him unwilling to discuss his feelings, which, he said, were located in his left leg and were a private matter. They found it hard to cope with a particular aspect of his behaviour, which he regarded as playfulness—namely, the shocking of female staff by creeping up behind them and pretending to strangle them. Although under close supervision, he would seek permission to go out to buy lighter-fluid for his cigarette lighter, and was disappointed and angry when it was refused, even though he was fully aware that the staff knew of his self-incinerating history. Gradually, the staff came to feel that much violence was hidden beneath his idealistic philosophizing and so-called playfulness.

At this point, two successive exploratory interviews were conducted and videotaped, and the following extracts illuminate the psychodynamics of his psychosis.

First interview

This extract begins 10 minutes into the interview. Anthony has been talking about his recurrent states of anxiety and fears of God leaving the world.

Anthony: I was anxious about being institutionalized or becoming a werewolf or possessed, you know.

MJ: What would possess you?

Anthony: What I was afraid of was becoming septic. Like gangrene, where once you had a healthy leg and then rot sets in and you just become cancerous and take . . . just suck the juice out of life without giving anything back again. It wasn't a possession, it was just about me becoming evil because I had such an unhealthy response to life that instead of giving out I was taking in and distorting it. I wasn't really doing it, but that's how I felt. I was becoming a bad influence, becoming destructive.

MJ: You felt you were going septic. That would be like gangrene or cancer?

Anthony: Yes. I would become cynical. Septic. Sceptic. You know, sceptic–septic. Sceptic is looking askance at experience. Sceptical, doubting it, not thinking it's very good— that's it, sceptic and septic, they're related.

MJ: They're not the same.

Anthony: Not the same, but related. I think sceptic is . . . what's that word . . . phonetically like septic. Or it has the same origins.

MJ: What would be the state in which something started happening inside you? You talked of it as a body getting gangrene or . . .

Anthony [*interrupts*]:   It's an emotion. My emotions are doing it.

MJ: How might it be if your emotions became gangrenous in that way?

Anthony: I'd have to be institutionalized. I'd have become very unhealthy and have to stop myself from becoming totally rotten.

MJ: And the rottenness would be an emotional rottenness?

Anthony: Yes, because I don't know what my emotions are like. I'm not in touch with my emotions. I think my ego has something to do with it. If I have an emotion, I get egotistical about it. I don't have emotions often. When I'm in a situation where I am aware of my emotions, I get egotistical buzzes. I'm pleased at having emotions. I think "God, I'm great, I've had an emotion". It's just a pleasure buzz, but it destroys the emotion, because the buzz becomes more important than the emotion.

MJ: Can you give an example of when you last felt such an emotion?

Anthony: Yesterday. I was full of hate . . . I hate the world for having been in institutions and never having lived a decent life. I've got a lot of hate inside me for Keith and for Emma and for disappointments in my life. This came out yesterday, and with the hate came emotional insight into people. This woman was prattling on about her shopping basket, and she approached us in a mild manner, being delicate because she doesn't want to expose herself to emotional violence. I don't mean that, but she doesn't want to be hurt by a rebuffal, so she talks about trivial things, so she can feel her way into bigger subjects, which is what a lot of people do. I got a buzz from having that perception. I regretted the buzz. I lost contact with the emotion.

MJ: How long have you felt you've been out of contact with your emotions?

Anthony: All my life. I think my emotions are very mature and powerful now.

MJ: Mature and powerful? But not available to you.

Anthony: They're not available to me, no.

MJ: Where are they then to be found?

Anthony: They're about there [*points to about three feet to his left, in mid-air*]. When I feel an emotion, I bring it from about there, and then into my body. My emotions are just there. There's a space which is isolated . . . my emotions are isolated from me by an intellectual barricade. It's just there.

MJ: Why there?

Anthony: I don't know. [*Irritated*] I don't analyse my emotions, you know. I accept them and get on with the business of living.

MJ: I see. Can you make contact with your emotions when you point to there and reach out to them?

Anthony: No, my emotions aren't physical. I don't reach out for my emotions in any case. I do it from a point inside myself. I become aware of a space and then of emotions. I never actually make that gesture.

MJ: Nonetheless, you feel they are on your left side rather than your right side?

Anthony: Absolutely. My intellectual and spiritual side is on my right. My emotions are on my left side. I feel that my left leg is the source of my emotions, of everything that I know about. I don't know anything about my heart. My left leg is my source of affection and love.

MJ: Your source of affection and love?

Anthony: And love, yes. And it's the source of my pain and my anger and my hate . . . it's the source of everything to me. It's a funny thing, because sometimes I don't feel my leg is connected to me. Sometimes I feel my left leg is . . . this sounds crazy talking like this; I don't believe this, I don't take it seriously, I'm just using . . . I know it's figurative, you know.

MJ: You know it's figurative.

Anthony: I know it's figurative. I know it's also true, but I know it's figurative; you know, it's a stupid way to talk, and yet that's the way I am, so I accept it and that's it. I feel that my left leg is . . . completely different to the rest of my body.

MJ: It feels true as well as being figurative. If we think about it on the level of its trueness, what would that experience be like? Your leg seems not to be a part of you in some way?

Anthony: Yes.

MJ: Could you describe it a bit?

Anthony: No. I don't want to. It's very precious to me. A lot of what I've told you is very private, and nobody talks about their private lives to that extent. It sounds ridiculous, but that's the way I feel. I can't go into that area. It's nothing to do with my emotional hang-ups. Perhaps you want to know about it in terms of science. I was trained as a scientist. Unless you go into nuclear physics, you don't have . . . I'm giving it away now . . . you don't have a sufficiently subtle process of understanding.

MJ: You feel that if I were to try to understand it, that would be a destructive attack on it by me?

Anthony: Yes I do. My left leg eludes analysis and always will, unless you chop it off and throw it away. I realize the futility of analysis. What's that noise? [Pause.] Oh, it's the camera. I'm being hostile here, because I haven't been told what's happening. I'm at your mercy. I would have thought I'd have been treated with more consideration. My left leg has nothing to do with my emotional content. I told you on the first day that I didn't want my sides to be altered.

MJ: Your sides?

Anthony: My left and right sides to be altered. We haven't talked about my emotional hang-ups, which is what I want to talk about. We've talked about shaking legs and my left leg. What am I to make of that? I'm here for healing, not in-depth analysis of my left leg.

MJ: Well, let's turn to your emotional hang-ups.

Anthony: Not unless you want to. If there's something else you'd rather talk about, please talk about it.

MJ: You've said that you feel you've never been fully in touch with your emotions, and that's what you'd like to happen. Could you tell me how it might be, if you were in touch with your emotions?

Anthony: Well I can be, you know. I went to sleep for two hours after lunch-time, and I came up here feeling great. I wanted to have fun. For me, having fun is a way of releasing aggression and violence and hate. But there's very few people can take me when I get into fun. It's very energetic. I feel all these angles and stepping on people's toes when I'm in that frame of mind. I felt sad and disappointed that there was no-one I could have any fun with. I know what that sounds like—a little baby. Maybe I am a little baby, but that's what I want to do. People wouldn't understand it. They would feel that it was violence.

MJ: What form would the fun take that people would think was violence?

Anthony: Just word games, approaching and backing-off— maybe like basketball, where you get rid of aggression, except you do it with words. It's also physical, touching people or whatever. Or strangling people. Giving people shocks. Pretending to strangle people, and making up. You need people for that.

MJ: I see. When you said you felt like a baby, I'm not sure what sort of experience that is.

Anthony: I wanted to have fun, and it was a selfish thing to want. I felt isolated. I had no-one to have fun with.

MJ: Do you think that is something you also missed out on earlier in your life?

. . . *Pause* . . .

Anthony: Yes. That sounds true.

MJ: That sounds true. Why was it the case?

Anthony: I don't know. I've never thought about it before. [*Pause.*] I know I was silent for the first two years of my life.

MJ: Silent?

Anthony: I didn't talk or do anything. My mother told me. I didn't say anything until I was two. I have some memories, but you know there's no real fun there. Things weren't right.

MJ: What's your memory of when things seemed to be alright last?

. . . *Pause* . . .

Anthony: I don't know. A long time ago. [*Pause.*] I don't think things have ever been right.

. . . *Pause* . . .

MJ: That raises the question of what effect you think your brother's death had on you. What do you think about that?

Anthony: I don't know. I get egotistical buzzes about not feeling grief about him. That's why I don't enter into relationships, or have feelings. I didn't want buzzes about affection or humour or love. I wanted to have them straight. I don't want to start getting pleasure out of grief. I really liked Keith, you know. The night before he died was the first time he'd ever been human to me. He never treated me as a person. But he commented on my trousers. It was such a nice thing to do. Then two people came to the door the following day and said that Keith and Alan had had an accident and they were badly shaken. We wondered how bad was the accident, but they didn't tell us, they just dashed off. I phoned up and had a hysterical breakdown over the

phone finding out about Keith, then we went round to my
aunt's and found out about Keith then.

. . . *Pause* . . .

MJ: What are you feeling?

. . . *Pause* . . .

Anthony: I'm just feeling sad. It's not a positive thing. I feel
very, very sad.

MJ: Not a buzz.

Anthony: No. [*Pause.*] I wish I could cry for him. I couldn't.
[*Pause.*] I went into a meditation, and when I came out, I
knew Emma had had my heart, you know.

MJ: You went into a meditation after Keith's death?

Anthony: No. Six or seven days ago. I felt good after it. Emma
no longer has my heart now. I loved her. But the next day I
realized it wasn't on, it wasn't going to happen.

MJ: Are you saying that you loved Emma, but you realized
that you weren't going to be together?

Anthony: Yes.

MJ: Did you fall in love with Emma after Keith's death?

Anthony: Yes. I spent a month with her in a caravan. I liked
her an awful lot, and liking grew into love for her, and
I've loved her for years. That was the summer after Keith's
death.

MJ: And were your feelings returned?

Anthony: No. She returned feelings of friendship, but not
love. She didn't love me. I scared her. The power of my
emotions scared her. I went overboard. That's what I do.
[*Pause.*] She loved me once, you know, but never properly,
not to the extent that she knew what to do with me. I think
she loved me, but she didn't know how to deal with her love
for me. I believe that.

MJ: You feel she loved you, but she didn't know how to
express it, or was afraid . . .

Anthony: She was afraid to express it. She was afraid of the
effect she had on me, because I trip badly. I took LSD and

had a bad trip, and after that when I saw her my perception of reality would change. That frightened her, that she could have such an effect on someone, and then I burned myself after I saw her the last time. I set fire to the dance hall. [*Pause.*] You know, she treated me like her husband, making me cups of tea and looking after like me a wife. There's an awful lot of evidence like that to imply that she loved me.

MJ: I see. And after you saw her, you burned yourself?

Anthony: It was just that she got in contact with my love for the world, and I felt I had to do something. It was the day I visited her. I went to the dance hall and started the fires. She knew that. I just went in and lit the fires. I didn't want to kill myself, though.

MJ: What did you want to do?

Anthony: It was a symbolic gesture. The same reason I burned myself in the first place. A gesture to God. I wanted to burn myself inside the building, but I hadn't the guts to do it. It would have been too painful. I just walked out, and the fire-brigade came.

MJ: It was a symbolic gesture to God, and also connected to having just seen Emma?

Anthony: Yes. It wasn't just seeing Emma, though. My mother was working in the chest clinic at the time, and she got out of the car, and I was getting buzzes from myself that I should burn myself inside the car at the time. I mean, those were absolutely dreadful buzzes. So, so bad. God. So bad. Oh boy. Boy. Christ. [*Becomes distressed.*] I was absolutely . . . it was just so bad . . . whole thing was so bad . . . oh . . . oh . . . just living with that all the time, for four years, I can't even believe it, it was so bad.

MJ: Living with the impulse to go into a place and burn yourself.

Anthony: Yes. Oh . . . oh boy . . . I hate that, you know I really hate that. [*Shouts, clutches head, rocks back and forth*] . . . oh . . . how could anybody do that to anybody, you know. I mean who the fuck did that?

MJ: It doesn't feel like you?

Anthony: No, it doesn't.

MJ: A terrible memory, but it's confusion, too.

Anthony: Aah . . . yes, I suppose it is confusion . . . oh . . . I
know I've felt that before, you know. I never felt so much
hatred for life for doing that, you know. I feel so much
hatred, it was something that I could never understand,
you know, about why. I mean I must have done something
terribly wrong to have to burn myself. I must blame myself
because I'm evil. I want to stop now, I've got to stop now.

*The interview continues for a few moments more and then
ends.*

Second interview

*A few days later. Anthony has insisted that he was not upset
by the previous interview, but then he remembered he was. He
and MJ discuss his self-burning impulses.*

Anthony: I was in such a bad state, and I felt the world was in
such a bad state, that it was highly likely God would leave
the world. I identified with the world instead of myself as a
person with hang-ups and emotional problems. At the time I
thought the world was getting much worse and that's why I
did it. I said to Frank, my best friend, that I did it to burn
the evil out of me.

MJ: So there were two possible explanations: one, that God
was leaving the world and the other—as you told Frank—
that it was to purify yourself of evil.

Anthony: Yes. And the world was filled with evil and violence
too, you know. The later fears I had that I was becoming
septic and cancerous pointed to the fact that I was absorbing so much of this poison into myself from the world. It all
turned in on me and became too much to handle.

MJ: When did you feel you were becoming septic?

Anthony: I thought that after I burned myself—about two
years after. It's still there; not so much, but it's still around.

When I'm in anxiety states, a whole load of alternatives raise themselves. One of them is, I'll become cancerous and start absorbing all the muck of the world instead of healthy feelings. Even healthy feelings turn into bad feelings. It's quite a bad mega-fear, you know. The last time I felt really anxious, I thought I was going to turn into a werewolf. I had feelings which corresponded to a werewolf.

MJ: What sort of feelings does a werewolf have?

Anthony: Well, they're very violent and aggressive, you know.

MJ: What do you do when you have those feelings?

Anthony: Run. I start thinking about something else. They're ghastly. I feel them in my left leg, you know, it's like a current of energy running up the middle of my left leg, and it has a kind of ambience about it. Another feeling I had was I was going to be permanently institutionalized. My father has a psychiatrist friend, and I thought I would be sent to him so he could look after me, because I felt I'd become so cold inside that no amount of warming up would help me. I would be institutionalized for the rest of my life, because I would be violent and aggressive. And then another fear was that I'd become a priest. That would be a cop-out of my humanity, my masculinity. The underlying theme of my illness is that I've been trying to smother my real emotions with love and affection. After a while the emotions come out and are hostile, and they turn on me. I can't forever repress my natural emotions, can I? That's why I'm here. I'll tell you something that astounded me in the summer. I felt in a tremendous amount of pain. I felt my body had been burned, tortured, brutalized, everything under the sun, psychologically tormented, and one night I was in bed and a young voice came out of my heart from under that weight and put everything straight by saying, "You're making a jackass of yourself". And then, you know, I was sitting in front of the house one day, looking at the sea, and I felt like a complete man, you know, and then about three seconds afterwards I felt like a complete baby. The child and the man can co-exist, I think, you know.

MJ: Were you able to talk to anyone about how you felt?

Anthony: No, not really. I used to talk to Frank, and to my mum about my thoughts on a Sunday. She would listen with a sympathetic ear, you know. My father talks to me about my madness. He asks me what I'm thinking and feeling. He's listened to me for seven years now. He doesn't understand the words I use, or my ideas, but I get on with both my parents well, you know, in a simplistic sense, although it's not simple at all. My father lets me be because my ideas have peaked and now I know what I'm doing. All my years of madness have culminated in my own philosophy now, you know.

MJ: What is characteristic of the years of madness you're referring to?

Anthony: A profound preoccupation with spiritual life. A quest. Why is life so painful? Why did this happen to me?

. . . Pause . . .

MJ: Why did what happen to you?

Anthony: Why did anything happen to me. When I said that just then, it was Emma that I was thinking about. She was the last straw. [Pause.] You know, my brother dying on me, and Emma and me breaking up, it isn't really that big a cookie, you know. It couldn't have caused me to burn myself or go through so many years of hell. It was God leaving the earth that did it. I don't want to explore it, you know.

MJ: Do you mean you'd like to know why you had to burn yourself but . . .

Anthony [interrupts]:   No, I wouldn't like to know. I do know. You see, either it's true that I burned myself because God was leaving the earth, or else I'm so screwed up about my idea and concept of God that there's something seriously wrong with me, and I've got to get it straight. I need to know which is which in order to live like a man.

MJ: I see. Perhaps we need to get clear what you're saying. There are two possibilities: either God is saying this world is too bad because of man's greed and violence, I'm leaving . . .

Anthony: Look what it's doing to all the earth . . .

MJ: Look what it's doing to the earth, I'm off. You, Anthony, feel that if you are a sacrificial victim God might not have to leave.

Anthony: Yes.

MJ: Or there's an alternative explanation, which would have to embrace another way of looking at these processes in the world. If we leave aside the leaving of God for a moment, in whose mind could the following situation feel real? Someone says, "the world is being so damaged by greed, so harmed, that that on which all humankind depends is going to vanish forever".

*rework
restate
reality
checking*

Anthony: That's unthinkable.

MJ: Yes. But somebody, namely yourself, is utterly dependent on and concerned with the well-being of the world.

Anthony: I love the world.

MJ: You love the world. You want to protect the world on which you depend, but the world is being so damaged that God is going to leave the world. Now there is another way of thinking about this, I think.

Anthony: Yes, I know, I felt that from you. I felt that maybe I was dependent on my mother and I didn't want to leave her, and maybe my mother was being so damaged by the world that I wanted to protect her.

MJ: Is that the first time you've thought that thought?

Anthony: Yes. Just now when you were talking, I thought of it. It's a rational, intellectual thought, though, not an emotional one, but I felt it.

MJ: Let's look at it, even though it may initially be from an intellectual point of view. There's an infant, a small child, who is feeling very afraid that his greed is going to harm his mother, and he also becomes afraid that unless he gets rid of himself, along with his greed which he feels is so destructive, then his mother will go away and leave him forever. Does that make some sort of sense?

Anthony: Yes, it does.

MJ: Right. So, what about your early history then, when you shared your mother with Keith when you were a baby? What would it be like, do you think, to have to share a mother with another baby who's only 11 months older than you? Perhaps you can imagine how you could have felt afraid of the damage that your jealous feelings might do?

. . . *Pause* . . .

Anthony: I think it's true, you know, what you're saying. I also remember being repulsed by my mother's breasts. I saw them once. [*Pause.*] You see, I think I was greedy . . . I took my mother's breasts . . . not because I was greedy, but because I loved her. If I'd taken enough, it would have felt alright to Mum, but if I couldn't, it would hurt her. I've never thought about it before, about being jealous of Keith or Mum being the earth, but she was. That was how I felt about her.

MJ: As Emma also then became.

Anthony: Yes, yes. I don't know if I can face this one, you know. I've got a whisper of it. I'm scared of my emotions. Especially about Emma. They scare the shit out of me.

The interview continues for five minutes more. Anthony leaves in a serious, reflective state of mind.

* * *

The first of these two interviews was dramatic, and the explosion of hatred and perplexity ("how could anybody *do* that to anybody!") was startling and unexpected. It carried a conviction and authenticity that were in complete contrast with his way of talking up until that point, and was so disturbing to him that he had to terminate the interview. His subsequent comment that he had never felt like that before was equally convincing. Before the outburst, he had talked in a manner that was patronizing and very much in control of the proceedings. When he talked of the "buzz" that brief contact with his feelings produced, he was momentarily excited. He subsequently stated that "all my years of madness have culminated in my own philosophy", and although this seemed to be an empty and defensive intellectualization, it was also an expression of his past attempts to understand himself in the absence of more satisfactory explanations. It is also likely that this interview was the first time his feelings had been seriously explored—or at least explored with success—since the onset of his psychosis. Despite his initial insistence that his emotions were a private matter (possibly a reference to the video setting) and that they were inaccessibly contained in his left leg, allowing himself to be admitted to the unit may have prepared him to accept some exploration. His reference to the prattling lady with the shopping basket trying to feel her way into bigger subjects seemed an almost direct criticism of my [MJ's] cautious approach, as well as his own prattling. It might have been possible to take this up as a healthy criticism of his own verbose self projected into me, but I was far from sure that this was happening. A subsequent criticism of me that he was here to explore his emotions and not to have an in-depth analysis of his left leg had some justification. My interest in the spatial quality of psychotic thinking had drawn me into exploring the location in space of feelings for which his left leg seemed to be the container.

In the second interview he was less defensive, and the events leading up to the self-burning impulses were clarified. The nature of his experience and the quality of his thinking and preoccupations were also explored. He had an intellectual awareness of his hatred of his brother as a rival, but no understanding of the nature of his underlying destructive impulses and his sense of guilt, for which he had sought a religious explanation. He claimed to realize that his reports of his experience were expressions of metaphor, but it seemed clear that although a large part of his personality was sane and intelligent, in the area of his conflicts his grasp on reality was fragile and his thinking highly concrete. He could recognize this, conveying that when he was anxious he experienced confusion between fantasy and reality.

It was striking to see how he used splitting and projective and introjective mechanisms to cope with the catastrophic events in his inner world. Damaged objects (representing the vulnerable mother of infancy) are projected into the world, where they appear as poisonous muck, which he then introjects, absorbing them and becoming poisoned himself. Both he and the world are then poisonous, and he begins to equate the inside of his mind with the inside of his body. Malignant feelings and motivations become synonymous with septic and gangrenous physical processes, vengeful objects become a devouring cancer, and, if the entire process possesses him, he will turn into a murderous, biting werewolf.

Despite his claims to sanity, it seems that he had often been living a waking nightmare, and that any attempt to make a loving attachment to another person appeared impossible. He felt his love to be destructive, and he had struggled to find an object to accept and contain feelings he believed to be omnipotently destructive. His massive use of projective identification seems to be responsible for his confusion between self and object, good and bad feelings, external and psychic reality, and the impairment of his capacity for symbolic thinking in the area of attachment and separation. The exploration of these processes in the first interview culminated in an interpretation in terms of developmental failure of the processes of infancy, and he showed interest in this reconstructive approach. As a small child, he had felt that his mother (earth) had been damaged by him and wished to abandon him totally, and he went on to provide what seemed like confirming evidence of the essential correctness of the underlying theory. By the time the second interview had ended, it was clear that he was willing to explore this new form of understanding. He felt hopeful and relieved at being understood, but his essential anxiety was not significantly diminished.

It was now possible to consider the meaning of his psychotic condition. His brother's death revived the split-off murderous feelings towards the infant brother and feeding mother, with the subsequent development of a dangerously powerful psychotic part of the personality, which was activated when he was confronted by the threat of loss of the mother of his infancy, or of her representative—his girlfriend, Emma. This suggested an encapsulated area of profound disturbance in his early relationship with his mother, the nature of which was not at all clear since the overt relationship appeared to be one of normal mutual affection. His self-immolation could be understood to be an expression of murderous jealousy, a violent attack on the mother–brother couple enacted in a drama in which he himself is identified with the offending brother. It is also possible that he was enacting the gratification of a sexually exciting incestuous phantasy.

The "self" who was the victim of the self-destructive behaviour was, therefore, not perceived by the patient to be himself, except perhaps insofar as there was a guilty self who was being punished. The compulsive repetition of the drama appeared to require that the self-immolation take place within a containing structure. Although this could be explained in practical terms, it suggested the possibility that the phantasy being enacted involved the representation of the mother's body—the "maternal space"—itself equated with the containing structure within which the occupant was doomed to die. As we shall see, developments in the course of subsequent psychotherapy supported this conjecture.

The foregoing formulations arose from the information gained from the history gathered on the ward before the interviews and from the interviews themselves. There could, of course, be other ways of understanding the material of the interview and of reconstructing the past. This particular way allowed for a specific formulation of his crisis and for a treatment plan centred on a trial of individual psychotherapy. He remained on the ward for several weeks while a search was made for a suitable psychotherapist. During this period he remained highly anxious and at times verbally aggressive and he resumed his attempts to shock the staff, with the result that they often felt uneasy and believed him to be on the edge of an explosive outburst.

A small dose of anti-psychotic medication was instituted, and interviews were held with his family. These interviews suggested considerable family psychopathology, not least involving a complex, disturbed relationship between otherwise well-meaning and close parents. The mother acknowledged that she had a tendency to depression and found Anthony's early years difficult. However, both parents were so disturbed by the prospect of further investigation that subsequent contact was deemed inappropriate. The following evaluation was then recorded:

"It is difficult to assess the risks that might be involved in attempting individual psychotherapy with this patient.

Although a large part of his personality is intelligent and intact, and up to a point able to make sense of psychodynamic formulations, the aggressive and destructive aspects of his personality that have never been contained and integrated are intense. The tendency towards expression in concrete thinking, sensation, and action is so powerful that severe negative responses to any psychotherapeutic alliance must be expected. We can also not be sure how much the anti-psychotic medication is holding further fragmentation in check. Against these dangers must be set the extreme likelihood of him drifting further into chronic schizophrenia, with eventual self-destruction."

Eventually a psychotherapist of some experience expressed an interest in him; at a preliminary assessment interview, she felt such an impact of a sense of latent violence, that she arranged for a male colleague to act as co-therapist, with sessions once weekly as an out-patient.

Follow-up

For the first four months of psychotherapy, the patient spoke in a detached way about his philosophic ideas and the mysteries of existence. At times he complained of a pain in his left leg, which had something of the quality of a hypochondriacal symptom. Gradually the therapy came to life, and he began to talk about his illness and his present and past life. A striking transference pattern developed, in which he would ignore the male therapist and focus his attention on the female therapist, at the same time ignoring any intervention she tried to make. The sessions were increased to twice-weekly, and his engagement grew. Eventually he began to speak about his burning episodes, which, he explained, were a protest directed against his family, whom he had experienced as having been quite unable to grieve when his brother died. His mother had been highly critical of him when he showed any sign of distress. Slowly, he began to realize in his therapy that being mad and being creative were not the same thing, and he began to reduce the intellectualizing talk. He found it difficult to exist in the non-psychotic world of ordinary human relations, but his intelligence and determination helped him to make good use of the therapists' support. He stopped medication, and a mild relapse of his psychotic disturbance necessitated admission for a few days and resumption of medication. This medication was continued for a further year, when it was permanently discontinued. He then took a job, found a girlfriend and continued therapy at what seemed a much more neurotic level. He married, his wife became pregnant, and he survived considerable anxiety during the ensuing pregnancy and confinement.

At this time the female co-therapist became ill, and a decision was made that he should continue the therapy with the male therapist alone—an arrangement that continued until the termination of therapy two years later. For some time he conspicuously ignored the topic of her illness, but eventually he began to ask after her health. This event ushered in a dramatic change, with the lifting of repression of a crucial memory.

He began to speak with great feeling about his mother and her profound grief reaction to his brother's death, and her total inability to cope with it. He remembered that in his third year his mother had given birth to a still-born baby, and he recalled how angry he had been at the loss of a sibling, and subsequently how concerned he was about his mother's depression and resentful that the event was never again mentioned. His father had remained detached, whilst his mother was absorbed in her grief.

It became clear why his brother's death had been so irreparably devastating to his mother. It had precipitated a pathological mourning reaction, reactivating the earlier loss, which had thrown her into a state of depression from which she had never recovered. It also explained why the parents had been so defensive and had made no reference to the event when they were seen at the time of the patient's admission. The therapist was now able to take up the wish to destroy the baby inside the mother as a fully understandable reaction at the time, a pattern that had continued to disturb him ever since, and which explained how this was enacted symbolically in burning himself inside a building. A partial explanation had been offered to him at the original assessment interview before the baby's death became known, and this had evoked deep feeling and intellectual interest. However, it was striking to see that it only became affectively real for him after a long period of working through in the transference, when the repressed memory could be released from repression. It was still unclear at that point why the destruction took the form of burning, rather than, for instance, jumping or self-poisoning. The patient supplied the answer, explaining that flames were an attempt to bring back to life a dead family and to purify the family for what had happened.

The impact of these realizations cannot be over-estimated. In one crucial session the therapist was rewarded by the patient bursting into tears, thanking him, and declaring, "You have given me some meaning. Now I understand why I did these terrible things." A fully satisfactory explanation of his psychotic disorder had finally been achieved. He had unconsciously held himself responsible for the baby's death in the womb, because of the rivalrous wish he had had at the time, which was in conflict with his love for his mother and his wish for a younger sibling. These wishes threatened to break through the repression barrier when his older brother died and were compulsively and repetitively enacted in a drama of complex identifications. The containing room represented his mother's womb, and the victim of the murderous burning was his guilty self identified with the rival baby. His early religious education had exposed him to the doctrine of the fires of hell as the fate of the guilty, and this may have contributed to the choice of fire as an appropriate method of self-purification.

At his own request, the sessions eventually became less frequent, and he gradually moved away into his own life, finally terminating the therapy at the end of four years. Six years later his marriage is stable, he has a successful work record, his wife has had a second child, and he remains well. Psychodynamically speaking, we can see how Anthony had begun to recognize his aggressiveness on the ward (masquerading as play) and that this confrontation continued in his therapy. Violent feelings, splitting, projective defences, fear of poisonous invasions and of becoming a werewolf, all receded in proportion to his overt acknowledgement of his self-damaging history and its emotional meaning, not least its unresolved rage and grief. By the time his individual therapy ended, his capacity to tolerate his emotions had expanded considerably, and as a result his intellectualization, excessive excitement, and feelings about his left leg as a container of emotions had all but disappeared. Anthony had become able to contain and tolerate in his own mind the pains of guilt and jealousy that had lain beneath his devastating behaviour.

CHAPTER THREE

Psychotic character:
"a bit of an old rogue"

A significant proportion of the clinician's work is concerned with attempts to assist individuals whose behaviour and symptomatology are the expression of
lifelong difficulties in forming and preserving close emotional
relationships. Such patients are regarded as suffering from
personality disorder. They present in many forms, often associated with diagnosable psychiatric illness such as hysteria (seen
more often in women), schizoid states (seen more often in men),
obsessive–compulsive disorder, or depression. They tend to
lead chaotic, unhappy lives and often cause emotional damage
to others. Psychoanalysts consider that such disturbances derive from failure in crucial phases of early emotional development, which leaves the individual without a coherent sense of
self or a capacity to manage impulses realistically. They are
often afflicted by feelings of futility, emptiness, and depression.
Although at times they function psychotically, these occasions
are usually responses to stress and last for no more than a few
hours or days, rarely leading to a diagnosis of psychosis.
Over extended periods, these patients may experience many
phases of disorganization, but they do not deteriorate, hence

they are designated as demonstrating "stable instability". Since they inhabit the border between neurosis and psychosis but belong to neither, they are classified as borderline personalities, and it is widely acknowledged that they are extremely difficult to treat. In recent years a burgeoning literature, psychiatric and psychoanalytic, has accumulated about them.[1]

Many of these patients were treated in the Maudsley unit, with varying degrees of success and failure, and much was learned over the years about the psychodynamic in-patient treatment of borderline personalities (Jackson & Jacobson, 1983; Jackson & Pines, 1986; Jackson, Pines, & Stevens, 1986; Jackson & Tarnopolsky, 1990). Since many of the characteristic features of these patients derive from psychotic mental mechanisms, the term "psychotic character" is regarded by many as an appropriate one (Frosch, 1983). The following case illustrates the problems and opportunities arising from an attempt to treat such a chronically disturbed patient within a psychodynamic milieu over a period of nine months.

RICK

Rick was 25 when he was admitted to the unit at the request of a psychiatrist who had known him and his troubled family for many years. He had referred Rick, several years earlier, to a psychotherapy clinic, where a psychoanalyst had assessed him and concluded that he had a profound borderline condition, veering towards psychosis and too disturbed for out-patient psychotherapy. The reason for now seeking treatment was a rapid deterioration in his mental state over several months, with the worsening of hypochondriacal and obsessive–compulsive preoccupations, symptoms that had first emerged during adolescence. These had a distinct psychotic flavour, and although he had managed to preserve some sense of reality, his behaviour had grown bizarre. He was compelled to cover his head when he walked through a door in case something should fall on him. He needed to check that he had not lost a piece of his skull in the bath-water. He demanded repeated assurances that he did not suffer from invasive cancer of the bowel, and he hoarded rubbish in order to avoid the possibility that he had inadvertently discarded something of value.

Routine history-gathering showed that he was a wanted second child, born prematurely and weaned early with some difficulty. He began to cause concern in his second year, when he was described as a sullen and resentful toddler, a fact not improved by his father's apparently punitive attempts to discipline and control him. By the age of 4, at the time of his mother's pregnancy with the first of two younger siblings, his aggressive behaviour at nursery school became so disruptive that his parents sought assistance from a child psychoanalyst, who saw Rick once, and then again when he was 8. From this early age onwards, Rick was never out of contact with the mental health services in one way or another, including periods of psychotherapy and special education. His schooling yielded little success, as he found it difficult to think or retain information, despite fairly high intelligence. (No evidence of cognitive deficits that might have contributed to these early learning difficulties was found during his stay.) His behaviour was disruptive and provocative at school and at home, but he was endowed with charm, a sharp, ironic sense of humour, and, above all, outstanding ability at football, and these provided him with a strong identity as a colourful school personality.

At home he was often violent, sometimes towards his mother, and during his adolescence he was in constant conflict with his father, who could not cope with his hypochondriacal complaining and obsessional behaviour. After leaving school, Rick led a mildly delinquent social life, using street drugs, fighting, and committing some quite serious motoring offences. Nevertheless, his passion for football remained undiminished, his skill in it grew, and he decided to embark on it as a career.

Rick's deterioration prior to his admission had begun 18 months earlier, when he was confronted with several life events that exceeded his capacity to cope, leading to escalating anxiety and massive intensification of the defences underlying his bizarre preoccupations. Rick was a sportsman of real promise, and he was, in many ways, an attractive, popular, and worldly young man. From a young age he had had a series of girlfriends with whom he became passionately involved, only to suffer tormenting doubts about their fidelity. He would turn against them, and his state of mind could become violent. In his late teens he made a girlfriend pregnant and arranged an abortion. To console her, he brought her a kitten, of which he grew very fond. Six months later, in a fit of anger, he drowned it, without subsequent remorse.

His sexual successes led to a further girlfriend becoming pregnant and another abortion, which was traumatic for them both. Success as a footballer had meanwhile gained him a budding national reputation as a striker in an up-and-coming team, but this had also led him into an extravagant lifestyle and financial difficulties. His vulnerability to rivalrous conflicts was exposed, and relations with his captain and team manager deteriorated. He began to lose his aggressive, goal-scoring ability, became increasingly unable to deal with his resentment towards authority figures (and also perhaps with his un-acknowledged feelings of homosexual temptation), and finally resigned from his team in a fit of acrimonious pique.

As investigation into his background proceeded on the ward, it became clearer that his family environment was cultured and talented, but unhappy and chaotic. His father, a scientist of some distinction and himself the son of a powerful, unstable father, dominated the family. Although a sensitive and creative person, he was subject to explosive bursts of rage and crushed the development of his wife, a depressed woman who, in her turn, had been dominated by a powerful and invasive mother. These relationships contributed towards a volatile and capricious family setting in which Rick's ties to his mother grew ever more intense. Her chronic depression led to serious dependence on alcohol and anxiolytic drugs and necessitated psychiatric intervention. By the time she had improved, her husband had turned to his powerful mother-in-law (Rick's grandmother) to assist him in domestic decisions and even in his scientific work. Rick's referring psychiatrist was of the firm opinion that the prime source of the family disturbance was the outwardly successful but seriously unstable father.

At the time of his admission, Rick was disabled by the preoccupation that he might have malignant tumours of the brain and bowel. He could no longer look after himself and was immersed in compulsive rituals, the foremost of which was to let food and rubbish accumulate in his flat over long periods—

up to a year in one instance—until it had become rotten, when he would plunge his hands into it to make sure there was not something valuable that had been left there, such as, for example, a gold ring or a crucial telephone number. Later, after some improvement, he transferred his obsessionality to close scrutiny of the contents of a vacuum cleaner, searching to reassure himself that nothing precious had been sucked up into the dust-bag.

After several months on the unit, his confused feelings became more comprehensible. His profound longings to be loved and respected by his father were in chronic, intense conflict with extreme possessiveness towards his mother and repressed murderous jealousy towards his displacing father and siblings. It seemed that the threat of return from repression of these murderously aggressive feelings had inhibited his sporting performance, goal-striking having become unconsciously endowed with the significance of an attack on the faithless mother of his oedipal phantasies and his rival father and siblings. He had been utterly unable to manage these emotional conflicts on a verbal level or by constructive, imaginative activity, and had been driven to enact them traumatically by impregnating girlfriends, killing the kitten, and antisocial behaviour. These psychodynamic upheavals mirrored the extreme power of his repressed infantile feelings and the original failure to negotiate the developmental task of separating from his mother, with the loss, grief, and rage this might bring.

Persistent therapeutic work by nursing staff reduced his obsessionality and omnipotent thinking, and gradually deeper aspects of his infantile fantasy life emerged. He took to smearing his head with clay in a state of excitement during occupational therapy classes. Occasionally he showed sensitivity in sculpting clay models. He began to participate a little in sports and eventually revealed how any personal sporting success used to release in him overwhelming excitement, with fantasies of himself as an adored national hero.

During his admission, Rick made predictably intense attachments to patients and staff and slow, turbulent progress in understanding himself. He became involved in rivalrous conflicts with other male patients and ultimately could not resist seducing a married, female patient, whom we shall call "Mrs D". At the time of the following interview, Rick had been on the unit for six months. Important work had been completed with his Primary Nurse, C, to whom Rick had developed a deep attachment. C had worked closely with the registrar, employing a cognitive–behavioural approach to Rick's problems whilst retaining a firm psychodynamic grasp of his behaviour. She had helped him to clarify situations that led to increased obsessionality and hypochondriasis. She had pointed out his inability to see anything other than hateful aspects of his father and showed him how denial of any loving feelings contributed to chaotic, fragmented thinking and aggression towards his father and others. He had understood this and, for the first time, had begun to behave constructively towards his parents at weekends, something that obviously surprised and pleased them.

He had recently learned that C was about to move to another post and would be replaced by another nurse. It seemed that his sexual involvement with female patient Mrs D was being used, at least in part, to control feelings he was threatened with by C's departure.

Interview

MJ: What sort of progress do you feel you are making?

Rick: I think I'm less . . . when I saw my father and mother before, I felt . . . I felt different with them. Sort of . . . I was getting on with my father's excitable, incurable romantic side. It was much easier. Is that what you mean?

MJ: Is that what I mean about what progress you're making? I have the impression that at the moment you feel tense.

Rick: You feel I'm tense now?

MJ: Let's put the question another way. What would you like to let me know about yourself?

Rick: I'm a bit of an old rogue. I'm a bit of a thief. Dr L [the headmaster of a progressive residential school] said once "You don't want to be a little Hitler, do you?" And I said, "No, sir". It was just before he died. It's been with me for the last 16 or 17 years. Whether I was born with this power career sort of thing or whether it happened later on, I feel it's got mixed up with being an old rogue. I know you understand. Maybe that's what Dr P [a previous psychiatrist] meant when I drew that picture for him of a rocket-ship. It was a penis or something. He said it's to do with power.

MJ: When Dr L said to you, "You don't want to be a little Hitler, do you?" was it that he meant that you have a bit of a little Hitler in you, but you don't want to become a person like that?

Rick: No, I think Dr L was powerful. He liked power. As you know, he was a very brilliant man. It sticks in my memory. I think he enjoyed exercising his power. In my stay . . . I had three years there . . . obviously there were people observing me very closely, I mean . . . I guess it was finally after I hit this man and broke his arm, and I think it was perhaps after that . . . the guy had been goading me for months, and I guess we were having a power struggle. I had a power struggle with my father. I guess that side of me he was talking about is a not very nice part.

MJ: You're saying that like Dr L, your father has power, so there were two powerful people out there who exerted power over you, and now you're in conflict. Perhaps you could tell me how you are getting on with your father? You have said that a side of your father is incurably romantic.

Rick: He has *joie-de-vivre*. Amusing. Youthful. Interested in beautiful things, and women . . . like ballerinas.

MJ: You have something of that in you, too, don't you? A love of beautiful things? We've heard from your occupational therapy instructor that you have a talent for making things from clay.

Rick: I did it before, when I was 13, for about a year, in 1968.

MJ: You also do other things with the potter's clay than make things.

Rick: What kind of things?

MJ: You don't know? You put it all over your head.

P [*laughs*]:   Yes . . . I did that today. I thought you meant a big penis or something.

MJ: You thought I was referring to you making a big penis out of clay.

Rick: I made this big phallic sort of thing . . . yes, no, I have covered my head and my face. It's a nice feeling. A rhinoceros turning over in the mud, and stuff. It's just sort of like . . . earthy, it's just a very earthy feeling . . . all in your hair. Same thing as when I worked on a building site. I got all sort of covered in it, if you like, covered in it and had a shower afterwards. Just sort of grime . . . feel you've done a bit of work.

MJ: It's pleasant to smear yourself with clay because it feels nice. But there's another question: how are you getting on understanding a different sort of activity which is related— the hoarding of all the food and things in your flat?

. . . *Pause* . . .

Rick: My flat is a little tidy.

MJ: That hardly answers my query: "how are you getting on?" I might say your flat's getting on a bit better, it's in better shape. But what about the owner of the flat?

Rick [*Blows nose. Pause.*]:   It's an obsession.

MJ: That's a label. It's an obsession, but it's not an answer to why do you do it—what it means.

Rick: It's beating myself up, really, isn't it? It's putting something in the way, so I just throw things away, and I feel angry with myself really, plus what you told me before in the first ward round. [*Pause.*] My mother and the obsessions.

MJ: Your mother and the obsessions. You link the idea of your mother with that behaviour?

. . . *Pause* . . .

Rick: Well the things are a part of my mother I'm hanging on to.

MJ: What you told me at that time was that you had to hoard all the food and other things, that nothing should be thrown away, and you'd rummage through it all to make sure that something good like a gold ring or a telephone number wouldn't be thrown away and lost. Do you still have that feeling?

Rick: It's a bit less, but I still check things. I can't just throw something away like normal people can.

MJ: What's the feeling that comes to you, needing to throw something away but not being able to?

Rick: I just want people to keep their distance until I've checked it's alright, you know. Then I can throw it away. I want to check it over, so it hasn't got anything still in it that I won't miss. My pockets, too, you know, I check my pockets to see that I haven't thrown anything out that's valuable. I empty my pockets.

MJ: I suggested that the valuable thing you don't want to lose is your mother's love. Instead of being able to face up to what it might feel like to lose your mother, you rummage through rubbish, and you do this because it's too painful to face the intensity of your feelings of love for your mother and about having to lose her. There's a power struggle going on: you've got to hang on to mother and continue to do so forever and never give her up to father.

Rick [*impatient*]:   My father's always incredibly obsessional. It's his strength. I mean there's not one second when he can leave it alone, leave . . . me . . . alone. He's fucking nuts. He should be in here. You should speak to my brother. He feels the same way. He's crazy. He's dangerous, you know; I can't believe he's a scientist, a so-called brilliant man. He's a sick man. I know I'm off the tracks, but he's a sick man. He drives me mad. Wash your hands, go and wash your hands. I say alright. He said it four or five times. You see him grinding his teeth . . . and the anger that he's got. He shouted at my mother, abusing her for weeping. My mother came to me later and said, "If I told him what I really thought about him, I'd have to walk out the front door". He shouted at her the other day, and I just told him what I thought of him.

MJ: He shouted at your mother.

Rick: I just said to my grandmother, *"You've* been married to my father. You leave me alone with my mother." And my mother looked at me aghast, and I said, "leave us alone". Grandmother suddenly became . . . her whole power, her life force suddenly became humble . . . you know, a big thing that's gripping my balls, there . . . I just feel she let go, she fucked off. She fucked off. She went into the garden, and my weak mother and I were left together. This had been my grandmother who has done all the cooking, and my grandmother has been strong and right, and my mother has been just lying on her bed all day long. Fucking depression, you know.

MJ: So your mother's married to father, and father's a little boy in love with his mother, under his mother's influence. No husband to your mother . . .

Rick: The provider.

MJ: He should just fuck off and leave you and your mother to get on with your lives together. Father can have grandmother, which is what he wants, and you can have mother, which is what you want.

. . . Pause. Rick cries.

Rick: My mother has been a manipulator all her life. How much I owe to her power. She's got aspects to her that I haven't seen and that have done a lot of damage.

MJ: I thought a little while ago you were cross with me when I told you about your crazy behaviour, and then you told me something about your father's crazy behaviour. I said you rummage around trying to find good things in shit—that's a bit of a crazy way to behave. You call it an obsession and give it a label, but I think you're afraid of thinking it's crazy, so you go on doing it. When I pointed that out, you got rather cross with me.

Rick: You told me once in a ward round that I was quite mad.

MJ: I think you are responding to my use of the word "crazy". What I mean by crazy is that there are things that don't make adult sense. Your behaviour makes sense if we think that you're trying to have your mother to yourself, and you insist that your father is just a little boy who ought to stay with his mother and not have anything to do with your mother. You want to take your father's place, and you are reluctant to give it up and get on with your life.

Rick: I want to do something like that.

MJ: But the question is, are you going to be able to give all this up and change? You see, I think you get confused between a healthy part of yourself, which truly feels sorry for your mother and would like her to have a happier life, and another part of you, who says, "Daddy's a little boy. I'm going to have Mummy to myself for the rest of my life." I think your concern for your mother is wholly admirable, but it's mixed up with a little boy who provides all his own pleasure by smearing himself with clay, wanting his mother to himself, has murderous feelings towards his father, and who tries to convince himself that father and mother have nothing to do with each other. You remain like a little boy who has to control fathers, take mothers away from fathers, have mothers all your life and break up in your mind the idea that there's anything good in your parents' marriage. I wonder when you will be able to face up to this? How are you going to help Mrs D, and not merely break up her marriage?

Rick: I don't want to break up D's marriage. I really don't. [*Cries.*] Are you saying to me . . .

MJ: What I said upset you. I have a feeling you are rather angry.

Rick: Yeah . . . I mean . . . I felt like saying you can do what you want with me, but there's no way you can open my head up [*angry*], never, not in a million years. I'll push myself through a window. You'll never open my head up. You're not going to put your fingers in my brain. You can do what you want with me, but I'm not having shock treatment, I'm not having no tattoo surgeon scaring me, I'll suffer like this for the rest of my life, there's no way . . . no way . . . I haven't harmed anybody, I'll survive in the bad state I'm in. Please, don't ever . . .

MJ: Open your head up?

Rick: Yeah . . . never . . . not even when I'm, you know, like, there's no way, no way, nobody's doing that, no.

MJ: You sound as if you felt that I was saying to you that you're crazy. What does open your head up mean?

Rick: Brain surgery.

MJ: What was it that made you think that I thought you should have brain surgery?

Rick: No way . . . never.

MJ: So where is the feeling about brain surgery coming from? It's not in my mind. You suspect that it might be in my mind. It's obviously in your mind, and it might help for us to try to understand what it means.

. . . *Pause* . . .

Rick: When I go to pottery, and I see people walking by with things on their heads trying to walk properly, I want to get to the bottom of what's causing the symptoms. My physical symptoms. My movement disorder. I have a movement disorder, and I just wonder what's causing it. Whether it's hysterical or neurotic or something wrong with myself, maybe it's a disease. I've had it for the last year, my balance is not functioning, my eyesight's not working, is not functioning. I'm scared, [*shouts*] I'M SCARED. Because I've been through a lot of anger and a lot of fear, and I know I'm hysterical. I'm neurotic and I'm hysterical and I'm crazy, but I, what I'm saying is that I don't want ever to have brain surgery for my obsessional behaviour, but I do want to be helped, but please, you know, if there's anything . . . there's no way, not a chance in hell, do whatever you want with me, I'll take whatever drug you give me, but I'm not going to have shock treatment or brain surgery, ever.

MJ: What's the movement disorder you're speaking of?

Rick: I had a movement disorder. My gait is weird. I told Dr L years ago. I've had central nervous system tests. Obviously they don't give you a brain scan or EEG, I don't know what they do. Yes, what could be causing my walking to go funny? Is it blood restriction from my neck? Is it . . . is it . . . I've got to face up to this, haven't I? That's one good thing. My gait being strange. This is the first ward round that I've ever talked to you about my physical symptoms.

MJ: You have mentioned before that you've had feelings that you're dead, that you had cancer inside you, but that's not what you're referring to?

Rick: My stool has been strange for the last year. Sometimes it's diarrhoea, sometimes it's very soft, it's not the same as it used to. Obviously my visual disturbances and my walking are the most primary. I feel I'm walking on a trampoline. Strange. Scary. Sometimes I don't want to get up in the morning, because I've got to walk. Does that worry you? I mean, I'm going to have the brain scan. Serves me bloody right, doesn't it? I'm a coward, and I've got to face up to this.

MJ: These feelings you're having now came out when I talked about you not wanting to harm Mrs D's marriage. I said you're being too possessive and overprotective towards your mother. It's possible that you're doing something similar with Mrs D.

Rick: It's all . . . it's not my right to do it, I see myself . . . trying to make her happy. I want to make everything alright for her. I'm running out of red carpet.

MJ: That's what you want to do for your mother, isn't it? You'd like to make everything alright for her. On the ward we want patients to be involved in their feelings about other people. Feelings are things to be discussed and understood, worked at. If somebody like Mrs D wants to deny her anxiety about her marriage and begin an affair with you, that's her business, but our business is to help her see that maybe she's not working at understanding her feelings of anxiety. She forgets them by getting caught up in a relationship, apparently perfectly well-meaning, with you, and you for your own reasons may be repeating with her some of the behaviour towards your mother, which means that you're not seeing the situation clearly. That's what I was trying to help you to see.

Rick: She's a bitch, isn't she? [Sighs.] I do love her, you know, I do love her. I love D, but I'm just definitely, you know, sort of, knock it on the head, it's wholly wrong.

You know I know what you're saying about feelings and everything. Sure. Blotting out her anxiety which she should be dealing with. And it is the same pattern with D like any girlfriend I've ever had. I've just got to make everything perfect for them, and then I get angry with them and angry with myself.

MJ: You want to make everything perfect for them, and then you get angry with them and angry with yourself for being angry with them.

Rick: It's just . . . when I saw her weeks ago . . . when D smiles, she's so beautiful.

MJ: She's so beautiful, you love her so much that if you start to hate her . . .

Rick: I don't hate her.

MJ: You get angry with her, and you then you get angry with yourself. You can't preserve your loving feelings. In this way being with girls is like being with your mother. You feel protective towards her and then get very confused when you get angry. You're frightened that your feelings become very destructive towards the person you love. These conflicts between loving your mother, then girls, and then coming to be angry with them and then yourself, are crucially important for you. You turn angrily against them, and you then just see it as a problem inside you, that it upsets your gait, that you feel that there's something wrong inside you physically. When I talked about Mrs D and you began to tell me that you weren't going to submit to operations on your brain, your attention turned to an awful process going on inside you that you think is going to destroy you instead of being able to see what's wrong with your feelings in relation to women. The problem is your fear of destructive feelings you have towards your mother and women—and towards your father. You don't want Mrs D to be the one you're angry with. Instead of being able to understand that your fear is of your destructive feelings towards her, you think you'll have to have an operation to have something cut out, or you're afraid that's what I'll think.

Rick: That's the nightmare I used to have nearly every night ten years ago. My father was coming home with a mask on, operating lights were on, doctors were holding me down saying this is really bad, this is the end, we're going to have to take this little bead out of your brain, which will make you into a respectable human being. I used to wake up screaming. He had a knife and was going to drill my head open, and . . . cut most of my brain out.

MJ: If we take that thing out, you'll become a human being. Was that what he meant? In the nightmare?

Rick: I believe it was that you'll . . . you know, that I won't hassle you any more.

MJ: Me?

Rick: Yes . . . I'm . . . disruptive, but then I'll be just like he wants me to be, calm and docile . . . he'll attack my burning desire to become famous at football, all my things that I might ever do more successfully than him.

MJ: You seem to feel that your father is envious of your achievements and doesn't want you to become more successful than him.

Rick: He's given us lots of money and presents . . . that's the way it is.

MJ: It must be confusing, that you think your father is filled with envy and jealousy and that gives rise to those terrible nightmares that he wants to take away from you the thing that keeps you alive. Perhaps you can't acknowledge your own feelings of envy and jealousy. Maybe that's why you turn on girlfriends because you become so possessive.

Rick: I think with D . . . as far as somebody else . . . I can't stand it. I ain't got no right cause she's married. I promise I'll stop, I will stop.

MJ: I'm not trying to cut something out of your behaviour with a knife. I'm trying to help you see that when there's somebody you love, in this case called D, the jealousy and rivalry you feel is so great that it makes you feel like a murderous little child.

Rick: She's got a beautiful, tender sensitivity . . . her eyes . . . this beautiful, soft jawline . . . she smiles, and her eyes are simply . . . she's just so lovely.

MJ: You remember ever thinking that way about your mother? When you were little. When you had her to yourself?

Rick: I feel scared, so anxious when D sucks her thumb, because I know she's . . . I understand she has to go through . . . she's got to go on her own, you know, without . . . I'm sorry, she should do it with her husband, and, er, I've just got to clear out of there, you know. And I know it'll be very hard to do, because we keep seeing each other every day, her big blue eyes and her beautiful smile.

MJ: And your murderous jealousy.

Rick: Yes.

MJ: When I said did you remember feeling that way about your mother, you didn't answer me.

Rick: I was alone with my mother . . . in Bournemouth . . . it was really like this . . . it was dark, and a radio programme was on in her room . . . I thought it really made me sad . . . my mother's been . . . she . . . it's so sad . . . I was so lonely . . .

MJ: I think at that moment you felt cast off by your mother, who ultimately is your father's partner, not yours, however bad the marriage.

Rick: I'm jealous of them?

MJ: What do you think?

Rick: Yeah. I think I am.

MJ: You see, your relationship with Mrs D could be potentially helpful to both of you if you can recognize how much she for you is a personification of your mother. I don't mean that your love isn't genuine, but I think it is the love of a child for a mother, a child who's never been able to love a woman properly since, because he does it in a fierce, passionate, possessive, and violently jealous way.

Rick [sad]:   She smiles like my mother used to smile. I know when D's happy, when she's not scared, and I suppose I want to keep things like that.

MJ: You can't bear the thought that you're going to have to give up your mother and face your jealousy. That is what you are expressing in your obsession. Hang on to something that could be precious, never let anything be thrown away. The precious thing is your mother that you love and you must hold on, never let her be free and be with your father, because you will be so murderously jealous. Hold on, hold on, power struggle, you're more important than father, you go on doing it, and with your obsession you never have to learn to know what you're feelings really mean.

Rick: I'm just going to have to be . . . I wish she wouldn't . . . be so nice to everybody else.

MJ: You want her all to yourself.

Rick: Yes. [*Cries.*]

MJ: You may have to stop. [*Pause.*] It's not my intention to upset you, but we now know what the problem is. You're going to need a lot of help to work through it so that you can make a relationship with a woman who you can love as you love your mother but who you don't have to be so murderously jealous towards that you have to break off the relationship.

Rick: You do like me a little bit, don't you?

MJ: You sound as though you can't believe that anybody could know about this destructive side of you and still think you're a nice person. You think I've been sitting here talking to you for a long time . . . that I would be doing it if I didn't think you were worth it?

Rick: No, no . . . I don't think you would.

MJ: Do you want to ask me something before we stop?

Rick: Yes, do you know what I mean by an old rogue?

MJ: It's where we came in, isn't it?

Rick: You understand what I'm saying? [*Pause.*] You know, a Terry Thomas[2] sort of character.

MJ: I don't know what a Terry Thomas sort of character is.

Rick: Bit of a cad, you know, bit of a bounder.

MJ: In your behaviour towards Mrs D?

Rick: No, I wasn't thinking of that. I'm with another man's
wife . . . I think what I'm saying is, if you get a good smack
in the mouth, you realize, shit, I'm out of order, that's what
I'm saying. I think I'm out of order in a lot of areas, and I
thank you very much for being so gentle with me. Thank
you for your love. Thank you, I really do thank you . . . for
not giving me the smack in the mouth sooner . . . how long
do you want me to stay in hospital for? I'm a paranoid
hypochondriac, neurotic, obsessive and hmm . . . I wasn't
shouting at you . . . I wasn't shouting at you. I hope you
know that. You do know that don't you?

MJ: Neurotic, hypochondriac, obsessional, crazy, all these
labels. I think you're someone who is highly sensitive to
rejection. You love your mother desperately, but so like a
child that your jealous possessiveness becomes quite murderous. That's what's wrong with you. What's right with you
is that you have talent and you have a capacity to love. If
you didn't have a capacity to love, you wouldn't feel so
jealous and so murderous. There wouldn't be anything to
feel so murderous about.

Rick: So the answer to that is to just let go of everything, to
become less jealous. If someone wants to dance with my
girlfriend, they can dance with her, is that what it is?

MJ: I think it will be a long time before you're able to deal
with your jealousy. The first thing you need to be aware of
is to know that it's yours. It belongs to you.

* * *

Until the time of this interview, there seemed to be good reason
to hope for a favourable outcome of treatment. In fact, follow-
up information showed an unfavourable one. The following
reflections on Rick's disturbance and the probable reasons for
his deterioration are based on a retrospective study of the
interview, his history, and on material that emerged during his
stay and after discharge.

   This was an emotionally powerful interview. In the discussion afterwards some of the staff, who knew Rick well, felt that
he was demonstrating a mixture of deep, sincere feelings, with
moments of shallow, placatory, ingratiating talk. They felt he

was often providing me with what he thought I wanted, and that he ended the interview with a flourish of false and sentimental gratitude for my so-called gentleness and kindness. I had also sensed the hypocrisy in his final comments and his underlying hostility and cynicism, and so the staff's responses made sense to me. It was clear from the beginning that Rick was conscious of the lack of privacy in the interview ("people observing me very closely"), and one might wonder whether anything genuine could be hoped for at all in such a contrived setting, given a patient with so evident an exhibitionistic character. Nevertheless, neither I nor the staff were in doubt as to the seriousness of some of his statements. For example, the sudden, shocking emergence in fantasy that I was considering him as a candidate for leucotomy had the quality of a brief psychotic outburst. The fact that this led to material about a recurrent adolescent nightmare of being at the mercy of his father further suggested a sudden psychotic transference. However much (or little) reality there may have been in his perception of leucotomy as a treatment for hopelessly obsessional states, the nightmare father was undoubtedly a terrifying internal figure. Its projection onto the external reality of his explosive, irrational, sometimes well-meaning actual father had deeply intensified his underlying view of his father as extremely bad and dangerous.

With hindsight it can be seen how the interview was influenced by the need to deal with a prevailing crisis, namely the affair with Mrs D, and this partly accounts for its confrontational quality. His parting comments, therefore, on "the lesson for today" could, in this context, be justified. Nevertheless, he also seemed to take the lesson seriously. The connection he made between his idealized mother, the serene face of Mrs D, and his repetitive pattern of destructive behaviour with previous girlfriends had the quality of the beginnings of insight—"I've just got to make everything perfect for them and then I get angry with them and angry with myself."

With the exception of the leucotomy fantasy, all the above material may be considered neurotic and understandable in the familiar terms of unresolved oedipal conflicts. However, behind this pattern lies material, the origins and pathogenesis of which are far more primitive and infantile. Freud's formulation that "the ego is first and foremost a body ego" helps to explain Rick's primitive functioning and to understand how he inhabits a borderline area between neurosis and psychosis. Rick's unconscious longing is to remain in a state of permanent ("symbiotic") possession of the idealized mother of his infancy, a powerful image persisting in the present in his inner world, which fuels his intense feelings of jealousy and much of his destructive behaviour. At this level of function his thinking has a space-centred quality characteristic of some schizoid mental processes (see Jackson, 1992). He unconsciously feels himself to be existing inside or outside a maternal space symbolized (by means of the mechanisms of displacement and identification) in a recurring danger situation such as going out of a room, and by hypochondriacal concerns about his own body interior. His "claustrophilic" desires co-exist with claustrophobic and agoraphobic anxieties. Consideration of factors like these may help explain the deep-seated nature of Rick's disorder and his inability to change. His obvious oedipal anxieties have developed on the basis of an early failure to separate from the beloved and idealized mother of his infancy.

Developmentally speaking, the concept of the body-ego denotes how mental life begins in infancy with unintegrated bodily perceptions that only gradually cohere to achieve mental representation and thus acquire direct and symbolic meaning. Eventually, at a more mature level of development, these bodily experiences become objects of reflective thought and patterns of affective relationships. Klein's theoretical extensions of Freud's work, derived from her studies of very young children, opened the way to greater understanding of the early stages of psychological growth. The infant's perceptions of a bodily nature occupy an experiential world of unintegrated parts, processes, and substances that, Klein suggests, pass between an inside and an outside of a vaguely conceived maternal space, long inhabited in the reality of intrauterine life. Out of this early part-object landscape will gradually emerge a sense of a personal body space and an integrated body image.

The thinking of the infant is at first of a magical and omnipotent kind, experience is literal and concrete, and only slowly do the means for symbolic representation evolve. If the pathways of normal development are arrested or weakly established because of difficulties in the mother–infant relationship (of whatever origin), this early level of unintegrated functioning persists. This is a pathogenic state and contributes to a vulnerability to later breakdown of a psychotic type. Such a psychosis may then appear as a breakthrough of persistently unchanged modes of immature thinking that cause impairment or loss of the capacity for symbolic thinking in crucial areas.

Although complex, controversial, and difficult to convey, such concepts have a practical usefulness in the attempt to understand the mental states and preoccupations of many psychotic and borderline individuals. In Rick's case, they helped to elucidate the meaning of some of the bizarre behaviour and thinking alluded to but not taken up in the interview. For example, the phenomenon of extreme retentiveness in the obsessional personality is well known and can take the form of bodily constipation or the more symbolized hoarding and accumulating of objects of personal significance. In a more advanced mental transformation of these bodily desires and part-object relationships, the pathological miser anxiously and triumphantly hoards money or gold. Less common is the prolonged accumulation of partially eaten food in receptacles by a psychotic or deeply obsessional individual who is not demented. More frequently observed obsessional sequences include the "threshold" anxieties that are aroused on entering or leaving a room, or when passing through archways or under ladders (the proverbial explanation for superstition around ladders is a concise illustration of the projection of phantasy onto external reality). Hypochondriacal concerns are also a familiar psychiatric symptom, often regarded as the (hysterical) conversion of anxiety into bodily symptoms, as in cases of dizziness, vertigo, and fears of falling (where there is an absence of organic disease). These may have a more paranoid and pre-psychotic significance if a patient's hypochondriacal preoccupations centre upon dangers perceived to reside within the interior of his bodily space. (The case of Carmen in chapter four illustrates the use of concepts of the "body interior" and "maternal space" in certain instances of psychogenic anorexia.)

Through an understanding of primitive thinking processes, meaning could be attributed to Rick's obsessional retentiveness, scrutiny of waste, concern with unsymbolized body products, and most notably his compulsive, anxious examination of faeces. Other puzzling behaviour also became clearer, like his fear of passing under archways and his excited play with dirt or liquid clay. As his scrutiny of (expelled) waste products gradually lessened, so the partial replacement of this concern by the sucking (incorporative) action of the vacuum-cleaner seemed to make dynamic sense. (For a graphic explanation of these phenomena see Hinshelwood, 1994, pp. 21–24.)

If Rick were ever to be effectively engaged in long-term analytic therapy, he might be offered interpretations about confusion between impulses of love and hate, of failure of normal splitting and differentiation into good and bad, and of unconscious phantasies of destroying his "bad" mother in the passage of thoughts through his mind, which are felt to be happening in his body. Above all, he would need great help to achieve a fully emotional insight into his desperate need to seek reassurance that the idealized mother, who holds out the promise of a blissful symbiotic relationship, should never be lost by exposure to the destructive, vengeful feelings aroused by her crime of loving another person who is not the "infant" Rick himself. This level of integration might eventually be achieved in such a patient through a long and patient working-through of the transference in a formal psychoanalytic treatment.

Rick's preoccupation with smearing clay on his head seems to represent a displaced form of anal masturbation ("rhinoceros in the mud") expressing a manic triumph over a potent, fertilizing father whom he loves and envies but with whom he has never been able to admire or to identify with. He must ignore any good qualities his father may have had because of the intensity of his vengeful hatred of the "combined parents", finding expression, in the smearing behaviour, in part-object terms. Clearly this developmental crisis has been made much more difficult for Rick by his father's psychological limitations, which derived from the father's own early emotional deprivation. Insights such as these might lead to Rick understanding his father more, to a lessening of his need for vengeance, and, ideally, to possible concern for his father and mother reflecting, in Klein's terms, the painful but more realistic developmental level of the depressive position.

In Rick's interview the truly pathogenic level of his destructive feelings remained largely untouched. For the same reasons
it was not possible, within the confines of an interview, to open
up an understanding of his longing to be seen merely as an "old
rogue", the son of another admired, eccentric "old rogue". The
concealed scale of these disturbances helps us to understand
why such an intelligent, talented, and truly likeable man as
Rick should have continued to live a destructive and in many
ways wasted life, despite numerous attempts to change course.
After the interview and ward round, Rick's relationship to Mrs
D became a good deal more normal, but his overall behaviour
continued to be provocative and disruptive. He increasingly
challenged the routines of the ward in a way that disturbed
patients and staff alike, and he proved unamenable to reason
or interpretation. It is interesting to consider that this bout of
disorder was comparable to the one manifested when he was
required to renounce exclusive possession of his mother at the
age of 3, when his troubled parents were compelled to seek the
help of a child analyst.

Follow-up

Eventually, after a nine-month stay on the unit, Rick departed,
pre-empting the discharge he knew was likely to come as a
consequence of his provocative behaviour, which the unit was
realistically no longer prepared to tolerate. With hindsight, it is
likely that Rick had been unable to cope with the loss of his
Primary Nurse, C, and had taken to idealizing Mrs D at the
same time. Censure of his behaviour with Mrs D had revived
profound feelings of anger and loss, which he then enacted
destructively. If this were the case, his departure would represent a failure of the capacity of the unit to contain the most
disturbing of his infantile feelings. Follow-up also revealed that
no permanent psychodynamic change could be claimed. His
obvious oedipal conflicts were based on a deeper and much
more serious unresolved tie to his mother, which involved
primitive splitting and paranoid fears of his father. Because
Rick hovered somewhere between hysteria and psychosis,

transference attachments (which were easily made) rapidly induced unmanageable anxieties and led to acting out. His
responsiveness was therefore deceptive, concealing as it did
extremely serious illness.

He maintained contact after his departure and was offered
regular appointments with a male registrar whom he trusted
and the female nurse who had replaced Nurse C. Over the
following two years, he gradually withdrew from contact with
the unit and embarked upon a career that represented a
further repetitive enactment of his basic conflicts. He made
a sudden sexual relation with a disturbed and emotionally
deprived young woman and appeared to accept responsibility
for the subsequent birth of a male child. This behaviour may
also have been motivated at some level by a reparative wish to
restore a baby to his damaged mother, but however much this
may have been the case, the consequences were disastrous. He
separated from the girlfriend, leaving her to seek the help of the
social services. He attended the hospital's family therapy clinic
with her for several sessions, only to disengage himself. His
hypochondriacal and obsessive–compulsive symptoms, which
had receded dramatically during his stay on the unit, revived,
and this led to an attempt to treat him with cognitive and
behavioural therapy. This was initially helpful, but he soon lost
any gains and was eventually considered to be consuming
valuable psychiatric resources to little or no avail. He was
offered supportive contact, which he declined, thus joining the
ranks of the large group of borderline patients who achieve
little or no lasting benefit from treatment or who break off
treatment prematurely even when they are benefiting from it.

Even though the therapeutic milieu did not meet Rick's
extreme needs, his fate raises the question of the amount of
time that is wasted trying to help such patients with methods
that, for whatever reasons, do not try, or fail to reach, the
deeper levels of disturbance that are responsible for their psychiatric condition. This is not to say that all such patients will
benefit from psychoanalytic assessment or long-term psychotherapy (although this may eventually prove to be the case to
an extent that is hitherto unappreciated), but, rather, that a
thorough grasp of the meaning of the patient's underlying

disturbance is a treatment component of the greatest importance. Thinking psychodynamically in this way can, in an appropriate setting, facilitate not only an understanding but an explanation of the behaviour and experience of complex, loving, and highly destructive characters such as Rick. Duly informed, the clinician can determine an appropriate treatment less ambiguously, and with greater understanding of its consequences.

CHAPTER FOUR

Catatonia 1:
psychotic anorexia

C atatonia is the term used to describe a disorder, the main feature of which is a recurrence of episodes of catalepsy. The actual term was first used in a psychiatric context by Kahlbaum in 1874 in a classic monograph entitled "The Tension Insanity" (Johnson, 1993). Catalepsy is a state of extreme physical immobility and mutism, lasting for minutes or hours at a time. A characteristic of catalepsy is the spontaneous adoption of postures, perhaps statuesque or stereotyped, and the automatic maintenance of bodily positions imposed by the examiner. Cataleptic phenomena may also include trance or stupor. The origin of catalepsy can be psychogenic (as in hypnotic suggestion), pharmacogenic (induced by certain drugs, including neuroleptics), or organic (neurological disease such as encephalitis lethargica).

The association of catalepsy with schizophrenic features led to the diagnostic category of catatonic schizophrenia (Bleuler, 1950) and later to hopes that such patients might respond to psychoanalytic psychotherapy (Rosen, 1953). Initial optimism proved unjustified, and it was found that most attacks could be cut short by electro-shock treatment, although recurrence was

usual. Catatonic schizophrenia was once commonly encountered in psychiatric practice and is now relatively rare. This is
probably due to the powerful symptom-reducing capability of
neuroleptic drugs and an increasing preference by clinicians
for more sophisticated diagnoses. Nevertheless, catatonia remains a common presenting problem and challenges the psychiatrist's skills in evaluating organic and psychogenic factors
in each individual case.

Inhibition of eating may occur in psychotic conditions such
as severe depression, or in association with a paranoid belief
that food is poisoned. In other cases it may reflect underlying
delusions about food, eating, and the body that have something
in common with the unconscious phantasies and delusional
perception of the body image of non-psychotic patients suffering from severe anorexia nervosa.

The first case in this chapter is that of a young woman who
suffered from a recurrent psychotic illness marked by catatonic
immobility, mutism, confusion, thought disorder, and episodic
anorexia. The second patient suffered from anorexia nervosa,
with characteristic preoccupations with weight gain and with
body size and shape. The life-threatening nature of the self-
starvation of the severe anorexic and the tenacity of delusional
beliefs about the body and its interior might suggest that
"anorexia psychosa" would be a more appropriate descriptive
term.

CARMEN

Carmen, a 28-year-old, dark-haired woman from a Spanish-
speaking country, was admitted in an acute psychotic state
characterized by extreme agitation and confusion. During the
previous week she had become inaccessible, with episodes of
postural immobility, mutism, weeping, and screaming. The
admission was her fourth since the onset of a remitting schizophrenic illness at the age of 16. In each of her breakdowns she
had exhibited similar symptoms, including marked catatonic
and paranoid features, and had recovered within weeks after
electro-shock and/or neuroleptic medication. Carmen had

complained that she could see black hair beginning to appear on her face, and that people on the other side of the street were noticing this sinister change. These delusional symptoms were followed by confusion, withdrawal, and the behaviour that led to her admission. During her first few days on the ward, little contact was made. She would not eat voluntarily and had to be fed with a spoon. Moderate doses of neuroleptic medication were administered, and she gradually emerged from her withdrawal. She went on to return to an apparently normal mental state. She talked about the strains of recent weeks, including how she believed her work-mates had been unfriendly to her, and how her family were pressing her to marry her fiancé too quickly. She wanted to marry but did not feel safe about doing so, and did not know why. The main pressure, she felt, came from her mother who was convinced that only a religious exorcism and marriage would cure her daughter (the family had emigrated when Carmen was 9 years old, and her mother's ideas were compatible with her indigenous culture). In family interviews, the mother displayed over-possessive behaviour towards her daughter, answering for her and making it difficult for her to say or think anything for herself. The father, ten years younger than his wife, seemed good-natured but passive. Carmen's siblings, an older brother, a brother a year younger, and a sister four years older, participated normally in the interviews.

Carmen's view of her current conflicts appeared rational enough, until an unstructured interview took place, when a quite different picture emerged. She spoke of the extent of her bizarre feelings during this and previous breakdowns. On these occasions she would feel unutterably slow and lifeless, sometimes unable to move or talk. It frightened her to think of it. A few weeks earlier she had learned of the death of a relative and was convinced it was her younger brother, whom she also knew to be alive and well, and the fluctuating state of confusion alarmed her. She felt so upset that she could not go to work, believing her work-mates would be so disturbed by her state that they would break down and themselves have to go off work. She was confused and frightened on the ward: she had wept a little and believed some of the nurses had burst into tears in response to this display of emotion. To let me know of her experiences would, she insisted, upset and anger me. Exploration of the delusional experience of her brother's death revealed a long-standing preoccupation with the subject of death. An earlier breakdown had occurred when she saw a corpse in a coffin in a church and believed that it was her younger brother. It was not possible to know whether seeing the corpse was an actual event, but her preoccupation with her younger brother was evident. She thought that her fiancé was having a sexual affair with her mother, but was confused because sometimes she thought her fiancé was her brother. In this fantasy concerning three couples in intimate relationship, her brother, fiancé, and father were not securely differentiated, and she seems to have been classifying them in respect of one thing that they have in common, namely intimate access to her mother or herself. Her suspicion that her younger brother was her mother's sexual partner may have been facilitated by the fact of the father being so much younger than the mother.

She thought that her first breakdown had occurred because she fell in love with a young man of whom her parents disapproved. Later enquiries left little doubt that this relationship was delusional in nature. Before her first breakdown, she had shown no sign of psychological disturbance, and her mother had appreciated her quiet and compliant nature, remarking, perhaps significantly, that as a baby Carmen was the only child who gave no trouble. She rarely cried and seemed quite untroubled by the arrival of her two younger siblings. After some weeks it was possible to record the following initial formulation:

"Carmen is suffering from a recurrent psychotic illness with paranoid, catatonic, and confusional features and associated severe disturbance of her sense of identity. It is likely that each breakdown was precipitated by efforts to establish emotional intimacy following the emergence of more mature sexual wishes. These led to confusion and anxiety, because they exist in conflict with deep, unresolved infantile attachments to her mother and jealousy of the one-year-younger brother. She fears that her aggressive feelings are omnipotently destructive, and projective mechanisms underlie the paranoid features.

Attempts to escape from her infantile identification with her mother have given rise to mild hypomanic periods. The impairment of ego functions in her psychotic periods leads to a failure of reality testing and an inability to differentiate memory from perception (with resultant mis-identifications). Similarly, past and present, internal and external reality, and self and other are confused. The most satisfactory diagnosis at present is probably schizo-affective psychosis with catatonic features."

The associated treatment plan included:

"Family work to explore the nature of the mother's influence, and help her become less possessive. We are probably dealing with a mutual symbiotic attachment in which the patient is unconsciously gratified by having her mother continue to treat her as an infant. Containment in the therapeutic milieu should help her to explore feelings and test the boundaries of her identity, and help correct her omnipotent thinking. Individual psychotherapy may be possible before too long, and her quick response to neuroleptics suggests that they will be helpful if future crises cannot be contained verbally."

Carmen made slow but steady progress. A Spanish-speaking psychiatrist saw her mother and helped her to understand the situation more fully, and the mother gave up her idea of exorcism. He also talked to Carmen in her mother tongue during a period of disturbance, but was unable to make contact. In a weekly psychotherapy session Carmen disclosed intensely aggressive feelings towards her mother and began to recognize feelings of guilt and jealousy towards her younger brother. Her periods of confusion and inaccessibility decreased, and she spoke of feeling like a robot and wanting to burn or electrocute herself by putting her fingers in an electrical socket. At times she seemed to be experiencing auditory hallucinations.

She had a past history of periods of extreme dietary restriction, in which she would suddenly adopt strict vegetarian practice. Her explanation was: "When you love somebody, you must stop eating meat or the earth will swallow you up!" She reported dreams, including some in which the earth opened up as a result of volcanic explosions. She made fragmentary allusions to a belief that she had been pregnant for a long time, by oral means. As she became more integrated, so her family urged her to leave the hospital and get married, and after six months she discharged herself. She remained on a moderate dose of anti-psychotic medication, and although her symptoms had receded, her departure was viewed by the psychiatric team as a "flight into health", and further disturbance was predicted.

She married, attended as an out-patient, appeared stable, and then a year later suddenly broke down and was re-admitted with the same symptoms as before. She refused all food and had to be spoon-fed. Her husband and parents were urged to remove any pressure on her to become "normal", and a new treatment plan was formulated based on intensive exploration of her deeper psychopathology, avoiding the use of medication altogether, if possible. I conducted four exploratory interviews with her in ten days, the last three of which were recorded on videotape. In the first meeting, Carmen was catatonic and mute, her eyes firmly closed. She was being spoon-fed on the ward, and some milk, which she had held in her mouth, escaped in a dribble. I spoke to her on the assumption that she could hear me, and maybe understand me. I told her I would see her the following day and that our meetings were to be videotaped. I did not seek her consent for this until later, when she had become able to consider it. Each of the interviews lasted about 30 minutes.

First interview

Carmen is brought to the interview in a wheelchair in a catatonic state, with one arm outstretched. Her eyes are, unusually, open, and she is blinking quite rapidly. Her primary nurse holds her hand.

MJ: Today you want to keep your eyes open. [*Pause.*] Do you think you remember anything about what I said yesterday?

[*Pause.*] Carmen, your eyes are open. Can you put your arm down now? I think your arm must be getting tired.

MJ touches Carmen's arm lightly: it descends. Carmen gives an anguished cry.

MJ: You make a sound when I move your arm, Carmen.

Gently touches Carmen's arm. Carmen cries out.

MJ: Like that. I think you're afraid of moving, Carmen. [*Pause.*] We want you to try to think and listen, but we know you're afraid, and we saw yesterday how you're afraid of crying, too. Now what we're doing at the moment is that we're taking some photographs of you so that when you get better, you can see them. [*Pause.*] Are you crying some more? [*Pause.*] You're trying hard to stop yourself from crying, I think. It's safe to cry, really. I don't think you think it's safe to cry, but it is safe to cry, and it would make you feel better if you can.

Muffled speech, in which Carmen seems to say: "Better" . . .

MJ: Yes, better.

Second interview
(three days later)

The interview has begun. Carmen is less catatonic and is beginning to be able to speak more clearly. She has just said the word "alright".

MJ: You say alright Carmen; what is alright? [*Pause.*] I think you know where we are. I think you know what's going on. I think you know who it is talking to you, and I think you know who it is who is sitting next to you. But I think you're trying hard not to know what's really happening.

. . . *Pause. Carmen sighs heavily.*

MJ: We're making a film of our meeting, because we think it's going to help you. We can show it to you some time later, when we think it will help you. But in order for us to help you, you need to try to help us. You need to try to help me

understand you. You see, I think you are capable of thinking, and you are also capable of talking, and I think there's a
part of you that is trying to prevent you, so that you shan't
be afraid.

. . . Pause. Carmen swallows hard.

MJ: When you swallowed just then, I think you may have
tried to swallow your words. The words you were going to
speak in reply to what I am saying. [*Pause.*] I think perhaps
you can even remember what happened when we last met in
here.

Carmen: I was in a state.

MJ: You were in a state.

Third interview
(three days later)

Carmen is now responding.

MJ: Can you tell us how you've been feeling? How are you
feeling now?

Carmen: I'm feeling a bit better . . . than I was.

. . . Pause . . .

MJ: What do you remember of the last time we talked?

Carmen: I've been leaving the thoughts to you . . . to . . .

MJ: You've been leaving the thoughts to me. Can you say a
little more about that?

Carmen: Somehow I wasn't able to . . . to find out . . .

. . . Pause . . .

MJ: Unable to find out what?

Carmen: What exactly . . . has been . . . [*Pause.*] . . . taking
place.

MJ: If you're leaving the thoughts to me, then it would follow
that it wouldn't be possible for you to know what was taking
place. I might be able to have some idea, but if you weren't

thinking yourself, you couldn't possibly have any idea, could you?

. . . *Pause* . . .

Carmen: Roughly, I . . . [*sighs*] . . . I know.

MJ: Roughly, you . . . ?

Carmen: I know . . .

MJ: Roughly, you know.

Carmen: What has been happening.

MJ: Roughly you know what has been happening.

Carmen: Yes.

Fourth interview (five days later)

Carmen's catatonia has significantly receded. She now seems merely slowed up in her mental and physical functioning. On the basis of previous explorations, the interviewer asks her about her past experiences of immobility and suggests that she might have been holding aggressive, angry feelings in check.

Carmen: Yes, partly it is anger.

MJ: It's partly anger. [*Pause.*] So now we know that one of the things you need to start thinking about so that you'll be able to recognize it and understand it, and to stand it, is your anger. You behave as though for you to be angry is very frightening.

Carmen: Well . . . some of the tension is . . . anger.

MJ: Some of the what?

Carmen: It's the tension . . .

MJ: Some of the tension is . . . what?

Carmen: Turns to anger.

MJ: The tension turns to anger. Does that not mean that the tension could turn into anger if you couldn't stop it?

. . . *Pause* . . .

Carmen: That's if you can stop it.

MJ: If you can stop it turning into anger.

Carmen: Yes . . .

MJ: If you can stop the anger, then you only feel the tension that comes with the anger. But you're afraid that the tension would turn into anger, because if the tension turned into anger, it must just turn into action, and you might do some damage.

Carmen: Well . . . I might.

* * *

In the first interview, I did all the talking. I felt that silence, however valuable under some circumstances, was not appropriate here. By speaking, I hoped I might be able to at least communicate to Carmen: "I am here, I am not going to harm you and I want to understand you." In attempting to grasp what she was experiencing, I had little to guide me save a belief that she was highly anxious and defending against some inner terror, possibly associated with the delusion of oral pregnancy. I thought that the setting of the audiovisual suite was probably affecting her, and that I might seem threatening to her. I had no way of finding out, as she was completely mute. Only her breathing, eyes blinking, and swallowing conveyed signs of activity. My suggestion that her blinking was a way of avoiding crying was a guess and, in retrospect, probably wrong. It was more likely to be, like her immobility, an expression of withdrawal from the external world (which was not properly differentiated from her inner world of phantasy). My comment in the next interview regarding the swallowing was probably correct in the light of the unswallowed milk of our earlier meeting, and the fact that she uttered her first clear words for days. I felt she was taking in what I said, and I spelled out our responsibilities. I thought that she was trying not to think, because if she did, she might realize what she was feeling, which would be frightening. She was trying to force me to do the thinking she needed to do for herself. She remembered this in the next session. I felt this was an expression of her own thinking, not a regurgitation of my words. Carmen was now talking and beginning to feed herself on the ward. By the final interview, she was behaving comparatively normally without medication. Although perplexed and strained, she was able to think clearly and appeared to confirm my conjecture that her catatonic immobility served the defensive function of protecting her against the threat of an outburst of aggression. Her statement that she somehow knew what was going on but was unable to find out seemed to refer to a conflictual, internal dynamic in which her capacity to think and know was being obstructed.

Subsequent brief periods of catatonic immobility and withdrawal attested to the fact that she remained a seriously disturbed young woman. Nevertheless, her improvement was maintained, and the exploratory interviews were terminated. A new treatment plan was started, combining an extended stay in the milieu, couple interviews with her husband, and individual psychotherapy. A psychotherapeutic approach had brought her out of her acute catatonia, but, as was so often the case, the unit did not have the resources to provide her with the long-term individual psychotherapy that she seemed to need. Low-dose anti-psychotic medication was resumed, to sustain contact, and time-limited psychotherapy on a supportive and exploratory basis was undertaken by a female registrar for 33 sessions over six months. Carmen gradually divulged her psychotic thoughts and confusions, and the nature of the pregnancy delusion underlying her catatonic states became more clear. She recalled many childhood memories and recognized her life-long jealousy of her younger brother, of whom she was deeply fond, but whom she had idealized. She acknowledged the value of the couple interviews and the understanding attitude of the ward staff. Her mother had, meanwhile, become less possessive. Carmen's relation to her passive father became more alive, and her sexual relation with her husband improved. Carmen also revealed in her psychotherapy something she called her "funny ideas". In her pregnancy delusion, for example, she could tell that the baby inside her was a boy, because he had black hair, but she did not know whether he was alive or dead. Also, her recurring fear of eating made her afraid of being seen eating by other patients. She often complained of severe toothache, but examination revealed no abnormality, and the complaint subsided. She spoke of feeling extremely strange, unable to understand her thoughts, and imagined that she was probably a man rather than a woman. This last delusion seemed to be linked to unconscious wishes to be her envied brother. It also revealed a failure in the development of that healthy identification with her father which helps a little girl transcend her primary identification with her mother—a failure that can undermine a sense of gender identity. The adult Carmen was trapped in a primary identification with her mother, which had not evolved any further. In this identification she was solely female. In her partial identification with her father, she experienced the superimposition of unassimilated masculine wishes. Both developmental phases had foundered, leaving Carmen without a secure female identity.

Four months into her individual psychotherapy, Carmen's therapist became pregnant. The patient then became pregnant in the minimum time possible. The curious situation had now arisen of a patient with a waning delusion of pregnancy, now pregnant, with a pregnant psychotherapist. Progress in the therapy ground swiftly to a halt. Although the staff were inclined to regard this as an act of sabotage, it seems possible that there was an element of re-enactment in connection with her childhood feelings about her mother's pregnancy. To imitate her therapist could signify rivalry and perhaps more deeply hostility towards a new sibling rival. Possessing a baby may also have indicated an unconscious reparative motive towards her mother. Carmen's therapist concluded her six months' stay on the ward, and it was decided that it would not help Carmen to begin again with another registrar for a further six months. Yet again there was no-one else available to provide the long-term therapy that she needed, and the treatment plan was revised to provide supportive contact from her primary nurse (who remained available to her) and from subsequent ward registrars. Three months later she left hospital and attended first as a day-patient, and soon as an out-patient. She was extremely anxious about the safety of her baby, and she reported nightmare-like dreams that seemed to express a terror that the baby would die. These included witnessing a huge submarine explosion, a baby in a box suffocating, and a baby close to death attached to a life-support machine. Her "funny thoughts" seemed to return, as did her anxieties about eating. Explaining these, she said, "I have to starve the baby!" then, "I have to starve *for* the baby!" These disturbances revealed more of her poor sense of identity and failure to resolve her infantile dependent tie to her mother. By now, sufficient evidence had accumulated to suggest that Carmen was threatened by a pattern of unconscious phantasies that led her to have to avoid acknowledgement of nutritional need and dependency on a primary object (representative of the mother of infancy) or of accepting a fully female role for herself. These two possibilities created dread that she would no longer feel herself to be her familiar self, but would become identified with:

a. a dangerous baby, endangered by a retaliatory, dangerous mother (the baby will destroy the mother with sucking and biting, and share the same fate); both baby and mother need to be protected from this, and only total control of eating can, in Carmen's mind, achieve this ("starve the baby . . . starve for the baby");

b. a menstruating female who can therefore become pregnant; this brings the dread that she will become a mother with a dangerous baby inside her, a baby felt to possess her own infantile biting and sucking impulses (cf. Rey, 1994).[1]

In cases unlike Carmen where bulimia accompanies anorexia or appears in the apparent absence of anorexia, one phantasy in particular may find expression in the form of a breakthrough of the impulses of a greedy baby that seeks to devour the mother, as though the only way to acquire anything good is to concretely "get inside" her. A process of mental (and physical) gorging and evacuating can then be repeated obsessionally, which may be understood dynamically as a phantasy of endlessly doing damage and then repairing it. This is similar to the obsession of Freud's "Rat Man", where the constant undoing was expressed in a more symbolic, less concrete form. Such complex behaviour derives from a failure to differentiate partial objects and process that are felt to be the same (cf. Segal, 1981). This form of understanding can illuminate many features of certain eating disorders. In the long-term psychotherapy of these patients, the fate of the therapist's "food for thought" becomes the object of interest. In Carmen's case, a full working-through of her unconscious conflicts did not take place, but important changes did occur. She relinquished her passive–aggressive dependency on her mother, a process that was helped by marital and family interviews. Her negative feelings towards her therapist as a sustaining figure found some expression, until the time of the pregnancy and the therapist's departure. Carmen's prompt pregnancy—most likely a response to the loss of her pregnant therapist—seemed also to be a re-enactment of her own displacement by her brother in the form of an identification with the mother–therapist. A reparative wish to replace a baby that she had in phantasy devoured or destroyed may have been also present, reflected in her insistence that loving required the renunciation of meat-eating, and the risk of being swallowed by the earth (mother). In the case of Susanna (the second case cited in this chapter), who appeared to suffer less severely than Carmen, psychotherapy uncovered hitherto hidden sadomasochistic character traits that acted in part as defences against psychosis. This illustrates how near to psychosis severe anorexia can be, whilst often remaining far less overt.

Rey (1994) has described how thought elements in a schizoid person like Carmen have a concrete, space-centred quality, which Freud identified as an essential feature of the unconscious system—the representation of *things* as opposed to *words*. Rey cites the case of a catatonic patient who explained that she had to remain immobile because her dead father was inside her, and she had to protect him from the dangers of collision if she moved. Such pathology may not be so uncommon. A middle-aged woman spent years trying to convince doctors that the dirt she believed she could see under her fingernails was evidence that her baby, in reality dead many years ago, was inside her body, decomposing and exuding through her fingers. Concrete spatial delusions of this kind are not unfamiliar to general psychiatrists. In Carmen's case, catatonic immobility protected her against the dreaded consequences of her aggressive impulses. Her shifting identifications suggested that at times it was her younger brother, felt as a real baby inside her, whom she had to protect. She feared that if she moved, she would kill him. In the light of this fear, her earlier and apparently suicidal wish—to put her fingers into electric sockets—may not have been suicidal. Self-damaging behaviour can often be an attempt to escape from deperson- alization into feeling more real (Hale & Campbell, 1991). If Carmen's unconscious phantasies about her brother were op- erational, as is likely, at the time she received electro-shock treatment, which "cured" her depression, the wish to electro- cute herself may have represented an unconscious attempt to bring life to the brother, felt to be dead or dying inside her. Long-term psychoanalytic psychotherapy would be required to verify a hypothesis of this type.

Follow-up

Carmen's pregnancy proceeded normally. A slow labour neces- sitated a Caesarean section, and she was delivered of a healthy baby girl. She felt unable to feed the baby, and with her mother's help bottle-feeding was established. The infant devel- oped satisfactorily, and the patient continued to attend hospital monthly.

All medication was discontinued, and two years later she had a second daughter, also by Caesarean section. She brought her children to meet the ward staff and reported that she was happy with her life and the role of mother. She was grateful for the assistance she had received but preferred not be reminded of her "funny ideas" and expressed no need of further psy- chotherapeutic help. Attendance at the hospital was duly terminated. Her general practitioner was contacted two years later (six years after discharge) and reported that he saw Carmen when she brought the children along with the "usual minor childhood ailments". Her second daughter had had temporary feeding problems, but he had no reason to think that they were anything other than a well-functioning family. A final enquiry 12 years after discharge revealed that there were no reports of further disturbance.

Carmen's outcome, though impressive, is clearly not per- fect. Although she achieved greatly increased mental integra- tion, there is no reason to believe that she has worked through all her conflicts sufficiently to guarantee reliable stability in the future. We do not know how she would have coped with a male child, or how her personal relationships have evolved. Given the complexity and depth of Carmen's problems, it is perhaps obvious how unrealistic it is to speak of "cure" of psychotic patients by psychotherapeutic (or any other) means unless the criteria used are strictly defined (see Cullberg, 1991). Carmen was and remains a vulnerable personality. Nevertheless, her psychoanalytically oriented treatment provided her with crucial assistance. Other treatments—pharmacological, psychological, behavioural, and social—contributed to the favourable outcome, but the decisive factor in her improvement was the combination of exploratory interviews and individual psychotherapy. Profound levels of disturbance were addressed and partly resolved. Unconscious phantasies affecting her sense of identity became more conscious and so freed her normal, non-psychotic self from their overwhelming influence. And, for the first time, she became able to think about her experiences. Her ultimate disinclination to pursue further psychotherapeutic exploration indicates a defensive preference to forget, but by that time it is likely that sufficient integration had occurred to maintain a durable, more symbolic level of functioning.

SUSANNA

The psychopathology of Carmen's disturbed body-image may be compared with a lesser degree of disturbance in Susanna, 30, who came from a very chaotic family. Intense rivalry existed between her six younger siblings, in particular between Susanna and a sister one year younger, who was her father's favourite. Her father exercised tyrannical rule. His depressed, inadequate wife took refuge in alcohol, leaving Susanna to look after each new baby. In her adolescence Susanna became disturbed, abused drugs, cut herself, and adopted an anorexic–bulimic pattern. Her disturbance appeared to go unnoticed by her family. She married a man who ill-treated her; she then left him, to train as a teacher. Her intelligence and capacity to remain fairly stable over prolonged periods enabled her to cope. However, her anorexia worsened, and at the age of 26 she was admitted to an anorexia unit for six months. Behavioural methods, re-feeding and group psychotherapy brought some improvement, but her symptoms eventually returned. An exploratory interview was requested and undertaken. The following extract illustrates Susanna's feelings about her body, in particular its shape and size.

Susanna has been talking about her failed marriage and her longing to form a good relationship with a man.

MJ: You want to get close to a man. What does that mean regarding the wish, say, to get married and have children? Where does that come in your mind?

. . . *Pause* . . .

Susanna: I don't know about getting married again. I just know I'd like to have a close loving relationship.

. . . *Pause* . . .

MJ: That's the first part of my question . . . you said nothing about having children.

Susanna: Mm . . . I used to obsess about it. Now, funnily enough, I talked to my mother one day quite recently, and I said, because my niece is due to have a baby this week, she's only 20, I said something to my mother about, you know I'm sorry I've never given you any grandchildren. And she said, I could never imagine you with children. Somehow it's sort of eased the load off me now, I don't think about it.

MJ: You don't have to worry about her disapproval of that. Other things, perhaps, but not that.

Susanna: Yes.

MJ: What was the obsessing about?

Susanna: The fact that I'm getting on in years and I haven't got many more left when I could get pregnant.

MJ: But what did the thought mean about having children? Did it mean you wanted to have them?

Susanna: I don't think I do, really. I don't think I could cope with children.

MJ: Did you ever think you wanted them?

Susanna: Yes, but I think it was an obsession.

MJ: What's an "obsession"?

Susanna: Well, extreme thoughts again.

MJ: Extreme thoughts? Could you say a bit more?

Susanna: Well, just going through a period when that was all I could think about, you know. Meeting somebody and having a child.

MJ: I see, that was really very important to you at some stage earlier in your life?

Susanna: I have been pregnant once, but I had a miscarriage. It still surprises me that . . . I was very sick at the time. I was drinking very heavily, and I was really surprised that I loved the changes in my body. I loved it, and yet I had, you know, extreme thoughts about my shape and everything, even at that time.

MJ: What were the extreme thoughts when you were pregnant?

Susanna: Well, I was just drinking and not eating at all. I loved the changes in my body, but I was just drinking and not eating at all . . . because I was still just wanting to be very, very thin.

MJ: What was it that you couldn't stand that made it so essential for you to be very, very thin?

Susanna: I just can't stand the feeling of fullness. My stomach seems to swell up.

MJ: Can you see it swell when you look?

Susanna: Well, I think I can. I see my stomach in the mirror, and it really does look awful.

MJ: Can you say something more about what it looks like that's so awful?

Susanna: It's like I'm pregnant, it's a horrible sight.

MJ: But when you actually were pregnant?

Susanna: Oh, I liked it.

MJ: You liked that, but it would be a real pregnancy, different from the awful body you see in the mirror . . .

Susanna: Yes. There'd be a reason for my body getting bigger.

MJ: Whereas for the other there would be no reason?

Susanna: No.

* * *

Although Susanna is not clinically psychotic, she has, like Carmen, a deeply disturbed sense of identity. She is threatened by an unconscious phantasy of being her own, endangered pregnant mother, an identification facilitated by her childhood displacement by six younger siblings. She dreads being trapped in this phantasy pregnancy because she believes it would become a permanent reality.[2] This dread exists alongside a normal feminine wish for a real baby, and the totally different nature of her perceptions of her body image in each instance is unusually clear. Whereas Susanna actively recognizes her state to be abnormal, can see no reason for it, and is sane enough to remain inquisitive about it, Carmen is engulfed by psychotic phantasies of a dangerous and endangered mother and baby when she is in a psychotic state. Her delusions then become her reality. Both cases merited psychotherapy and made good progress. Susanna, less ill, needed no hospitalization and was an out-patient for twice-weekly psychotherapy. She proved to be an extremely difficult therapeutic proposition, revealing more varied characterological disturbance than her presenting anorexia, and at one point she passed through a period of near-psychotic disintegration. She had the good fortune to have a psychotherapist who persisted with her, and after five years she achieved considerable stability. It is worth emphasizing that severe psychopathology per se is no indication of a bad prognosis for psychotherapy. Both Susanna and Carmen suffered severely, but each possessed a reasonable amount of healthy functioning in the normal part of their personality. This fact is often a far more accurate and reliable guide to future outcome than diagnosis. Similarly, a patient's capacity to make use of psychotherapy may be gauged by the degree of contact achieved with an experienced interviewer during an assessment.

CHAPTER FIVE

Catatonia 2:
imitation of Christ

DAVID

D
avid, a trainee priest, was 25 when the exploratory
interview to be described was conducted. He had
broken down two years earlier with a schizophrenic
illness and was treated with ECT and a maintenance dose of
anti-psychotic medication, which his mother supervised. Some
months after his discharge from hospital, his mother went
away for a fortnight, and David failed to take his medication. As
a result, he relapsed into an acute catatonic state. Mute, immobile, refusing food, and demonstrating automatic obedience,
maintenance of imposed position of limbs, and the "waxy flexibility" typical of catatonia, he was admitted to his local
hospital as an emergency. After observation and intra-gastric
feeding, he was again treated with ECT and eventually emerged
somewhat from his state of withdrawal. Attempts were then
made to encourage him to talk about his experiences, but they
were unsuccessful. He showed no emotion apart from smiling
in what seemed to be a quite inappropriate way and demonstrated many characteristic symptoms of schizophrenia,

117

including listening to hallucinatory voices. When questioned, he would say he was quite happy, but his train of speech was regularly interrupted by thought-blocking. He disclosed a fear that his thoughts were being broadcast and that they could be heard by others.

A more detailed study of the events leading up to his first breakdown revealed a complex background of psychological disturbance long antedating his first breakdown. He was the second of ten children of an apparently happy, comparatively liberal Roman Catholic family. He had a particularly warm and close relation with his mother and a brother who was one year younger. Although never close to his rather authoritarian father, relations seemed reasonable. A quiet but sociable child, David surprised his family early in adolescence by announcing that he wanted to be a priest. He was accepted for training and acquired a theology degree, but his anxieties and a tendency to withdraw into himself concerned his teachers enough for them to suggest psychological counselling. Toward the end of David's training as a priest his father was murdered by armed robbers in an attack on a large supermarket where he worked as a security guard. Subsequently, David became deeply preoccupied by a coming visit of the Pope to London. He was eventually advised by his tutors to take a year off college and to reconsider his choice of a religious career, due to the obvious turmoil and confusion he was suffering. He returned home extremely withdrawn and took to spending hours in a penitential posture in front of a religious picture. This led to his first referral for psychiatric treatment. The acute relapse during his mother's subsequent absence produced similar behaviour, in retrospect recognizable as the stereotyped posturing of catatonia. It extended to long periods of lying immobile in a crucifixion position. A request was received on the unit for him to be assessed for his suitability for psychotherapy. Shortly before the interview, he had disclosed a guilty secret to the referring psychiatrist. He believed that during the visit to London of the Pope he had stolen the crucifix that hung round the Pope's neck. This theft had provided him with special access to Our Lady, the Virgin Mary. At the time of the interview, he had been stabilized on a moderate dose of anti-psychotic medication.

Interview

MJ: Hello, I'm Dr Jackson. I understand from Dr B something of your trouble, and our aim today is to see if we can help you and if so, in what way. How are you feeling?

David: I feel fine at the moment.

MJ: Mm. Can you tell me what you're thinking?

David: I was just thinking what this is all about. Why am I so special that I should be chosen to take part in this?

MJ: Can you tell me your thought about being so special that you were chosen for this?

David: I thought it might be to do with something I'd said before . . . about my problem . . . I heard voices.

MJ: You thought the doctors would think that that would make you in some ways an unusual sort of person?

David: Yes. I don't think it's really that unusual. I think it's quite normal.

MJ: What does hearing voices mean for you?

David: It's just an experience of prayer . . . during prayer I'm in communion with other people. Because of that I hear one or two words now and again. That's all. Things like . . . "clumsy".

MJ: "Clumsy."

David: "Spoilt brat" [*laughs*].

MJ: "Spoilt brat."

David: Yes.

MJ: What else?

David: "Exceedingly happy."

MJ: "Exceedingly happy?"

David: Yes.

MJ: Where do the voices come from? Do you recognize the people who are producing the voices?

David: Yes, I do. Well, it's not really who they are or what they

say that matters. It's the help they give. They're in communion with me, and because of that they're helping me.

MJ: The voices are helpful.

David: Yes.

MJ: Does it help to hear someone say "you spoilt brat?"

David: Yes, because it makes me check myself and discipline
myself.

MJ: Yes, I see. And what is the evidence for you being a spoilt
brat? Are you a spoilt brat?

David: Yes, spiritually . . . because we're all sinners, and it's
just . . . something . . . I said or did.

MJ: Something that you said or did. Something you can recall?

David: I can't recall it now.

MJ: What sort of person would usually be addressed as a
spoilt brat?

David: I am.

MJ: Yes, but how old are you?

David: Twenty-five.

MJ: Twenty-five. What would be the age of a person who's
being addressed as a spoilt brat? Twenty-five? Or is perhaps
"spoilt brat" a term that would be more addressed to a child,
rather than to a grown-up man of twenty-five?

David: Yes, but we're all children of God.

MJ: Yes . . . I see. You're saying there are two sorts of
children, the children of God, and the children of man,
of parents—but adults, too, are children in that they are
children of God.

David: Yes, but children are still the children of God, too.

MJ: Mm: there are children of mothers and fathers, with
brothers and sisters, and children who can be children of
God and when they grow up they can be children of God,
too. Two realities. Children of parents, whom the parents
might call spoilt brats, and children of God that people

might call sinners as some people have been saying you are. Would you say it was fair to put it that way?

David: Yes.

MJ: Can you identify who they are who've called you a sinner?

David: It's the priest. In our town.

MJ: You have been to him for confession?

David: Yes.

MJ: And does that help?

David: Yes. It helps because my sins are forgiven. The priest can do that by the power of God. It helps me pray and love God more.

MJ: I see. You confess your sinfulness and your sins; the priest, then, being able to minister the power of God, helps you be forgiven, and then you are more able to pray.

David: Yes. There's a special grace from the confession that gives you help to pray and to love God more.

MJ: I see. So, the idea, if I understand you correctly, is that you'll find yourself in a state of grace, and you'll then be closer to the love of God. Now what sort of state is that, where prayer would be leading to? To put it in perhaps a crude way, what would your ambition be if your prayer was most effective?

David: Union with God.

MJ: Can you describe what that state would be?

David: The highest form would be contemplation, I suppose, meditation or contemplation.

MJ: The highest form. What would that involve?

David: I'd be praying all the time.

MJ: Twenty-four hours a day?

David: Except when I was asleep.

MJ: What would be the content and nature of your prayer?

David: It could be very simple. [Pause.] Repeating a mantra, something like that.

MJ: I see. Now, could you tell me a little about your sins, your actual sins? It's a private matter for the confessional, I know, but if I were in the confessional, what sort of thing might I be hearing about?

David: You'd be hearing my faults. I can't tell you them, because it's private.

MJ: Yes, it's private, and I've no wish to invade your privacy, but perhaps we might also think about why it is important to you that it has to remain private.

David: I feel there's a difference between psychiatry and religion.

MJ: Yes. So let's say you don't feel able to be open with me about your sins, and they're going to be dealt with in a separate area by the priest. There are psychiatrists who you feel might help you in some ways, and there's religion and the priest, and only there is it possible for you to make known what your sins are.

David: Yes, because there's grace involved, you see. There's a special grace given in confession to enable you to confess your sins. That's the priest's work. It's the care of souls.

MJ: And the reward is the grace that's given by him alone?

David: Yes.

MJ: Right. So I wonder if we can now see something about why you feel I shouldn't find out about what you regard as your sins. If I find out, then it's going to interfere with a process that's very important to you, namely confessing your sins, and in return getting the grace. It's important it should all stay in that area, because from there you get the grace that enables prayer that brings you into a happy state.

David: Yes.

MJ: I, representing psychiatrists and people here who are trying to understand you, shouldn't have access to that particular part of you, namely the system whereby something inside you says you're a sinner. You go to the priest and confess, you get grace that allows you to pray and that brings hope that ultimately your troubles will be over.

David: Yes.

MJ: A tight, organized system . . . not safe to put it in jeopardy.

David: No.

MJ: So, would you agree that your system doesn't in fact need understanding, because it's already understood? You understand everything about it you need to understand.

David: Yes.

MJ: And you feel there's no other way of dealing with your problem of feeling sinful, other than the way that you've decided is the proper way.

David: Yes.

MJ: Right. Now, I wonder whether you think that a Catholic priest would say that there are areas which he feels are within his sphere and his competence, and there are areas which perhaps he would acknowledge are for the psychiatrists to help with.

David: Yes, I do think that.

MJ: So what would you think if I were to say that psychiatrists may have a way of helping you understand your experience that might not be couched in religious terms, but would not be anti-religious? That I, for example, might be able to understand something about your feelings of sinfulness and help you understand them, better than you can understand them yourself so far using your system?

David: Yes, I can see that could be possible.

MJ: Alright. Now, you're feeling that you are better than you were a few weeks ago. What would you say your state was a few weeks ago? It certainly wasn't a happy one. Anything but blissful.

David: Don't know, really. I was ill.

MJ: You were ill. Did you have a virus? Did you have influenza? What sort of ill?

David: Mental illness.

MJ: Have you got any idea of what was wrong with the way your mind was functioning? [*Pause. David reflects.*] I think that one of the things that may have been going wrong was your feeling of guilt. Could it be that it was so great that it couldn't be coped with by your system, so something else had to happen.

David smiles and shifts in chair.

MJ: You smile. What are you thinking?

David: I know that it was to do with my feeling of guilt . . . that's the point, you know . . . you're . . . you've . . . [*Pause.*] . . .

MJ: Hit the nail on the head?

David: Yes.

MJ: Bit of a relief, perhaps.

David: Yes.

MJ: So the trouble, we can agree on, is your sense of guilt.

David: I think so.

MJ: So we would now have to say: what is it you feel so guilty about? To answer that, we would have to acknowledge that the system you're sticking to is no good. It's not going to work. Perhaps we have to find something more in human terms, rather than divine terms, to help explain why you feel so guilty. What you are guilty about, I assume, includes what you would regard as sexual sins, and you're afraid of them coming into the open, partly because you'd lose the protection of your system and partly because you would feel embarrassed.

David: Yes.

MJ: Nevertheless, I think you realize that there is a lot at stake, don't you? We're talking now about something very important: your mental health. So you're going to have to put up with a bit of embarrassment. Does that make sense?

David: Yes, it does.

MJ: So what is it that you feel about your sexuality that makes you feel guilty? Why is it you can't have sexual feelings or masturbate without feeling that you're a great sinner, when both these activities are normal?

David: They're normal but they're sins. Masturbation is a sin.

The Catholic church says it's a sin, so long as its done with full knowledge and full consent.

MJ: Okay, let us say then that masturbation is a sin. What are you going to do with your sexual feelings?

David: Well, I have to cope with them normally. If I'm not able to cope with them, then I'd have to accept that the priesthood is not for me.

MJ: If you accepted that the priesthood was not for you, what would it mean for you?

David: It would change my life completely, because that has always been my ambition and still is my ambition.

MJ: So, if you were to face the painful decision that the priesthood was not for you, and let's say that your priest and your teachers even agreed with you, there then arises the question—what would David do then?

David: I'd have to go on living, of course. I may possibly get married.

MJ: Get married.

David: Yes.

MJ: What would you think about that? The possibility of getting married?

David: I've never thought about it.

MJ: So here you are at twenty-five, and you've never thought about getting married. Did you ever think when you were younger that you might eventually grow up and become a man, a husband, and a father?

David: Not serious thoughts, no.

MJ: What does your mother want you to be?

David: She wants me to be a priest.

MJ: You feel it's a vocation.

David: Yes, I heard talks by priests, one talk in particular by a priest who visited our school and who talked about missionary work, and that inspired me. It made me think more seriously about my vocation.

MJ: What was it about the missionary work that was so inspiring?

David: He talked about a leper colony and their work there helping the people.

MJ: Helping people who were damaged, incapacitated.

David: Yes.

MJ: Yes. Can you look back and remember when you first started to be come concerned to be helpful? Was it before that, or did it all come suddenly when you heard that inspiring address?

David: Oh, it was before that. When I was at home I used to help my mother.

MJ: Help your mother.

David: Yes. I used to help with the washing-up and cleaning the dishes and cleaning the house.

MJ: You were helpful to your mother.

David: I think I was helpful, yes.

MJ: Do you think that in a way could be the forerunner of your wish to be helpful to other people, such as the lepers?

David: Yes, I do.

MJ: So if we go back in time and think about your childhood, we're talking not of a child of God but of a child of your mother and your father, and you're helping your mother. I wonder if at that time you remember ever feeling that you had a special relationship with your mother, or that you wanted to have one?

. . . *Pause* . . .

David: I feel very close to my mother . . . [*David becomes tearful*].

MJ: What are you feeling?

David: I feel happy just to think about her.

MJ: You feel happy just to think about her. It seems to me that you are on the verge of tears.

David: Well . . . [*David smiles*].

MJ: You smile. You smile with happiness, and you're on the verge of tears. You don't think you are on the verge of tears?

David: I don't know.

MJ: When you think of your mother and the happiness of being so close to your mother, and the thought of your very special relationship with your mother, you feel happy. You have a lot of emotion inside you, but you're not exactly sure what you're feeling.

David: No. I know it's happiness alright.

MJ: It's happiness, yes. Happiness because your relationship with your mother is so special, to you and to her. You're happy. She's happy. You're helping her. She's loving you for being helpful. That is a happy state that you would like to go on forever.

David: Yes, that's right.

MJ: If you were to lose it, what would you feel?

David: I'd feel sad.

MJ: And you'd cry.

David: Yes.

MJ: Perhaps we can understand now why you never gave thought to growing up to become a man, or to marry and have a wife and family of your own. If you did that, you'd lose this happy, eternal relationship with your mother, and you'd start to cry just like you're trying not to cry at the moment.

David [*cries openly*]:   I never thought of it that way before.

MJ: I know you didn't. [*Pause.*] I think maybe it is important that you think of it like that. I think that if the thought of growing up and having to leave your mother becomes real then it must start to feel like a terrible hurt. A grief.

David: It does.

MJ: Yes. Up until now the thoughts you have had about it you have fitted into religious terms, and I'm not saying that they are wrong or misguided, but I think it's possible that a person can use them to protect himself. In religious terms, you have grace given by the priest for your confession, a special relationship with Our Lady that will go on for ever, and one which will be blissful and happy and will keep you safe from all sin and misery. You weren't able to think about it in the rather more simple, human way we're now considering.

David: It makes sense. But I don't know whether it's true or not.

MJ: No. I'm not asking you to accept that it's true. I'm sure it's true myself, but that doesn't make it true for you. I am asking you to use your intelligence to consider a different way of understanding your thoughts. So far, you have only been able to fit them into a religious framework. If you can take them seriously in a human way, too, quite a lot of things may follow. You've had other thoughts that might become understandable. For example, you feel you stole something from the Pope.

David: I stole the cross of the church from the Pope. Or, rather, I prayed that I would be united with the cross.

MJ: You prayed to be united with the cross.

David: Well, I said that . . . I asked to be united with Christ on the cross of the church, crippled as I am by the death of my father.

MJ: Crippled as you are by the death of your father.

David: Yes. I believed that I . . . my sickness . . . I felt ill at the time . . . mentally ill, if you like, I believed it was due to my father's death . . . I was crippled inside in some way. That is what I believed.

MJ: Because of your father's death you become in some way crippled inside, and you used the cross to pray?

David: Yes.

MJ: And you prayed that you could be united with Christ suffering on the cross. It's as if you felt you had something inside you.

David: Something that prevents me from being myself. I'm not living fully . . . I'm not living an ordinary life like normal people.

MJ: Like a man who gets married? Did that come into it?

David cries.

David: No, it didn't.

MJ: No, but it's very upsetting to think of it.

David: Yes, it is.

MJ: Can you say what is the upsetting thought that made you cry?

David: Great need, I suppose.

MJ: Great need.

David: A need to be married.

MJ: Need to be married. A longing feeling.

David: Yes.

MJ: A longing, and thinking what it would be like to have a wife who you could love and who would love you.

David: Yes, it's mostly that that I think of.

MJ: Different from having a mother who you can help forever.

David: Yes.

MJ: So you see, you felt your father's death in some way helped to cripple you inside. You felt you couldn't actually ever lead a normal life. The only solution you could think of was a religious one. If you could find the cross, you could become the suffering Christ yourself; you would then be reunited with God, and then you would cease to be a crippled person. It would become possible for you to then become a normal person again.

David cries.

The interview continued for several more minutes, during which the theme of David's feelings of loss and martyrdom were discussed.

* * *

The interview was moving, both for the observers and the interviewer. The contrived setting of the audiovisual suite and one-way mirror, an interference in the authenticity and spontaneity of a patient's responses, seemed to have little effect on David. As soon as he felt understood, he lifted his defensive "flattening of affect" in a dramatic way and accepted a reformulation of his problems that did not undermine his deeply held religious beliefs. These beliefs had lent themselves to a psychotic enactment of the role of the suffering Christ. The beliefs themselves were not abnormal, given the values of his family and community, but he had used them without insight as metaphors to express his psychological confusion regarding questions of desire, punishment, and forgiveness. There was abundant evidence in the interview of David's reparative motivations, which had played a part in his wish to be a priest and had endowed him with intellectual honesty and determination. They contained echoes not only of his wish to help his mother, but also a clear longing to take his father's place. His oedipal desires were only too obvious. Stealing the Pope's cross as a symbolic expression of a wish to steal father's penis and possess mother forever could hardly be more transparent. Its obviousness attested to David's psychotic vulnerability, but this needed to be set against his reparative feelings, representing mental health and a potential to function at a more integrated level. His quick responses to ECT and medication also demonstrated an affective element in his disturbance and the possibility, therefore, of a good long-term prognosis.

During the interview, David showed no obvious sign of psychotic functioning apart from the long-established flattening of affect that lifted during the session. His psychotic state had been stabilized with neuroleptics and continued nursing care, and he seemed to be acting as would anyone who was looking back at a period of severe confusion. However, the interview, although deeply moving, did not allow a reliable evaluation of his vulnerability to further psychotic developments. His delusional beliefs were not strongly challenged, the circumstances surrounding the fantasy of the theft of the cross were not explored, and the possible contribution of medication to the flattening of affect remained unclear. Psychotherapy and further assessments of his dynamic state would be needed to assess with confidence his progress in working through his pathogenic conflicts.

David's psychotic experience was the regressive revival of immature and omnipotent ways of thinking in which normal object-relationships were replaced by wish-fulfilling delusions and identifications. A sane part of his mind continued to function but could not resist encroachment by psychotic thought processes. His breakdown was, from a developmental perspective, a breakthrough of the unfinished business of his past life. When his unresolved preoccupations broke through and overwhelmed his capacity to differentiate between inner and outer reality, he became "mad". David's oedipal rivalry with his father, and no doubt with his younger brother, were not in themselves psychotic. His wishful delusion and identification with the suffering Christ definitely were. A sane religious individual who performs rituals involving repentance and punishment for sins, which can include the adoption of stereotyped postures, is aware of the element of imitation and can relinquish it when the ritual is completed. In the spontaneous postural stereotypes of catatonic schizophrenia, there is no such awareness. The imitation is an unconscious identification. The death of David's father was almost certainly a crippling blow, yet alongside this sense of loss it signified the fulfilment of David's unconscious hostility towards him, which had the significance of a repressed parricidal wish. His sexual guilt thus had deep roots and required his mother to be highly idealized, an immaculate virgin. At the same time his unconscious hostility to his actual parents who created so many children after him was split off from awareness. In his mind they were experienced as damaged and impoverished by his attacks. His love for them also appears to have been strong and generated valuable concern and reparative wishes, which found expression in his selfless devotion to the poor and sick.

Follow-up

The interview ended on an optimistic note. David expressed great relief and appreciation about having understood, for the first time, the meaning of his breakdown. He said that he was looking forward to digesting and following through what he had learned. He returned to the care of the referring psychiatrist with the opinion that he was a suitable case for long-term individual psychotherapy. This could not be provided because of a lack of resources, but he was offered supportive therapy, which he pursued for several months. He developed a very strong positive transference for the female psychiatrist who conducted the therapy. He worked through some of his disillusionment about his career and, with the agreement of his religious teachers, he abandoned it completely. He acquired a job appropriate to his intelligence and education and resumed the sporting activities and social life he had renounced years before. Medication was terminated, and after six months he discontinued therapy voluntarily. At this time he seemed to be in a normal and optimistic state of mind, and no further treatment was pursued. Contact with the psychodynamic unit was lost.

However, it was learned that two years later he had a brief period of depression, had been admitted to a mental hospital, and had been given ECT. Ten years after the interview he was observed to be free of psychosis, but still apparently unduly attached to his mother. It seems likely that when he became depressed an opportunity was lost to help him to continue his development. The main psychodynamic change in David was the alleviation of his sense of guilt and the partial resolution of conflict between heterosexual desires and his pathological use of religion. Becoming a priest, although an expression of compassion, was imbued with a rivalrous identification with the father of his infancy and childhood. His father's death had activated unconscious guilt, necessitating the search for an identificatory solution—that of becoming the crucified Christ who takes on the sins of the world and displays them to a punitive/forgiving Father. This omnipotent phantasy contains reparative aims in that the father is kept alive in David's mind.

After renouncing a religious career, David expressed his social concerns through charitable work, doing "the right thing for the right reasons", as he put it. Although his "imitation of Christ" contained a definite cultural component, his proclivity for forming psychotic identifications suggests a profound developmental failure. In the assessment interview his inhibition ("flattening of affect") was lifted and the paralysing tie to his mother introduced. His brief period of psychotherapy could not address these psychotic anxieties in any depth but was enough to allow him to accept his heterosexual nature. He worked through his career confusion and began to live more realistically. Later, his profound disturbance reemerged as a depression. Loss of contact with his unit and conventional treatment devoid of psychodynamic content are likely to have precluded the chance of much further emotional development.

CHAPTER SIX

Manic–depressive psychosis

Manic–depressive psychosis is an affective disorder producing periodic disruption of apparently normal moods by pathological depression or elation. Although a single manic state in a lifetime is not uncommon, manic–depressive illness is usually seriously disabling, hard to understand, and often difficult to treat. Before the advent of mood-stabilizing drugs, the most effective treatment was ECT, which is still occasionally used in dangerous crises as a life-saving strategy. Impressive anti-depressive and anti-manic medication, and compelling evidence for a genetic component in the illness, have focussed attention on biological aspects of the disorder. Even when allowing for such genetic influences as a necessary causal factor, there exists an equally compelling case for the parallel study of developmental psychology if a *sufficient* causal explanation is to be found.

Psychoanalysts have long contributed to the understanding of factors involved in the predisposition to manic–depression, to the precipitation of episodes, and to its psychodynamics. Abraham (1911, 1924) and Freud (1917e [1915]) laid the foundations for the understanding of the nature of pathological happiness and unhappiness. Recognizing the extreme abnormality of the affections manifest during attacks, Abraham began with the simple statement that in such states hatred paralyses love. The hatred is unconscious and, like the love it paralyses, has infantile origins. It represents a severe developmental failure in the normal process of individuation. In particular, emotional attachment is dreaded because of extreme sensitivity to the loss that may follow. Jealousy and its precursor, envy, may be present in highly destructive form, often very difficult to detect. Immature processes of identification that are normally left behind persist and are regressively reactivated under external stress or internal fears of loss of the loved object. The prototypical object is obviously the mother and, in later life, "security figures" who are invested with maternal significance.

Freud discovered a form of identification in melancholia (psychotic depression) in which aggression aroused towards the "bad" object is turned upon the self—a process that is also a part of normal mourning. The extravagant protestations of self-hatred by the severe depressive can be understood as a defence that preserves the loved object (felt to be too vulnerable) from aggressive feelings (felt omnipotently to be too dangerous). At the same time, the mechanism serves unconsciously to protect the subject from the full impact of loss, as the object continues to exist in the guise of the suffering self. Melancholia was thus recognized as a form of abnormal mourning. From these beginnings Freud developed his concept of the superego, the unconscious conscience. He recognized that in melancholia the superego possessed extreme harshness, which he regarded as an indication of its infantile origins. So unremitting is the savagery of the melancholic superego that it not infrequently leads to suicide (dynamically, an act of self-murder). Many studies have since illuminated the origins of this pathological conscience and the reasons why an infant may even experience a normal mother as similarly vulnerable to aggressive feelings (see Klein, 1935; Rosenfeld, 1963; see also Jackson, 1993a, for a review of major contributors). Freud recognized that mania was in many respects the opposite of melancholia. Deadness and immobility is replaced by liveliness and overactivity, severe depression by pathological elation. Sexual impulses, often of a childlike kind, are regularly present in mania. Freud also observed the switch from depression to mania and recognized its defensiveness, expressed as massive denial. Melanie Klein had a special interest in the psychodynamics of manic–depression and studied, in particular, the attitude of triumph, contempt, and control in the mind of the manic individual. This gross form of devaluation is reserved for an object who arouses feelings of need and dependency in the subject, and for the healthy, dependent part of the subject's own personality. The underlying developmental failure responsible was further illuminated by Bion's concept of maternal containment, to which we shall return. The degree of developmental failure in the manic–depressive, however severe, lacks the extreme unintegration characteristic of schizophrenic psychoses. Furthermore, the manic–depressive's wish to spare and preserve the object attests to a comparatively advanced level of development. Despite the fact that schizoid features occur in a significant proportion of manic–depressive patients, most typical sufferers are potentially able to function at times at the level of the depressive position (see Glossary) given the right therapeutic conditions, which is why well-conducted psychotherapy can achieve good results.

Manic–depressive patients are widely regarded by psychiatrists as unsuitable for psychotherapy. This attitude is understandable, given the high risk of suicide during the depressive phase and the difficulty in managing psychotic behaviour during the manic state. However, many psychotherapists have come to believe that a large proportion of such patients could benefit from psychotherapy under the right conditions. The case of Nicola is an example.

NICOLA

Nicola, a doctor, was 30 years old when admitted to the unit for assessment[1]. She had spent all but a few months of the previous five years in mental hospitals, incapacitated by a cycling

manic–depressive psychosis. The breakdown that preceded her
admission to hospital on the first occasion had occurred whilst
she had been required to attend to late abortions soon after
graduation. She had made numerous serious, often near-fatal
suicide bids in her life, the first at the age of 14, and she had
responded only briefly to medication and over 50 ECT treatments. She suffered persistent persecutory hallucinations of
voices ordering her to kill herself, and she was regarded as an
unusually resistant case. Leucotomy was considered as a last
resort. Psychotherapy had been ruled out because of the
prevailing psychiatric view of its potential for self-harm, which
in her case seemed reasonable. There had been an attempt to
initiate psychotherapy at the beginning of her illness five years
earlier, but on the eve of her first appointment she made a
serious suicide attempt, which led to the abandonment of any
further attempt to use psychotherapy.

Nicola was admitted to the unit under intensive nursing
surveillance. Preliminary exploration of her history revealed a
highly disturbed family background. She was the eldest of
several siblings of a devoted but fragile mother, who was herself the sole survivor of several siblings who had died peri-
natally of Rhesus incompatibility. Her father was subject to
hypomanic episodes, and a paternal aunt and grandmother
had suffered from manic–depressive psychosis. Her father was
capricious and unjust in his behaviour and subject to violent
rages. Her childhood was marred by chronic domestic tension,
culminating in the divorce of her parents during her adolescence. Her illness began as a severe depression, after a distinguished graduation from medical school, and this led to the
first referral for psychotherapy. At a conscious level she had
been eager to begin therapy because she had long had disturbing dreams which she could not understand. Later, when she
was finally able to embark on psychotherapy, she showed un-
failing interest in the meaning of her dreams, and this often
helped sustain treatment. I [MJ] undertook the psychotherapy
myself, on a twice-weekly basis, though in periods of crisis I
would see her more frequently for a shorter time, and sometimes daily during periods of crisis. The excerpts that follow are
from sessions that took place some months into the psychotherapy.

First session

Nicola is depressed and withdrawn and sits motionless in her chair. She is dressed in pyjamas and dressing gown and has bandages on her wrists from a recent suicide attempt. She had smuggled a razor-blade onto the ward and cut herself badly. This was one of many attempts and followed an incident in which another patient had set fire to herself, resulting in serious harm. This had activated a hypomanic response in Nicola, followed the next day by depression and suicidal behaviour. The following excerpt begins 5 minutes into the interview and finishes 15 minutes before the interview ends.

MJ: Do you remember what we talked about last time?

Nicola: No.

MJ: I'll remind you: you told me of a dream in which you were in Euston Station, and a terrorist had planted a bomb but it was too late to escape. It exploded, and you were caught under the rubble. You were crying out, but nobody could hear your voice. Do you remember? [*Pause.*] You were caught under the rubble, trapped, all hope was gone, and you told me you felt that you had destroyed your psychotherapy and any chance of my being able to help you.

Nicola: It's true.

MJ: It's true that was the way you felt, yes. You felt as you seem to be feeling now. Hope is gone. What you seem to be saying to yourself is that I can't possibly help you.

Nicola nods.

MJ: That must also mean that you feel that the psychotherapy is finished. [*Pause.*] I think that you are listening to a side of yourself that is telling you that everything is finished. I also think that you are perhaps listening to voices that are telling you that you should kill yourself because you're so bad.

Nicola nods.

MJ: That is happening at the moment?

Nicola: Yes.

MJ: Do you remember in your dream that you were complaining that you couldn't have a bath because it was full of demolished rubble?

Nicola [*nods*]: Yes.

MJ: You were complaining to your mother that there was no room for you in the bath because it was full of rubble. I think you are feeling as you felt in the dream. There is nowhere safe for you. Everything's demolished and turned to rubble. No hope. You can cry out as much as you like, but you feel nobody will hear you. But what you don't seem to be noticing is that I am hearing you and that the psychotherapy is not over, however wicked you may feel yourself to be.

Nicola: Nobody can help me.

MJ: Nobody can help you. What would you call the activity of the staff who are busy keeping you alive? Is that help? They are quite determined to do all they can not to allow a patient to be killed. They are determined you should stay alive and for the psychotherapy between you and me to go on. Nothing gets put right if something in you says you're so wicked that the only thing you must do is die. Dying doesn't make the trouble better. Not only is it not dealt with, you may even be afraid that you'll go to hell and your trouble will go on . . .

Nicola: Hell can't be worse than this.

MJ: Hell can't be worse than this. Yes. You know, you have told me that there have been times when only the thought of eternal torment in hell stopped you from killing yourself. I can believe that nothing feels worse than being in a situation where you're constantly being told that all hope is gone. That is absolute despair. Would that be the right word?

Nicola: Yes.

MJ: Yes. Nobody feels despair unless they've once had hope. Where has your hope gone? You can't answer that question at the moment, I know. You have no hope. I'm the one who has to have the hope. I believe it is a perfectly logical hope to try to keep you alive. That is our task. Your task is to try to listen to me, instead of listening to the side of you that's trying to demolish our work, turning anything hopeful into rubble, even if necessary by telling you lies.

Nicola: I don't think it is lies.

MJ: You don't think it is lies. I understand that's the way you experience it. What you can't remember is that in the past you've been in this state of mind, even worse, and you've managed to stay alive. You've passed through it, you've recovered, but now you've gone back into it again. That is how this happens. Do you recognize it?

Nicola: I don't know that it's the same.

. . . Pause . . .

MJ: When you say to me, "I don't know that it's the same", you've taken an important step. You've shown something called curiosity, and when you show curiosity, there's a chance that you can have hope. I think your responsibility is to try to carry on with that thought, and tell me in what way it's not the same. You have nearly died many times. The nurses have managed to keep you alive until your state of mind has changed, but this time you think it's not quite the same.

Pointing out progress — reinstil hope

Nicola: Perhaps there was some hope before.

MJ: Perhaps there was some hope before. [*Pause.*] I wonder if you can recall—I can recall—that when you started your psychotherapy with me, you were in the same state. You had no hope. Then you got some hope. You began to be interested in how your mind works. Now you feel hopeless again. This is how your mind can change. Do you remember telling me what happened when you drank too much a few weeks ago, and something inside you told you you should lie down on the road in front of a car, and how that's always there, in the background?

Make her remember make her think

Nicola: Yes [*nods*].

MJ: It makes you feel hopeless. Now, if that is always there in the background, how can we deal with it unless it comes into the open? It's inevitable that it should make you feel hopeless when it comes out, because it's very upsetting. [*Pause.*] If you remember, something very upsetting happened to you. It had to do with Mary setting herself on fire, do you remember? You were very upset. You became manic and spoke with contempt about any efforts to understand your feelings. I think you were frightened that you would have to do to yourself what Mary did. It was a catastrophe, and you felt that you might have to be the same as her. It's difficult to admit now how frightened and upset you were.

Nicola: I thought I had no feelings about it.

MJ: That would make sense, you know. I think you were so upset and frightened that you had to get rid of those feelings from your mind. You became manic. You laughed and joked about it all. When you get rid of feelings from your mind, there's no room in your mind for anything human, only for accusations that you're terrible. An upset person doesn't hear voices telling her how wicked she is. An upset person is alive and feels very upset that something awful has happened; feels something painful that might be called grief.

Nicola: She was very nice.

MJ: She was very nice. You liked her. But you tried to destroy your feelings of upset, and now your voices say that *you* have to die. Mary is, in fact, going to live, and I'm hoping that we can bring her back to the ward before too long. [*Pause.*] It is very important that you live, and not follow the same path as somebody who has to do something so terrible to themselves. The nurses have to keep you alive. I have to see you. Your responsibility is to admit to yourself how upset you can feel. We can see now why you have been ill for so long. Whenever you have certain feelings, you try to get rid of them, explode them, tear them up, and say you're too weak to feel upset. You must die instead. Your dreams tell us how this side of you prevents you from making connections with feelings that are upsetting, but human. It tells you that you are bad and that you should die rather than face feelings of loss and sadness. It's by turning away from your feelings that you feel abandoned and in despair and you lose hope.

. . . *Pause* . . .

Nicola seems to be more engaged. Her eyelids move rapidly and her breathing rate increases. She appears to be concentrating.

MJ: Can you remember the dream you had last night?

Nicola: I'm at home.

MJ: You're at home.

Nicola: And on the radio there's a bomb alert.

MJ: On the radio there's a bomb alert.

Nicola: So I went to shelter in the cellar. Then I remember the
cats.

Just repeating — making her do the work — not jumping ahead

MJ: You went to shelter in the cellar with the cats.

Nicola: No, I forgot about the cats. —   *She corrects him!*

MJ: You forgot about the cats.

Nicola: So I went up into the garden to call them in, but while
I'm doing that, the bomb goes off, and the house is reduced
to rubble. The street, everything is rubble.

MJ: House reduced to rubble, street reduced to rubble.

Nicola: My skin is burnt.

MJ: Your skin's burnt.

Nicola: And peeling off.

MJ: And peeling.

Nicola: So I think I must go and find Adrian [her husband].

MJ: You look for Adrian.

Nicola: So I walk into the city. Everywhere is ash and rubble.

MJ: The city's been reduced to ash and rubble.

Nicola: And I find the street where Adrian's office is, but the
building is just rubble.

MJ: You find the street where Adrian's office is, and the
building he's in is just reduced to rubble.

Nicola: So I try to dig, dig in the rubble to find him, but I'm
burnt and its too painful. I can't do it. [*Pause.*] That's it.

MJ: You're alive, you're trying to find him, but it's too painful.
Too painful to try to see if you can rescue your husband
who's buried in the rubble.

Nicola: Yes.

Interpretation
she paused,
he feels she's
ready

MJ: You had a thought about it? You were going to say some-thing. [*Pause: Nicola does not reply.*] Isn't your dream about what I have been saying? Always you're threatened by some-thing trying to explode and prevent you feeling your feelings.

Nicola: Yes.

MJ: You love your cats, and you're trying to preserve some-one you love from exploding, destructive processes. Somewhere, submerged in the rubble, you are struggling to see if there is life left in your husband, your partner. I would also say, in the partnership of the psychotherapy. You are doing something to help that aspect of yourself that might be alive, but it's very painful. Some feelings are too painful to bear, but in the dream you are prepared to try, even though you have to give up in the end. You go on digging, painful as it is. You have to, I know. The consequence of not digging, of getting rid of feelings that are too upsetting, like about Mary, your cats, your husband, or of getting rid of feelings that you think are destructive, is that the voices then tell you to kill yourself.

* * *

The purpose of the following brief excerpts is to demonstrate the dramatic switch from depression to mania and back again. In the first excerpt, Nicola is slumped in her chair, withdrawn into deep depression. She had apparently drawn her husband into a collusion to blame the nursing staff for having failed to pre-vent her from cutting herself. High-level complaints against the staff followed, which put me in the position of having to defend the nurses against criticism by the hospital managers. I was irritated with her, and although I attempted to conceal it, I did not succeed.

Second session

Nicola: You sound angry.

MJ: Me . . . ?

Nicola: You sound angry.

MJ: I sound angry. [*Pause.*] I think you're listening to me now, if you think I sound angry. You're also opening your eyes a little more. Now, if you think I sound angry, why then do you think I should be angry?

* * *

This was the first verbal acknowledgement she had made to me in a week, and it came as a considerable surprise. When I recovered my composure, I acknowledged my anger and the reason for it. She spoke briefly about regretting the self-cutting, and shortly afterwards the session came to an end.

Immediately after the interview she cried, admitting to herself and her primary nurse how upset she was. Within 90 minutes she had become acutely manic. She came to the interview on the following day in an over-active state, wearing a purple T-shirt and fluorescent yellow trousers. She was manic and aggressive, talking excitedly and contemptuously.

Third session

The following day. Nicola, MJ, and the ward psychiatrist are present.

Nicola [*to psychiatrist*]:   What are you doing here?

Psychiatrist: I shall be sitting in for a while.

Nicola: Why? I want to know why.

MJ: Do you think you could talk to me?

Nicola: I don't know. I'm very angry with you.

MJ: Can you tell me . . .

Nicola [*interrupts*]:   Because you're keeping me in here against my will.

MJ: You feel there's no need to be here.

Nicola: No, there's no need to be in here.

* * *

Fourth session

Two days later. Nicola strides into the room, grinning.

Nicola: You don't mind if I smoke, I hope? Is there an ashtray around? No ashtray? Oh dear, I'll have to throw it on the floor. [*Sits down.*] What are you grinning about?

MJ: Well, your grinning is very sad, actually.

Nicola: My grinning isn't sad. I'm quite happy.

MJ: I think you're trying to make yourself feel happy so you won't feel sad, really.

Nicola [*shouts and points*]:   Why didn't you come and see me at 1:15? And why couldn't I go over to the Institute?

MJ: Good question. Have you got any ideas?

Nicola: Because I've run away, of course.

MJ: We didn't have enough nurses to make sure that you wouldn't run away. So I've had to come to see you here [on a locked ward].

Nicola: Well, that's a shame. I'm sure you didn't enjoy the trip.

MJ: I think it would be easier for you to think that I didn't want to come and see you than to think that I actually did want to come to see you.

Nicola gets up and walks round the room.

MJ: I understood that you wanted to speak to me on the telephone.

Nicola [*shouts*]:   Yes I did.

MJ: Could you try sitting down for a minute?

Nicola sits.

MJ: Do you remember . . .

Nicola: I don't know what I wanted to say now. I've forgotten.

MJ: Your mood has changed. You weren't quite so excited then as you are . . .

Nicola [*shouts*]:   I'm NOT excited. This is a myth. [*Gets up, walks around.*] I must have an ashtray. Can you get me an ashtray? [*Walks around looking for an ashtray.*]

MJ: I think it might be preferable to drop it on the floor than to go wandering around in the valuable time we've got.

Nicola: Oh yes, I'm so sorry, of course. [*Pause.*] I don't like doing it. It's messy. [*Pause.*] You don't seem convinced.

MJ: I think it's one thing to make a mess on the floor, but another to make a mess of your mind.

Nicola: My mind's perfectly alright.

MJ: I don't know if you recall the last time we met here.

Nicola gets up, walks around.

MJ: You said the only trouble with you was that your psychotherapist had the delusion that there was something wrong with you.

Nicola [*raucous laughter*]: It's not only my psychotherapist. It's the doctors and nurses as well! [*Sits down.*]

MJ: Can you remember your dreams?

Nicola: I didn't have any last night. I didn't sleep the night before. [*Leans forward, shouts and points.*] I didn't have any last night because they dosed me up with Haloperidol; can you tell them to stop dosing me up with Halperidol? They gave me 20 milligrams last night. I don't like taking it.

MJ: You remember the . . .

Nicola [*interrupts*]: Well, can you or can't you?

MJ: I think it would be easier for you to try to regard me as the one who prescribes the medicine rather than the one who tries to prescribe the sanity.

* * *

The fifth session is similar to the fourth. Nicola walks round the room, occasionally sitting. She laughs manically and is dismissive and contemptuous. The atmosphere also seems to be sexualized, with Nicola approaching MJ, standing in front of him in a provocative manner.

In the following, sixth, session Nicola has come down from this mood of pathological elation and is barely able to speak.

Sixth session

Three days later. Nicola sits crumpled and withdrawn.

MJ: Can you tell me how things have changed, since we last met?

. . . *Pause* . . .

Nicola [*whispers*]:   I feel quite desperate.

MJ: You feel quite desperate. Do you remember when we met last what your state was then?

. . . *Pause* . . .

Nicola: No.

MJ: Do you try to remember, or is it that you try not to remember?

. . . *Pause* . . .

Nicola: I try to remember . . . but I can't.

* * *

These excerpts began with a session in which the patient was deeply depressed, listening to voices telling her she is wicked and must kill herself. This was precipitated by the self-injury of another patient to whom she had become attached. Her extreme sensitivity to feelings of loss had already been observed in relation to departing nurses who meant something to her. The defensive–destructive organization in her mind turned against the healthy dependent part of her personality, promoting the idea of suicide and serving to avoid attachments, which could lead to the mental pain of envy, of jealousy, and, above all, of separation and loss. Her profound reaction to her friend's self-harm illustrates Freud's early contention that melancholia is an abnormal form of mourning. The patient spoke in a low, almost inaudible voice. My repetitions of her comments served to confirm that I had heard correctly, and also to provide an intermission to think of an appropriate response. The reason for my repeated intervening was that when Nicola became so depressed, active contact seemed the only way to reach her—as though her interest needed to be stimulated and her normal self forcefully contacted, for example through repetitive themes that emerged in her dream life. Making contact during the sessions, in the face of such depression and despair, required careful attention to the feelings aroused in myself. Anxiety, guilt, despair, irritation, and inadequacy felt during sessions needed careful scrutiny in order to differentiate between personal responses to a difficult, frustrating situation, and countertransference communications that could yield information about the patient's internal conflicts.

The concept of her mind being organized into different parts made her less difficult to understand. At certain points, for example, I felt she could become provocatively manipulative, yet I would press ahead in order to support the sane part of herself—her fragile but functioning ego—against the propaganda of her archaic superego. Nevertheless, it was often difficult to know what was going on between us. This is inevitable, and it is important to be prepared to tolerate states of ignorance and uncertainty, possibly for long periods, in such work. With this extremely ill woman I had accepted from the outset that we were committed, for better or for worse, to an extremely difficult struggle with her pathology. This commitment proved to be of some value when, later, a trial of strength developed between her psychotic self and me. The intra-psychic nature of this trial of strength involved her using me for a time as a container for her sanity, hope, and capacity for reflective thinking, whilst she expressed a good deal of her insanity. I explained what was happening to her in order to avoid an idealization in which I became the sole representative of sanity in a world of madness. This was indeed the case in one sense, but if the prevailing situation were to have been accepted concretely by the patient, it could have led to the disowning of her destructive motivations, or to her simply condemning her psychotic self as evil. A deeper recognition by her of why psychotic defences arose in the first place was required.

The manifest content of her dreams was usually a direct expression of thoughts about devastating destruction, and the endangered state of her loved objects. Valuable documents are torn up, she drops a precious vase that has been entrusted to her, railway stations and bridges are blown up. In the dream that I recalled in the first session, the rubble-filled bath symbolized the containing maternal space whose contents, the siblings of her early life, had been destroyed, expressed in the transference as my mind, creatively occupied in providing her with food for thought. The theme of attacking my work at those times when it was good became increasingly familiar as the therapy proceeded and evoked in me a feeling of being secretly derided, manipulated, and demolished. This "negative therapeutic reaction" could be understood as a manic triumph over the therapeutic work and its containing function, with which her healthy self was struggling to cooperate. A formulation like this helped to explain the dramatic switch from depression to mania within the course of an hour and a half. When she succeeded in provoking me into losing my customary level of reasonable calm, my "human" personal response had a dual consequence. Her healthy self saw this as proof that I cared personally about her,[2] and she was briefly able to express deep positive feeling associated with a memory of some past loss. Within an hour and a half her omnipotent self had launched into a celebration of envious triumph and took over control of her mind, until the manic mood had run its course one week later. This process was the basis for the dynamic switch from deep depression to mania. Switches on such a scale are of particular theoretical interest (Pao, 1968), and biochemical studies have been inconclusive. Less dramatic changes, from depression to hypomania, sometimes occurred during a premenstrual period but were more often precipitated by psychodynamic factors and were often foreshadowed in dreams.

The subsequent two excerpts following the switch show her in a typical manic state. She seems to be projecting her sane self into me, and I try to restore her contact with the disaster that is taking place beneath her manic belligerence. Her not entirely convincing determination to show that it is her therapist who is mad is also pointed out to her. The final excerpt shows the collapse of the mania three days later and the return of the depression.

There are very different dynamic states that earn the label "depression". The depression in the first excerpt is an essentially paranoid state of inner persecution, characteristic of psychotic depression. This may be accompanied by "true" depression, which is the expression of despair and disappointment, linked to feelings of deprivation, abandonment, and loss of self-esteem. The depression in the final excerpt appears to be of this more "true" type than that in the first excerpt, perhaps the result of some sane recognition that her belief in her abundant good health when manic was in fact serious pathology. Bion's (1957) concept of "psychotic part of the personality" and Rosenfeld's (1971) definition of "destructive narcissism" were, for me, the key concepts to allow understanding of her desperate resistance to help and growth. A manic undercurrent discernible in some of Nicola's depressive phases confirmed for me the subtle domination of her personality by the psychotic part of her self, which exerted its imprisoning effect through secret, triumphant contempt and denigration of the sincerity of the therapeutic work and her participation in it.

Follow-up

Despite the transitory nature of the breakthrough illustrated in the sessions, a continuing improvement took place in Nicola, and her work in the therapy became more productive and reliable. Her mood swings began to flatten out, and she came to recognize and tolerate feelings of extreme emotional pain. As she became more aware of, and owned, her hatred, envy, and contempt, the persecuting voices receded, appearing only at moments of extreme stress. After two years of twice-weekly psychotherapy, conducted within the therapeutic and containing environment of the ward, she was discharged on a low dose of medication. The genetic contribution to her mood instability suggested that maintenance on lithium medication would be advisable for a long time—perhaps indefinitely. By the time of her discharge, she had experienced a normal mental state for several months, but there was no reason to think that this improvement would remain stable under all circumstances. She was eager to continue to work at her problems in further psychotherapy, and it proved possible to arrange for her to continue in long-term psychoanalytic treatment. She made further progress, punctuated by a few relapses, one of which involved a brief period of hospitalization at her own request. Her marriage improved, she negotiated a miscarriage without severe consequences, and she then had a successful pregnancy. Five years after leaving hospital, she has returned to work—albeit work of a non-medical nature—and is successfully raising her child. Her increased integration and insight are likely to mean that if a relapse occurs in the future, it will be more manageable. There also seems little doubt that psychotherapy has prevented a successful suicide.

Her long-term psychotherapy was by no means trouble-free. She was capable of evoking great anxiety by powerful acting out, and on several occasions needed to be admitted briefly to hospital when her hallucinations threatened her safety. In the first phase of her treatment, threats of suicide were commonplace, but it seemed that the survival of her therapy (past and present) meant more to her than dying, and she admitted how important her experience on the unit had been to her. Understanding her psychotic states could be facilitated by thinking of them as analogous to dreams. In them, there often occurred a woman persecuted by her mother for a mortal sin she had committed—the killing of babies in the wombs of their mothers. As a result she should take her own life. This archaic superego was of unprecedented ferocity. The entire murderous/murdered drama was experienced repeatedly in the transference to her therapist. In reality, many children on her mother's side of the family, going back two generations, had died prematurely, and this tragic background had affected the whole family. Work on her superego was unceasing and productive, not least because she eventually experienced her therapist as a separate object able also to survive her murderous attacks. When, after five years, she became pregnant, she felt a frightening impulse to stab a knife into her stomach as the voices were telling her she was not fit to have a baby. By this time she had some understanding of separate, enduring objects, of dependency, and therefore of a need to keep the baby alive. With the help of good maternity staff she had a normal delivery of her baby. After the birth, murderous impulses towards the baby required continuous interpretation and succeeded in extricating her from her identification with the cruel, murdering mother. She began to appreciate the child's love for her and even to take pleasure occasionally in her relationship to her therapist. Hospital admissions ceased. Mother and child are doing well, and her husband has played a supportive role throughout. Her therapy continues, towards termination.

CHAPTER SEVEN

The treatment setting

The clinical vignettes presented in the first six chapters refer to work that took place on a small, experimental unit of 11 beds, which shared a ward with a general unit of a similar size. The units together made up an acute admission ward known within the Maudsley as Ward 6. The experimental unit made use of a psychoanalytic perspective in its treatment plans, whilst its partner functioned on more general psychiatric lines. The two units dealt with a wide range of disturbances, and since most of the nursing staff served both units, a beneficial mutual influence evolved. An increasing psychodynamic attitude developed on the ward as a whole, whilst the provision of a firm psychiatric base for work of a psychotherapeutic nature came to be appreciated.

Contexts and credos

The psychodynamic philosophy of the unit regarding the nature of functional (as opposed to provenly organic) psychoses and their treatment could be summarized using a number of theoretical and clinical observations repeatedly confirmed over time. For example, psychotic conditions and severe disorders of character with psychotic features often called "schizoid" or, more recently, "borderline" conditions, affect individuals who are predisposed by reasons of constitutional vulnerability or adverse environmental conditions in infancy and childhood, or both. Many psychotic symptoms and delusions reveal meaningful content and are an expression of profound intra-psychic conflict. An acute psychotic attack may often be understood as the final stage in a struggle—perhaps lifelong—of a vulnerable individual to adjust to the world of external reality in the face of overwhelming and unresolved emotional problems of relating to the self and to others. This struggle has its roots in infancy and early childhood and in a failure, in varying degrees and for differing reasons, to experience a sufficiently stable relationship with the mother or primary object. The development of a normal core to the structure of the personality and a capacity for making and sustaining emotional attachments have been impaired, and it is frequently the demands on the adolescent to change and grow that precipitate the first overt breakdown.

Acute psychotic breakdowns have often presented themselves on the unit as the breakthrough of hitherto repressed or variously disowned wishes, impulses, and phantasies ("phantasies" being *unconscious* desires) into conscious life. The revival of these primitive modes of thinking reveals literal, concrete, non-symbolic, and action-centred thinking that possesses the quality of "unlabelled metaphor". As such, it offers a hope and an opportunity that, given sufficient residual health in the patient and proper therapeutic assistance, a more advanced level of integration and functioning may be achieved from this inchoate, but at least accessible, material. The above observations gave rise to a set of convictions that became a type of credo underpinning the unit's daily work with psychosis:

1. All patients, irrespective of diagnosis, are entitled to the best possible assessment of their mental state and of their assets and disabilities.

2. All patients have the right to be listened to and understood at as deep a level as is possible. Psychoanalytic concepts such as unconscious phantasy, conflict, mental defence

mechanisms, primary process thinking, transference, countertransference, and repetition–compulsion facilitate this understanding. Destructive motivations are to be differentiated from self-preservative aggression, and constructive, reparative impulses are to be recognized for what they are.

3. Disturbed experience and behaviour have meaning in terms of the patient's internal and external life. Biological aspects of a disorder must be attended to, but an effort to understand the patient's emotional difficulties plays a central role in formulating any treatment plan.

4. All patients, irrespective of diagnosis, should be presumed to be potential candidates for individual and/or group psychotherapy (whether or not the facilities exist) until it is proved otherwise. The majority of patients, including many who are unsuitable for psychotherapy, benefit from some form of psychological treatment, and frequently from a psychodynamic approach.

Although psychodynamically minded psychiatrists would agree with some or all of the above requirements for the treatment of psychosis, they are less likely or able to apply them in their formulation of treatment plans. Psychoanalysts, meanwhile, are unlikely to be given the opportunity to implement them, at least in the United Kingdom. We believe that bringing the two disciplines closer together is desirable if efforts to effect comprehensive and lasting change in the psychotic personality are to succeed. It was Freud who first recognized the potential of the application of psychoanalytic thinking to the understanding of psychosis. He was initially pessimistic about the suitability of psychotic individuals for psychoanalytic treatment, regarding them as too withdrawn from reality to become usefully engaged in the analytic dialogue. Subsequently he thought that certain patients could be helped, and he wrote with an acute awareness of the need to reconcile psychoanalytic thinking with clinical psychiatry. Referring to the interest of analysts in the subject of psychosis, he observed:

> . . . so many things that in the neuroses have to be laboriously fetched up from the depths are found in psychosis

on the surface, visible to every eye. For that reason the
best subjects for the demonstration of many of the asser-
tions of analysis are provided by the psychiatric clinic.
[Freud, 1925d, p. 60]

Freud was in no doubt that it was in the future application of psychoanalytic concepts to clinical psychiatry that the
possibility of helping the psychotic patient was to be found.
Analysts, he said, have never relaxed their efforts to come to an
understanding of psychosis, and this had yielded great theoretical gains:

> . . . mere theoretical gain is not to be despised, and we may
> be content to wait for its practical application. In the long
> run even the psychiatrists cannot resist the convincing
> force of their own clinical material. [Freud, 1925d, p. 61]

The early work of Freud and of subsequent generations of
psychoanalysts with regard to psychosis gave rise to a new
epistemology. We possess today compelling and coherent ways
of explaining psychotic thought processes and otherwise in-
explicable, bizarre human behaviour. These insights are not
merely intellectually satisfying—although this they are. They
make practically possible the dynamic engagement of the psychotic mind with the mind of the clinician, and hence the
inclusion of a psychotherapeutic component in the management and treatment of psychosis. In many cases the scene
can also be set for successful longer-term psychotherapy.
This knowledge can also help workers to achieve confidence in
their ability to understand psychotic patients, even if the
patients themselves prove resistant to treatment (Jackson,
1991; Jackson & Cawley, 1992).

Interestingly, there is a significant proportion of psychotic
patients, sometimes presenting in a highly disturbed state,
whose disorder is neither disintegrative nor deserving of a bad
prognosis. If treatment plans are tailored to their needs and
capacities, they become suitable for long-term psychotherapy
(not necessarily full psychoanalysis) and often do well. This is
emphatically so with acute, first-attack patients who have a
history of relatively good adjustment. There is evidence that
some such patients recover with little or no treatment, whilst

others benefit greatly from psychoanalytic psychotherapy. Obviously, these patients must be distinguished from those with long-standing previous pathology who tend towards chronicity and disintegration, and who are often better served by cognitive and behavioural methods in conjunction with rehabilitation. However, each case, of whatever degree of severity, needs to be assessed on its merits, as there are many chronically psychotic patients capable of making productive use of psychoanalytic psychotherapy if it is skilfully integrated into cognitive and behavioural programmes.

Much prevailing psychiatric practice is directed at the removal or suppression of symptoms using anti-psychotic medication, followed by speedy discharge and a return into the community. This may be adequate treatment for some, but for others it can mark the beginning of a cycle of recurrence and eventual chronicity. This represents a failure to elucidate the meaning and significance of breakdown in the context of the patient's relationships and life history. If, by contrast, the psychiatrist can take the opportunity to try to understand how and why the crisis has occurred, then any subsequent attempt made to shorten or avoid hospital stay could represent a great advance in care. The worst outcome of a failure to grasp the significance of breakdown in an accessible patient is the production of a secondary handicap—of essentially iatrogenic origin—following on the consolidation of psychotic mechanisms.

People and practice

The ward's 22 beds, divided between the two units, were occupied at an average rate of 80–90%. There were usually 18 nurses assigned to cover two day shifts and one night shift, seven days a week. The staff/patient ratio was 1:1.5. When a patient was discharged, the ward's policy was to maintain contact during the transition to care in the community. For the first weeks of discharge it was usual for patients to continue to attend the ward several days a week. They maintained an involvement in the life of the ward, including therapeutic groups, and this proved to be of value not only for them but in sustaining a therapeutic atmosphere during times of change.

About two-thirds of general psychiatric patients who were admitted were residents of the local catchment area. Selection procedures were the same for both units. A principal source of referral was the hospital's Emergency Clinic, a 24-hour walk-in assessment centre serving the whole of London. Forensic, drug-dependent, and psycho-geriatric patients were directed to specialized units; others were received into the hospital's general intake units, including our own. A small proportion of patients (about a quarter) were directly referred to the unit from other psychiatric units in the United Kingdom and, occasionally, from other countries. Most of these were psychotic, severely neurotic, or personality-disordered patients who had already received extended treatment elsewhere. For these direct referrals we operated a selection procedure. Study of psychiatric notes, an interview with the patient, and discussion amongst the staff took place to decide whether or not the patient would benefit from a psychotherapeutic approach. An effort was made to clarify the patients' expectations and determine whether they could tolerate cramped dormitory accommodation whilst attending groups and occupational therapy and complying with the requirements of primary nursing. Assessment of these patients was undertaken only when a place on the unit was available, which was rare. As a result, many apparently suitable patients had to be turned down. A small waiting list was sometimes maintained with patients who, for the time being, were seen as out-patients. Powerful family conflicts were often disclosed during this waiting period, and these demonstrated the significance of involving the family from the outset. In the case of patients with severe personality disorder, it was important to consider whether admission might precipitate a severe regression with acting-out behaviour that might prove too difficult for the unit to contain. The goal of the unit was to suit treatment procedures to the needs of the individual patient within a psychoanalytic perspective, as part of a long-term programme. Early discharge was not a primary consideration. The average length of stay settled at around nine months as staff became confident of their methods and convinced of the limitations of "quick turnover" care. A few patients with very severe personality disorders stayed for longer than a year, and readmissions, although not common, were sometimes predictable and even desirable for the successful working-through of important conflicts in personal relationships. Over 13 years the unit treated some 150 patients. ICD-9 (ninth edition of the *International Classification of Diseases*) diagnoses of the first 112 were: schizophrenia (27), other psychotic conditions (15), personality disorders (34); the balance comprised a miscellany of conditions, including anorexia nervosa, neurotic disorders of varying severity, and hitherto unsuspected organic disorders. The resources on the unit were far from ideal, with a continuing struggle to retain more experienced nursing staff. One consequence was that episodes of violent behaviour had sometimes to be dealt with by locking the door of the ward, using heavy medication, and even by transfer to an intensive-care ward. The occupational therapist and social worker had only a half-time attachment to the ward and were under pressure from the demands of other units. There were no financial or staffing privileges, and the ward was run as a conventional general ward, with the operational constraints this implies. In cases where individual psychotherapeutic treatment was undertaken, this was usually carried out by successive psy-chiatric registrars in training. Their lack of experience was compensated for by their enthusiasm, but their departure at the end of the six-month rotation period was disturbing for patients and staff alike. Although resources were limited, by comparison with the conditions under which some psychiatrists work in the United Kingdom, its facilities could be regarded as generous.

Application of "nursing process" procedures (Ritter, 1989), with an emphasis on the attachment of a primary nurse to each patient, permitted intensive nursing care reminiscent of the psycho-social model practised at the Cassel Hospital in London, although our unit was not a therapeutic community and the patient population and psychiatry practised were different. Each patient on the unit was cared for by a primary nurse and two associate nurses—an arrangement that usually overcame the unavoidable absences of individual nurses working a shift system. Experienced supervisors were provided by the hospital's out-patient psychotherapy department, which also provided individual or group psychotherapy for a few selected patients following discharge. The services of a family therapist became available latterly, and this work strengthened the view that early involvement with the family of the acute psychotic patient helps to shape an effective treatment plan (Räkköläinen, Lehtinen, & Alanen, 1991). A controlled study of elective referrals showed that where families were involved from the outset, there occurred a decrease in the need for hospitalization and an improvement in the patient's integration into ward life (Davison, unpublished paper).

First contact with family members was usually made by nursing staff. Whenever possible, the unit psychiatrist would then interview the family and obtain information necessary for formal assessment of a case. Where more detailed or prolonged family involvement was required this was undertaken by the social worker attached to the unit. From time to time the provision of nursing staff was stable enough to allow the organizing of pre- and post-discharge groups to assist the passage of the patient into the community. On discharge, a nurse who had known the patient—but not usually the primary nurse—was assigned as key worker with the aim of maintaining contact for as long as necessary. This provided a safety net during crises, a trustworthy listening ear, and the possibility of brief re-admission to the unit on a "guesting" basis if the key worker felt it necessary. This arrangement proved particularly useful to patients who had proceeded to individual out-patient psychotherapy, in that it supported the psychotherapist in the treatment of individuals who might otherwise have been regarded as too difficult to treat. Certain patients eventually received long-term psychoanalytic psychotherapy and a few (six in 13 years) were referred for formal psychoanalysis. Continuity of contact on the ward and after discharge came to be regarded as essential for all patients, but this often proved difficult to provide.

Special attention was paid in the milieu to elucidating the nature and meaning of tensions that developed in relationships between patients and staff. The identification and clarification of conflicts helped to explain the difficulties patients had long experienced in their personal relationships, which had often played a part in the development of their illness. A large group, consisting of the whole ward community of patients and available staff, met at the beginning of each day, and small groups were conducted twice-weekly by doctors and nurses under supervision. The small groups were relatively unstructured, dealing principally with immediate questions, such as why patients had needed admission, tensions on the ward, the setting and maintenance of boundaries, and occasionally with fundamental issues, such as mistrust, rivalry, attachment, and loss. A weekly staff group took place, the aim of which was to discern conflicts between staff members, though not to provide psychotherapy for the staff. These conflicts were often found to have originated in the pathology of patients as well as the personal attitudes and difficulties of the staff. The staff group could provide valuable diagnostic information as a result. More broadly, the group was able to help staff cope with pressures from external sources within the hospital and the National Health Service during a time of rapid change, conflict, and frustration. Attempts to work in new ways, which were quite different from conventional practice, caused problems for the staff, but with the help of the staff group such strains could be addressed, if not always resolved.

The function of the nurse was continually re-defined, as were the objectives of treatment and the patient's care plan. A formulation of different "levels of psychotherapy" (Cawley, 1983a) proved to be a valuable framework in this respect. A minimum level of supervision was regarded as essential, to help manage the burden of conflict, responsibility, and the impact of transferences onto the nurse. Conflicts of roles between doctors and nurses, males and females, occupational therapists and social workers were inevitable and, where possible, were discussed openly in an effort to reduce them to manageable proportions. The nurses operated primarily as reality-oriented figures, accepting patients as far as possible in a non-judgemental manner, whilst attempting to arouse their interest in the meaning of behaviour and subjective experience, and how these can relate to past and recent life. The philosophy of the ward in respect of psychotic disorder was that it signified a problem of adaptation to life circumstances and was not simply the consequence of inevitable misfortune, biological or

otherwise. Although the nurses did not aim to be psychotherapists, their work was often psychotherapeutic, and in many
cases they succeeded in enabling patients to assume increased
responsibility for their condition and future. The work of the
unit had a positive impact on the hospital as a whole. A post
was created for a senior unit nurse to become a specialist in
psychodynamic liaison throughout the hospital, which improved the unit's relationships with other hospital disciplines.
Another senior unit nurse undertook an extensive revision
of hospital nursing practice (based on the unit's methods) by
rewriting the Maudsley nursing handbook, adding a more
psychodynamic perspective (Ritter, 1989). The traditional pattern of "nurses care, doctors treat" was largely abandoned by
the unit as a result of its experiences, and when its new system
of shared responsibility for the therapeutics of psychosis went
well, which was certainly not all of the time, there occurred an
impressive state of cooperation by all members of the team
and, on certain memorable occasions, by all patients too.

CHAPTER EIGHT

Integration

Our aim in this book has been to demonstrate the value of a psychoanalytic perspective in the understanding and treatment of psychotic disorders, and of the importance of making emotional contact with afflicted individuals from the first opportunity. We have illustrated the significance of a psychodynamic evaluation when breakdown occurs or appears imminent. The greater the sensitivity of the assessor to the patient's emotional reality and the better his understanding of psychodynamics, the more profound and accurate will be the evaluation. A treatment plan may then be formulated and implemented in accordance with the patient's needs and capacities, which may vary at different times. Such a plan coordinates psychodynamic, psychosocial, neurobiological, and pharmacological methods so that each occupies its appropriate place within a comprehensive, fluid grasp of the patient's problems.

An attempt to reach a patient emotionally from the earliest moment involves: exercising empathy, discerning the non-psychotic part of his personality, attempting to understand his life (external and internal, present and past), searching out the meanings of his disturbance in relation to his history and prevailing phantasies, considering his experience of the interviewer and of providing him with the experience of being understood. Such a formidable list indicates a specialized activity in which competence can only come with training and experience. However, even in inexperienced but supervised hands, a basic knowledge of psychodynamic principles coupled with an attitude of respectful curiosity and a belief in the patient's resources and reparative capacities can prove to be of great benefit. If this attitude is carried over into long-term individual psychotherapy with an experienced therapist, impressive results can follow (see Levander & Cullberg, 1993). By comprehending the psychotic person's experiences in *his* terms, we discover an existential coherence and emotional logic to his communications. These may be confused or hard to follow, but they are his own ways of expressing his crisis. If we succeed enough in understanding him, we reach *levels of meaning* that offer significant explanations of the phenomena under observation. "Understanding" in the way we describe takes many forms, not least, for example, acceptance, tolerance, and the withstanding of the patient's communications. It is shorthand for the practitioner's progressive recognition of the patient's experience, its relation to his life story, and the way he has needed to control his severe underlying anxieties. Control requires the use of unconscious mental defence mechanisms to deal with otherwise unmanageable feelings arising particularly when he tries to achieve emotional closeness to others. In severe psychotic conditions these mechanisms have been active since infancy and may have led to structural changes within the personality. These can appear obvious when the onset of psychosis is early, or they may be slow and insidious, or present as limitations of personality that may not be obvious. Any improved awareness of his life problems and the causes of his limitations will help the patient integrate the meaning of his psychosis. The search for meaning and understanding may be thought of as an attempt to help a sane and cooperative part of the patient's mind to acquire an interest in how his mind works. We must try to find out why a part of his mind has become psychotic and why he maintains a prefer-

ence for the psychotic world, with all its confusion and sometimes terror, to the pains of the world of dependent relationships. Important contact can sometimes be achieved at the first
encounter, as we have demonstrated, depending upon the evo-
lutionary stage of the psychosis. If a high degree of integration
is subsequently acquired as the result of long-term individual
psychotherapy or psychoanalysis, the quest for self-knowledge
can become an enduring motive for the patient and an un-
swerving ally of sanity.

The notion of seeking out a sane part of the personality may
sound didactic, referring as it does to a patient's cognitive
appraisal of his mental life. However, if employed in a trustworthy, long-term therapeutic relationship, it should never
have the quality of intellectualization. It is a dialectical, educa-
tive interplay between cognitive, emotional, and unconscious
mentation and a reflective state to be pursued according to each
patient's ability. Intelligence and psychological-mindedness are
widely recognized as prerequisites for the acquisition of "insight" (see Glossary for comment regarding this elusive concept). Clinicians would be wise to remain open-minded about
any particular patient's potential for insight, as it occurs more
frequently than is realized. Even with chronic patients it is not
uncommon for the interviewer to be asked such questions as
"Why do I have such crazy ideas?", or "I know I am pregnant,
but I am a man and can't be. I can't stand the confusion!", or
"Why do I see my mother as a cockroach instead of something
else?". Unfussy explanations, perhaps using the analogy of
dream-like thinking invading waking life, can be extremely
relieving, as well as help the patient begin to integrate inner and
outer reality.[1] The degree to which psychotic patients appreciate a clear framework to begin understanding their experiences
should not be underestimated.

Much has been written about the clinician's need for understanding and the importance of the psychotherapist's attitudes
of warmth, empathy (see Ping-Nie Pao, 1983), and concern.

It is widely recognized that treating the psychotic is a very
different matter from treating the neurotic. However, the difference in the severity of pathologies should not be allowed to
induce unnecessary caution. For example, the psychoanalytic

dictum that direct interpretation of symbolic processes is inadvisable and hazardous need not be true for many psychotic patients. The advocates of supportive psychotherapy argue—understandably—that it is safer to help the psychotic individual to acquire a sense of existential security rather than reveal unconscious symbolic meanings (see, for example, Killingmo, 1989). Yet some psychotics deeply appreciate interpretations of hidden meanings, and they often respond with constructive understanding. Provided that these communications are offered in a clear way to the sane part of the mind at an appropriate developmental level, they are safe. The reason they are safe, and often highly effective, is because they are directed towards a more realistic and sane component of the mind capable of promoting thinking and emotional contact, whilst avoiding an assault on the psychotic part of the personality. Haphazard or uninformed use of interpretations of symbolic meanings can, of course, risk doing very severe harm. Experienced therapists know that as integration proceeds, so the neurotic patient's capacity for absorbing complex symbolic understandings increases. What is less well known is that this is also the case for many psychotic patients—again, provided that interpretations of unconscious, symbolic life are addressed to the part of the patient's mind that is sane.

Pathogenesis of schizophrenia: defence and deficit

The concept of a psychotic and non-psychotic part of the personality has far-reaching implications and an extensive theoretical history. Detailed consideration of this subject is beyond the scope of this book, but an outline of some of its theoretical premises is necessary to explain our emphasis on the interplay between destructive and reparative motivations in psychotic conditions. The work of Melanie Klein has fostered developments in theory and therapeutic approach which depart from the classical psychoanalytic position (see Spillius, 1988). Her elaboration of a psychology of infancy, her extension of

Freud's concept of the death instinct, her views on destructive envy, the early superego, and the emergence of reparative impulses in the depressive position have been extended by her followers, in particular by Segal, Rosenfeld, and Bion. (The originality of the work of Fairbairn also lay in this theme.) Rosenfeld's concept of destructive narcissism created a new understanding of the opposition to change that is frequently encountered in borderline and psychotic conditions, and of the negative therapeutic reaction first described by Freud (1923b)—of which the case of Nicola in chapter six provides an example. Bion's concepts of attacks on linking and containment offered an original approach to the pathology of thought and of thinking. (The difficulty in thinking experienced by Carmen in chapter four seemed to be an example of psychogenic thought blocking—see Grotstein, 1981a; O'Shaughnessy, 1992.) Elaborations of the notion of a psychotic organization as a dynamic structure within the personality of borderline and psychotic subjects have cast light on the pathogenesis and psychopathology of these conditions (see Steiner, 1993) and have provided a theoretical basis for the use of more active and confrontational techniques with certain psychotic patients in assessment and treatment.

In classical psychoanalytic theory, the schizophrenic is considered to have a "deficit" in ego functions that is ultimately inaccessible to psychoanalytic treatment and arising from an innate handicap or disturbed early object relationships. "Conflict" theorists, by contrast, consider that the psychopathology of schizophrenia is explained, like the neuroses, on the basis of impulse and defence,[2] as the pathological outcome of an attempted resolution of intrapsychic conflict.[3] Such a resolution may itself subsequently serve as a deficit in ego function, and a number of hypotheses have been put forward to explain this process (see Higgitt & Fonagy, 1992; Killingmo, 1989). The schizophrenic group of psychoses may, in the light of contemporary psychoanalytic (and neuro-physiological) research, be thought of as arising from an interpersonal or intrapsychic activation of a profound susceptibility originating in a variety of sources. Innate susceptibility may be of genetic origin, by way of mechanisms not yet properly understood, which may, in turn, be complicated by intrauterine or perinatal pathology such as infection or trauma. Pathogenic disturbances in the early environment may be biological and/or psychological in nature. Psychological causes of deep sensitivity are to be sought in disturbances of the early mother–infant relationship. Theories of *bonding, attachment, containment,* and *separation* enable these latter factors to be considered. Whilst psychoanalysts have in the past proposed a variety of explanations of psychosis based on Freud's economic and structural theories,[4] Klein gave priority to far earlier stages of development. Segal (1981) has presented a succinct summary of the Kleinian view of psychosis:

> It is our contention that psychotic illness is rooted in the pathology of early infancy where the basic matrix of mental function is formed. By projection and introjection, splitting the object into a good and a bad one followed later by integration, introjection and identification with good objects, the ego is gradually strengthened and it acquires a gradual differentiation between the external and the internal world; the beginnings of superego formation and relation to the external objects are laid down. It is at this time also, in the first year of life, that symbol formation and the capacity to think and speak develop. In psychosis, it is all these functions that are disturbed or destroyed. The confusion between the external and the internal, the fragmentation of object relations and the ego, the deterioration of perception, the breakdown of symbolic processes, the disturbances of thinking; all are features of psychosis. Understanding the genesis of the development of the ego and its object relationships and the kind of disturbance that can arise in the course of that development is essential to understanding the mechanisms of the psychotic. [p. 133]

We have included in the Glossary definitions and comments on basic psychoanalytic concepts, including those relating to psychosis, but for a fuller inquiry the comprehensive texts of Segal (1964), Greenberg and Mitchell (1983), Spillius (1988), Hinshelwood (1989, 1994), and Petot (1991) are recommended.

The recovery of imagination

The "Unimaginable Storms" of our title, taken from Yeats' poem, is a metaphor for psychotic mental storms that signify an all-consuming, immediate engulfment of the rational mind. Such a massive loss of contact with reality can induce panic anxiety and a disappearance of the sense of continuity of existence as an identifiable self. Not all psychotic individuals endure this extremity of distress, but those who do survive a quality of existence that is difficult, if not impossible, for the more sane person to imagine. If some form of representation of the psychotic experience can be achieved in the imagination of the afflicted subject, then an emotional distance can be established between the inundated self and the storm, and reflective—*symbolic*—thinking about the psychosis becomes possible. When psychotherapy succeeds, the individual recovers, or discovers, the capacity to think about experiences symbolically. He may come to understand that what he regarded as reality was, in fact, metaphor. For example, the belief: "I am the Messiah" may be comprehended as: "I wished to be omnipotently powerful, bigger than my father, because only in that way could I hope to gain control over my overwhelming feelings of powerlessness and inferiority". Or, "I am the Devil" may be recognized as an omnipotent belief that certain aggressive wishes are omnipotently destructive and generate unbearable guilt. Similarly, paranoid delusions may come to be seen as arising in the mind rather than emanating from the radio, passers-by, or distant stars.

The patient's dream life, in itself a visually observed experience involving a degree of distance, may begin to provide a helpful focus for a search for meanings. Acquiring a manageable psychological space to permit thinking to occur can be supported non-verbally through the use of graphic or plastic materials, in creative art work, in body movement, dance, or music. These media facilitate a point of departure for rational understanding and transformation, via the imagination, of upheavals that would otherwise need to remain under psychotic control (see Barnes-Gutteridge, 1993; Rycroft, 1968; Segal, 1991). When such growth processes occur, the psychosis becomes contained, its levels of meaning become approachable, and the individual can feel some rational control over his mental life. Unmodified, psychotic processes create a susceptibility to a quality of anxiety, sometimes like nightmare, variously described as "unthinkable anxiety" (Winnicott), "disintegration" (Kohut), or "nameless dread" (Bion).

Schizophrenia and neurobiological deficit

The fact that modern techniques of brain imaging and methods of neuropsychological investigation have confirmed the high incidence of neural and cognitive deficits in schizophrenia and schizophreniform states, and such findings as imbalance of hemispheric functions, has unavoidable implications for psychogenic (or psychosomatic) theories of schizophrenia.

Although it is likely that cognitive deficits may sometimes have a psychogenic origin, as Klein and Bion's work implies, as yet it is not known how often this occurs or how responsive to psychotherapy these defects are. It seems more appropriate to postulate that structural pathology creates a range of handicaps in its own right but also plays a varying part in interfering with the maturational programme of personality development. The early detection of handicaps in childhood[5] would indicate a need for remedial treatment, and detection at the evaluation stage of psychotic illness in adult life would suggest a need for specialized educational intervention. One generalization that seems to be accurate is that schizophrenia presents as a group of psychological disorders, often manifesting various degrees of brain pathology. There seems to be a case for differentiating sub-types of schizophrenia according to the presence or absence of brain pathology, of genetic influence, and of disturbed family relationships in early life. Pao (1979) has provided a useful classification, ranging from those with a normal or moderately disturbed early family environment who are in principle suitable for psychotherapy, through to those with severely disturbed backgrounds who are less accessible.[6] He also describes a group who have progressed from a less severe category into chronically deteriorated schizophrenia as the result of inadequate treatment or institutionalization. (The essentially iatrogenic nature of a significant proportion of chronic schizophrenia has been pointed out, for example, by Pylkkanen, 1989, and Cullberg, 1991.)

The Finnish approach

The dangers of generalizing about the causes and treatment of schizophrenia and the risk that the needs and capacities of the individual can be overlooked have often been pointed out (see Schultz, 1975). Comprehensive approaches that combine individual psychotherapy with group, family, pharmacological, and other treatment methods within the hospital or the community are the least likely to make these mistakes. Two countries in which such approaches have long been adopted in the public sector are Norway (see Ugelstad, 1979, 1985) and Finland (the most detailed and accessible account of this work is to be found in the *Nordic Journal of Psychiatry*—Alanen et al., 1990). A high level of conceptual clarity and sophisticated practice has been achieved since The National Schizophrenia Project in Finland was launched in the 1980s. This work has given rise to the "need-adapted" treatment model for schizophrenia and related psychoses (Alanen, Laakso, et al., 1986). (This model has been tested with favourable results on a large number of schizophrenic patients, with long-term follow-up—see Lehtinen, 1993.) The Finnish group responsible for this highly original approach so convinced their government of the cost-effectiveness of the use of psychoanalytic psychotherapy in mental illness that it is now widely available in Finland and usually publicly funded (Pylkkanen, 1989). A Nordic multicentre prospective cohort study of 65 first-attack schizophrenic patients was launched in 1983, and 57 of these were followed up in great detail (Alanen, Ugelstad, Armelius, et al., 1994). This important study worked towards a comprehensive and integrated model for early schizophrenic disorders within a psychodynamic perspective, providing individual psychotherapy for all the patients with varying combinations of other treatment modes. The results were impressive. The application of such comprehensive treatment is now long established in these countries, and in Norway a multicentre organization for research and treatment has been founded with official government support (The Centre for Psychotherapy and Psychosocial Rehabilitation of Psychosis—SEPREP).

From a psychoanalytic–anthropological point of view, early studies of pathological family interaction as a contributing factor of schizophrenia were first initiated by anthropologists in the 1950s (Bateson et al., 1956; Bowen, 1961; Lidz & Lidz, 1949; Wynne & Singer, 1965). This work reported on the high frequency of distorted and deviant patterns of communication in the families of schizophrenic patients, which had pathogenic significance in many cases. With further developments in systems theory and its application to the understanding of family dynamics, the place of family conflict in the aetiology of schizophrenia and of family therapy as a significant treatment component became accepted (for a concise account of this development see Falloon et al., 1984). However, the findings by workers in these fields were vulnerable to generalization, which led to certain partial truths mutating into misleading oversimplifications—for example, the unrestrained use of notions such as the "schizophrenogenic mother", or of a purely sociogenic theory of schizophrenia (in the later work of R. D. Laing), or of the opinion that family therapy theories rendered psychoanalytic therapy redundant.

The Finnish model itself began as a psychotherapeutic one but, like many other Western mental health systems, fell prey to an idealization of family therapy, which resulted in a decrease in interest in individual psychotherapy. For some time family therapy, along with other strategic, psychodynamic, and educational approaches, focused on systems of transaction within the family members which were considered to provide sufficient psychological analysis—*ergo* treatment— for psychotic patients. Eventually a more balanced position re-emerged in which crisis intervention with the family (in some cases developing into family therapy) was combined with individual psychotherapy and other modes of treatments in suitable cases. Contemporary British health policy of transferring the care and treatment of mentally ill patients from the hospital to the community has been motivated principally by short-term financial and ideological considerations. The former derive from the unacceptable cost of the large mental hospital population, the latter from a rising antipathy towards traditional public mental hospitals. The anti-psychiatry movement of the 1960s sought to liberate chronic psychotic patients from the adverse consequences of mental institutions, whilst creating an environment in which the original meaning of the term "asylum" as a place for refuge and recuperation might be realized. The study and development of therapeutic environments has received increasing importance in recent years (see Mosher & Burti, 1989), but regrettably this has often occurred at the expense and devaluation of what was most valuable about the traditional psychiatric hospital (for a review of the development of therapeutic environments see Werbart, 1992a; for clarification of the difference between psychoeducative and psychotherapeutic treatment philosophies of associated treatment units, see Werbart, 1992b). The Finnish model has used a comprehensive model that supports the therapeutic role and potential of the psychiatric hospital within a broader mental health policy. At the same time, it has shown how a hospital can serve as a base and a support for community services (see Alanen, 1992). Finnish hospital-based psychosis teams today provide a quick response to psychotic breakdown, including evaluation and the implementation of a psychodynamic need-adapted treatment plan (which takes into account future treatment in the community). The consequences have been a substantial reduction in the number of hospital admissions, more rational use of medication, prompt involvement of the family, reduction of the length of admissions, and a greater differentiation of patients who do not need admission or who need only a few days, from those who may need months (see Lehtinen, 1993; Räkköläinen et al., 1991). Although community-based teams play an indispensable part in the system, there has been a recognition that the hospital base is essential for the containment and management of most psychotic patients.

If the gulf between psychodynamics and biology is to be bridged, it is important to differentiate accurately between different theories, theorists, and applications by theorists to the understanding and treatment of psychosis. To avoid a polarization between "scientism" and environmentalism (an illusory and wasteful conflict), respect for contributions from differing disciplines must be accorded where they are merited. We have stressed that biological, social, and psychological methods have their own concepts, languages, and methods; bridges between them can be difficult or impossible to build. Engel (1962) suggested that nature is organized in a hierarchy of functionally interdependent dynamic systems, each requiring a distinct theoretical model. This is a valuable perspective and implies that neurobiology is essential but not sufficient to account for the creation of mental phenomena. Psychological theories such as psychoanalysis are needed to account for the dynamic complexities of the mind and of human interaction. These can include pathogenesis and the treatment of disorder, even in conditions with organic substrates like schizophrenia (for a critique of dualistic and interactionist theories of the body–mind relationship, see Robbins, 1992), but they do not explain their organic origins. Robbins cautions, however, that hierarchies do not represent reality. They are different disciplinary ways of conceptualizing a reality which is always larger and more complex ("God did not create the world along the lines of a University's departmental structure"—Cancro, 1986). With regard to hierarchical claims by neurobiology to explain mental functioning, he concludes:

> Neurobiological theory may properly attempt to account for both normal and disordered mental functions, and for the effects of thinking and meaning on the nervous system, including the effects of psychoanalytic treatment, but it must respect that these are not reducible to biology. [Robbins, 1992]

The history of the over-emphasis of biology in the explanation of mental events has been accounted for in the following terms:

> For many years, the psychological models of psychoanalysis dominated theory. With the exception of the early efforts of Freud and very few others, this theory was devoid of biological content. It may then be a form of justice that current theories are exclusively biological and devoid of psychological content. Although this may represent a form of cosmic equity, it is also scientifically regrettable. The biological theories suffer increasingly from reductionism.

Psychological phenomena cannot be reduced directly to biological phenomena . . . psychological concepts such as love are not going to be isomorphic with a molecular cluster. [Cancro, 1986]

In the light of these historical disagreements, perhaps it may prove simpler to build bridges between theorists than between theories. For example, the delineation of three different etiologic and phenomenological types of disorder within the schizophrenia group would seem to offer an opening for like-minded workers in each field of research to share their understandings for the benefit of practitioners and psychotic patients alike ("Render unto Caesar . . .").

Fast-food psychiatry

The need-specific approach to treatment introduced by the Finnish workers has demonstrated that many patients spend unnecessarily long periods in hospital and that admission rates can be reduced without diminishing the quality of care. If the quality of care in hospital is poor, time spent there can be of little long-term value, and at worst it is a damaging experience and a waste of money. Short-term government policies, the unconsidered pursuit of quick cures, and cost-cutting programmes have accelerated the decline of public hospital psychiatry—a situation that is being increasingly criticized. In the United Kingdom, the Mental Health Act Commission describes inner-city mental hospitals as "crumbling madhouses" (see *The Times*, 11 December 1993). In Australia, the failure of hospital care and of community provision for the severely mentally ill has been branded a national disgrace (*British Medical Journal*, 6 November 1993). Bad hospital psychiatry can also, of course, give good hospital psychiatry a bad name, but allowing for this, the preservation and improvement of hospital psychiatry has been impaired by poor government commitment over many years. Similarly, gross inadequacies in community care for the mentally ill are now widely recognized, in particular for psychotic patients previously installed, for better or worse, in mental hospitals. There is a view that the remedy is merely to increase funding. The desirability of such a move may seem obvious, but on what should the funding be spent? If spending is not accompanied by a coherent mental health policy (currently absent), which includes recognizing the role of the psychiatric hospital as a unique vehicle capable of adopting an integrated approach towards a psychotic patient, the quality of care for patients will remain inadequate or continue to decline. The task of defining a coherent mental health policy in the United Kingdom has not been achieved, even by professionals. This prevents successive governments, public servants, and the public themselves from recognizing and understanding what is needed to provide the best treatment and care of the mentally ill.

It is not only psychotic patients who suffer from an underfunded, strategy-starved, and increasingly impersonal mental health service. Psychiatrists, psychologists, nurses, and social workers often work under tremendous handicaps in their attempts to assist psychotic patients. Psychiatrists frequently spend more time in administration than talking with patients. "Burn-out" is common and serious, and a proportion of psychiatrists make no secret of their regret at having chosen psychiatry as a career. Beneficial advances in the knowledge of neurobiology and pharmacology can, if misused, lead to adverse, iatrogenic consequences for patients and clinicians. For example, where an inadequately trained or hard-pressed psychiatrist confines his first contact with a psychotic patient to completing check-lists of symptoms, making a diagnosis, and prescribing the appropriate medication, the patient is receiving second-rate care, and the clinician is learning little. Similarly, the value of psychiatric diagnostic classifications, as exemplified by *DSM 3R* (see under "Schizophrenia" in Glossary), varies entirely according to the aims of the user. The relentless pursuit of greater diagnostic precision, and of concern with form at the expense of content, can distract from recognition of the *meaning* of disturbed experience and behaviour, which may be crucial for the outcome of treatment. Lest we, the authors, appear excessively partisan in our advocacy of psychotherapy, it needs to be said that psychotherapists remain by no means beyond reproach where matters of clinical rigour are concerned. Psychotherapists may have something to learn from the intellectual discipline of traditional descriptive psychiatry—the so-called "medical model"—and the painstaking application of phenomenology to clinical work if they are to shake off a reputation for imprecision. (Comprehensive treatment of these topics is to be found in Cawley, 1983b; Clare, 1986; Mullen, 1986.) Considering the complexity of the material confronted, it is not surprising that the formulations of psychotherapists can become vulnerable to loose or confused thinking. This is not, however, an excuse for lack of rigour. Good psychotherapy will always possess an inherent uncertainty in its approach, which is a hallmark of respect for the human mind: yet psychotherapists need to cultivate clarity of thinking, conceptual accuracy, and technical precision as much as any other clinician. A plea should be inserted here for psychiatrists and psychotherapists never to forget the patient's personal history, including his responses to past treatment—if only to avoid a repetition of past mistakes and further ineffectual treatment. (This injunction does not apply to moments during the course of psychotherapy when it is important that the therapist should not be constrained by his knowledge of the patient's past history.) At the same time, it should be recognized that traditional psychiatric procedures such as history-taking, whilst essential, can readily be used by a clinician as an intellectual defence against genuine emotional engagement with the patient: this is an impediment and a danger for all psychiatrists, not to mention those in their charge.

Although the cases we have presented appear at times dramatic, such patients are commonly encountered in the daily work of the public hospital service, and they offer ample opportunity for mental health workers to increase their understanding of psychotic states. If these patients are approached from a psychoanalytic perspective, as we have done, many issues, theoretical and practical, arise. The advantages to the patient of detection of psychosis, imminent or overt, at the earliest possible moment cannot be overestimated, and a skilled psychodynamic assessment is of enormous help in achieving this. All the patients we have described in this book were chronically ill by the time they were referred to us—a situation that could have been avoided in many cases had an earlier psychodynamic assessment taken place. Recent innovative developments in the work of early intervention teams are achieving success in this respect. Other efforts to help families adapt to the care of schizophrenic relatives have emerged in recent years, notably through education. With only a little psychodynamic knowledge to complement their understanding of the patient's character, families can often make good sense of the schizophrenic condition. It has also been established that high expressed emotion ("E.E.") in the family has an adverse effect on schizophrenic patients, and training of the family in stress management can redress this. However, if, as may happen, relatives are only advised that their child has a disease like diabetes to which they must adapt, and that they can take comfort from the fact that the illness is in no way their fault, the opportunity for deeper investigation of the psychodynamic nature of the stressful emotions evoked in the patient may be lost, and with it the understanding of the patient's psychotic thinking and behaviour. Although reassurances can help some families, they are unlikely to resolve the guilt that many relatives feel, often quite unwarranted, nor will they illuminate the unconscious elements in parent–child relationships that may be more complex than "blame" or "guiltless" imply. As Lehtinen has remarked, psycho-educational approaches stress the importance of continuous depot neuroleptics, whereas the Scandinavian need-adapted approach goes further: "medication is not used to cure an illness, but is explicitly prescribed to help a behavioural pattern or experience, and its effect is analysed in those terms" (Lehtinen, 1993). The same author has made the trenchant observation that when the concept of mental illness or disease is over-used on first contact, it may contaminate (in a manner analogous to a computer virus) all subsequent transactions with a schizophrenic patient. Seeing the patient as a passive victim of a disease process can infantilize him and deprive relatives of better understanding, which may sometimes be superior to that of the professional. The frequent adverse consequences of approaching the patient from an exclusively biomedical point of view were long ago described as "closure"—a labelling of the patient by all concerned as totally different from other people (Scott & Ashworth, 1967). It can also serve to conceal the part the patient may be playing, for whatever reasons, in creating and maintaining stressful situations. An interesting comparable approach can be seen in the philosophy of Alcoholics Anonymous. Participants are told that they have an incurable disease from which they will not recover and to which they are or have been innately vulnerable. However, treatment is based on a firm confrontation of their individual responsibility for the management of their condition, and for the cultivation of a lifelong search for increased self-awareness and psychological insight.

At the present time, when many in-patient units are being reduced in size to accommodate brief admissions for rapid neuroleptic medication and early discharge, there is a case for re-stating the importance of those units whose work seeks to promote fundamental change in patients. Such a claim does not imply that all patients should have psychoanalytic psychotherapy or necessarily spend a long time in hospital. However, if a skilled psychodynamic assessment of a patient is made on first contact, it becomes possible to make an informed selection from a range of treatments (if available) most fitted to the patient's disabilities, vulnerability, and potential psychological assets. Medication, individual psychotherapy, group-, couple-, and family therapy, psychosocial, behavioural, and cognitive methods might all be employed at various stages as the patient becomes able to benefit from them. This method, used by the Finnish group, gave rise there to hospital and community-based psychosis teams able to differentiate with some precision those patients who did not need admission from those who needed brief or long stays. These psychiatrist-led but non-authoritarian teams offer an improved role for the clinical psychiatrist of the future and an opportunity to promote a more integrated psychiatry. Many psychiatrists today see their specialized skills undervalued and some of their roles usurped by other professionals.[7] Fragmentation of identity and disillusion within the profession would be less likely to occur if general psychiatrists were encouraged to acquire a deeper, more rounded grasp of the psychodynamic components of severe mental illness. Part of this understanding would involve some form of training in psychodynamics (already mandatory in some countries) as without this the psychiatrist will not be properly equipped to fill his unique place amongst fellow-professionals in the mental health services.

Although it may seem obvious to psychotherapists and psychiatrists who practice psychodynamic methods that the approach to psychosis we have described is therapeutically potent and economically cost-effective, financial providers will need to be convinced.[8] Outcome research presents unique difficulties in a field where controlled clinical trials may be misleading or inappropriate,[9] and individual case studies rarely carry widespread conviction (see Milton, 1992, for a critical review of literature relevant to outcome research in psychotherapy). Much reported work fails to take account of the different levels of skill, experience, and psychotherapeutic ambition of the individual psychotherapists involved in the study; of criteria used in the selection of schizophrenic patients; or of the settings within which work took place. A useful clarification of psychotherapeutic aims differentiated insight-oriented (EIO) from reality-adaptive supportive (RAS) psychotherapy, and served as a reminder that different patients have different treatment aptitudes and different requirements (Gunderson et al., 1984; Stanton et al., 1984). However, impressive results have been recorded of insight-oriented psychotherapies (e.g. Fenton & McGlashan, 1987; Karon & VandenBos, 1980; Sjöström, 1985), and recent Swedish studies in case-finding and in the identification of predictors of good and bad outcome for psychotherapy have been well received (Cullberg, 1991; Cullberg & Levander, 1991; Levander & Cullberg, 1993). In the psychodynamic treatment and rehabilitation of schizophrenic psychoses the work of the Finnish group is now well established, not least for its outstanding cost-effectiveness (Lehtinen, 1993). The fact that this advanced work is being done in Scandinavia is a reflection of a long history of concern for the individual and the high quality of social welfare systems.[10] Changing social trends are forcing revision, and a reduction in welfare provision is taking place, as in all developed countries. The large population of psychotic patients needing long-term treatment and support is potentially at risk, but it is to be hoped that the flexibility and sophistication of the Scandinavian approach will minimize this. The devastating impact on families who receive little or no support in their care of a chronic schizophrenic member is gradually being recognized, following many years of psychosocial research.[11]

Undoubtedly, the quality of overall care for the psychotic patient will only be improved by increased financial resources: however, the quality of clinical care by the individual practitioner is largely independent of financial considerations. Every patient should have the right to tell his life story from the first time of contact, if possible, and the practitioner has an obligation to encourage him to do so and to learn to listen with as high a degree of understanding as possible. For example, a genuine but non-colluding interest in the content of a psychotic patient's delusions can offer entry into the nature of his preoccupations and their place in his life history. Simple comments like, "How has it come about that you now believe that you are Hitler?", "What was happening in your life at the time?", "What do you think it might mean that you are experiencing spiders crawling round inside your head?", or "I wonder what it must be like for you to be uncertain whether you are a man or a woman?" can lead to relief and often useful developments and enable the patient to feel you are on his side. If no other interest is taken in delusional content than to establish a diagnosis, crucial opportunities are lost. If we do not discover why the patient needs delusional explanations for his distress, it is unlikely we shall ever succeed in helping him find better, more realistic ones.

Public interest in psychodynamic understanding and psychological disturbance has grown over the years. In Britain the major training bodies offer public lectures in the concepts of psychoanalysis and on individual topics of special interest. Presentation in the media varies from occasionally excellent to staggeringly naive. Tragic cases of self-damaging, violent, or bizarre behaviour are often portrayed as mere failures in care by the community, with no interest in the origins and meaning of the psychotic behaviour. The conclusion drawn from these tragedies tends to be that patients should receive more supervision to ensure they take their medication. This may be needed in many cases, but it cannot be taken for granted that the treatment these patients have received has been based on an accurate, skilled assessment of their mental state and needs.

Conclusion

It may take time before the treatment pendulum, which has swung in recent years in the direction of biology, will come to rest at a point where collaboration between biological, psychosocial, and psychoanalytic thought is achieved. Integrating the treatment modes available to help the severely mentally disturbed patient would create a welcome complementarity. This would not mean equivalence. The relevance of each treatment would be assessed according to its power to increase understanding of the psychotic patient, reduce distress, improve the quality of his life, and stimulate mental growth processes. Applied sensitively, conditions for improved object-relationships and a more established sense of self would be created. This objective is neither utopian nor beyond the capacity of daily psychiatric practice to achieve. Even if the necessary resources do not exist, we are obliged to provide the best treatment we can. The approach that we have presented could make considerable improvements possible in ordinary circumstances, given some integrated planning by collaborating professionals.

Psychiatry today is an extremely demanding discipline. Its practitioners carry a heavy burden of responsibility for difficult and often potentially dangerous decisions, and they are obliged to do good work each day in the face of psychotic and psychopathic behaviour. Psychiatrists are under pressure from many quarters, not least from the effects of inadequate resources. The perspectives we have brought to bear might suggest that there exists a large-scale failure in psychiatric provision for psychotic patients, a failure that has not been properly realized. Some would argue this is the case. Our aim in this book has been to demonstrate how the present difficult situation can be improved by those people with an immediate opportunity to effect change—clinicians themselves. If the dimension of unconscious mental processes and the inherent meaning of psychotic experiences can be taken into account in our daily work, then much psychiatry, including research into the outcome of treatment, will no longer run the risk of lacking substance. The care of psychotic patients may suffer immeasurably if attention is restricted to diagnosis, symptom control with medication, return to the community, and time-limited stress counselling for relatives. Where concern is absent for the relevance of delusional experience and its unconscious formation and a developmental approach is not acknowledged, a grasp of the psychotic patient's world is unlikely to be acquired. Understanding the meaning of psychotic experience and behaviour permits the clinician to bring to the psychotic individual the depth of understanding all human beings, normal or psychotic, need and deserve, and without which life is impoverished and, at worst, meaningless. The proper application of psychoanalytic concepts to psychotic patients in a contained, well-managed setting yields profound benefits we ignore at our patients' expense.

We have described the setting in which the work we presented was carried out, and how the work represents the application of psychoanalytic principles within the context of general clinical psychiatry. We have drawn attention to centres in Scandinavian countries where these principles have been applied with a high level of sophistication and encouraging results. Such work has not received the attention it deserves outside Scandinavia, and we believe it offers both a cost- and treatment-effective way forward for the care of psychotic patients. If the motivation exists, and the resources, beneficial changes in patients will not be difficult to achieve. In addition, the use of experienced psychotherapists, medical or non-medical, as members of hospital and community teams could make a major contribution to treatment (see Hobbs, 1990). At the very least, an experienced psychotherapist should be on hand at the assessment stage. Nurse training in psychodynamics could revive interest in a creative career in psychiatric nursing—an interest sadly declining in the public sector. A psychodynamic perspective on psychopharmacology would improve the quality and sensitivity of prescribing and maximize the potential of these essential, potentially dangerous, and often misused drugs. We do not suggest that all mental health professionals become psychodynamic psychotherapists, but we believe that they should acquire some understanding of what this knowledge is, and of its potential contribution to hospital and community psychiatry. Education can be acquired in different ways, at different levels: the most important single item in a training in psychotherapy is a period of personal psychotherapy. This can be recommended to all interested workers, as there is little to match first-hand experience of the process. If it proves successful—perhaps even profound—it provides the worker with a unique deepening of sensitivity to the pain and suffering experienced by a high proportion of psychotic patients, a recognition of the fact that "normal" people also have psychotic characteristics, and what it is like to experience painfully acquired mental defences being questioned. An invaluable consequence of successful personal therapy for the mental health worker is a heightened capacity to understand the experience of *countertransference*. For example, it is easy to feel irritation, even flashes of hatred, towards a difficult or impossible patient. This can be a countertransference reaction. In an in-patient setting, staff have to cope with such feelings every day. Only by distinguishing which feelings originate in and belong to the patient (and are perhaps being unconsciously forced into another person) and which to oneself is it possible not to take these emotional assaults personally in a way that inhibits work. When a psychotic patient has the good fortune to meet such a sensitive, psychodynamically informed professional helper, his experience of the treatments subsequently made available to him, not to mention the clinical encounter itself, is likely to be a very different and more valuable one. We hope that this book will contribute to the search for a fully comprehensive model for the understanding and treatment of psychotic individuals and be of some value to those engaged in a personal and professional search for a more integrated perspective.

GLOSSARY

For those who find some of the terms we have used confusing or who do not have access to more formal psychoanalytic texts (e.g. Hinshelwood, 1989; Laplanche & Pontalis, 1973; Moore & Fine, 1968; Rycroft, 1968; from whom we have borrowed extensively), we offer a brief glossary of terms to be encountered in this book and elsewhere, with related comments.

Claustro-agoraphobia

Pathological fears of closed or open spaces are relatively common and, like many other phobias, may respond to behavioural methods of treatment. However, some cases are resistant to such treatment and can prove extremely disabling. This disturbance can be explained more or less satisfactorily as the expression of a state of mind brought about by the excessive use of projective identification, which confers a particularly severe quality of anxiety. This dynamic can be described as a phantasy of *being trapped inside an object*, or else of being threatened by psychic disintegration when outside it, as a result of its total loss.

Containment

The term "containment" is often used loosely, and it is therefore important to be clear about what is being referred to, about whom, and in what context. Broadly, it signifies actions necessary to protect the acutely disturbed patient from harm to himself or others, usually involving admission to a suitable containing structure—typically, a psychiatric hospital ward—where he will find people who will try to "contain" him. This means controlling dangerous or self-destructive behaviour; reassuring him as far as possible by words and behaviour; talking with him, if this can be done, in order to understand what he is experiencing; and, if these anxiety-alleviating measures prove insufficient, administering appropriate tranquillizing medication. When the acute disturbance subsides, a further level of containment then becomes possible, facilitated by the understanding, withstanding, accepting, and enquiring attitude described. A final sense of the word is to be found in the process whereby the helper may at times detect that the patient is attempting to recruit him into acting a role in his inner drama. This definition of containment refers to being able to accept and emotionally digest the patient's projections in the service of understanding him. Elucidation of the drama being revealed in the therapeutic relationship can help him to recognize, tolerate, *work through*, and ultimately find improved solutions to the (often unconscious) inner impulses and desires being lived out. Nursing staff can play an important part in this revelatory process, and it requires them to differentiate between *regressive* behaviour that is undesirable from that which represents material the patient is unwittingly bringing to the specialists to be helped. The concept of containment in this sense of a potentially growth-promoting process has been elaborated in detail by Bion in his "container–contained" theory (see Bion, 1970).

Delusion

In psychiatric usage, a "delusion" is a false but fixed belief that is impermeable to reason or logic (see Hingley, 1992; Roberts, 1992). The circumstances that give rise to it are incompletely understood. Grandiose, persecutory, or erotic delusions are characteristic of schizophrenic, paranoid, and manic psychoses, and delusions of unworthiness of psychotic depression. Persecutory delusions, sometimes constructed around a fragment of truth, may represent the retaliatory consequences of destructive envious and acquisitive wishes (see Freeman, 1981). Delusions may appear in the psychotherapeutic transference and, depending on the circumstances and the skill of the therapist, may bring psychotherapy to a halt or, on the other hand, may be worked through to provide a unique learning experience for the patient.

Depressive position

Klein asserted that the normal infant has, by the age of three to six months, reached sufficient mental maturity to be able to integrate the previously split and opposing versions of his mother (good-providing and bad-withholding). Before this, his feelings of love and hatred have been dealt with by primitive defence mechanisms—principally, splitting and projective–introjective procedures. This early stage is the *paranoid–schizoid* position, and the later one the *depressive* position. The latter can be regarded as a maturational achievement, the "stage of concern" (Winnicott, 1958). The first stage is accompanied by persecutory guilt, where concern is for the survival of the self, the second by depressive guilt, where concern is for the object. Attainment of the capacity for depressive anxiety is considered a necessary quality for the forming or maintaining of mature object relationships, since it is the source of generosity, altruistic feelings, reparative wishes, and the capacity to tolerate the object's ultimate separateness. It is not a once-and-for-all achievement in which the paranoid–schizoid mode is left behind, but, rather, a dialectic (or diachronic) relationship between different levels of integration, continuing through-out life. Increasing maturity brings a growing capacity to function at the level of the depressive position. Such growth does not bring an idealized freedom from unhappiness but, rather, brings new and different burdens, albeit of a human sort, and a potential for freedom to make responsible choices. It is not the resolution of a dilemma . . . "one is stuck with it, with all its advantages and disadvantages, unless one regressively flees from it into the refuge and imprisonment of the paranoid–schizoid position or through the use of manic defences" (Ogden, 1990).

Envy

The envious wish to possess what the object is seen or believed to have, and that the subject does not have, may generate admiration and a desire to emulate and acquire through personal effort. This constructive, life-affirming im-pulse represents the positive face of envy. In the case of destructive envy, sometimes referred to as primary or infan-tile envy, there issues a wish to deprive the object of his possession or to spoil it by devaluation or other hostile means. Klein regarded envy as an innate element in mental life, first directed at the mother's feeding breast and at the creativity this represents, and she considered it to be a basic pathogenic factor in mental illness, in particular at the core of schizophrenic psychopathology. In contrast to *jealousy*, which involves three parties, envy reflects a two-party situa-tion. The envied object is hated, not because it is bad, but because it is good but is not in the possession of the envious subject. This carries profound implications for mental life (see Joseph, 1986). Primary envy, according to Klein, leads in infancy to phantasies of invading and colonizing the in-terior of the mother's body, which is felt to be the container of good things, and of destroying those contents that are felt to be bad or undesirable, such as other babies. Normal mental mechanisms, primarily splitting, projection, and in-trojection, permit development to proceed in infancy, in the process generating feelings of love, trust, and *gratitude* which overcome envious hatred (see "Envy and Gratitude",

Klein, 1957). An individual is rendered vulnerable to psychosis in later life by the varying degrees of failure of these normal developmental steps. This view of mental life, and of psychosis, has by no means been accepted by all psychoanalysts. (A detailed exposition of sources of evidence in favour of these concepts and an examination of the disagreements has been provided by Hinshelwood, 1989.)

Identification

Contrary to the popular sense of this term as a process of recognition, "identification" refers to a mental process whereby the subject comes to feel himself to be similar, the same as, or identical with another person in one or more aspects. It may be a complex state and take different forms. He can achieve this by extending his identity *into* someone else (projection), by borrowing his identity *from* someone else (introjection), or by fusing or confusing his identity *with* someone else (at times believing similarity to mean equivalence).

"*Projective identification*" refers to an unconscious belief that a part of the self or inner world, usually unwanted, can be disposed of by re-location into the mental representation of another object. This is usually regarded as a primitive form of the mental mechanism of *projection*, different in that it may involve behaviour by the subject towards the object in a way that will allow him to confirm his omnipotent suppositions. The projectively identifying mechanism can be used for purposes of denial (of disposing of unwanted elements), or of controlling the object or of communication. In the latter case, the therapist is required to attend to his own non-rational responses to the patient's communications, his *countertransference*, which will constitute an important source of information about the patient's state of mind at that moment. Many psychoanalysts hold that projective identification is a primary form of communication between mother and baby, comparable with the *attunement* described by workers in infant observation research (Stern, 1985).

"*Introjection*" is a process of taking something into the mind (*internalizing*) which can sometimes be felt as a bodily event (*incorporating*). Such elements may then be integrated, temporarily or permanently, into the ego and felt as being part of the self, thus completing the process of *introjective identification*. Since projective identification depletes the self and distorts perceptions of the object, what is introjected may also be a more or less distorted version of the actual object. Differentiation of what belongs to the subject and what to the object is held to be a fundamental process of infant mental development and is often a major sorting-out process in psychotherapy later in life. Introjective identification is the basis of much normal learning, and normal projective identification underlies a mature capacity for *empathy* (the ability to imagine oneself in another person's place without losing awareness of one's identity). By contrast, *pathological* projective identification is conducted with omnipotence and violence (Bion, 1959), leading to a confusion of self and object and susceptibility to psychotic developments.

"*Splitting*" is a term used to depict a normal mental activity in which the ego strives as part of its development to effect distinctions and differences. Pathological splitting is an extremely primitive defence thought to precede developmentally many others, including repression.

Identity

One of the characteristics of maturity is the possession of a strong sense of "identity"—the stable conviction of being an individual distinguishable from all others, and an enduring sense of existing intactly in space and time. Psychoanalytic theory holds that a sense of identity has its roots in infancy on the basis of processes of identification, which gradually evolve in the course of development into a capacity for object relationships. Many psychotic symptoms develop on the basis of a fragile sense of personal identity, and certain personality disorders are characterized by a "*diffusion*" of identity.

Insight

This complex concept has several referents. In everyday usage, "insight" refers to self-knowledge, or self-awareness. In psychiatry, it refers to the capacity to recognize that disturbing thoughts and feelings are subjective and can be tested against reality—a capacity that is more or less absent in the psychotic. In clinical practice, the assessment of insight is of central importance. Insight can be considered as a continuum, with different mechanisms responsible for impairment in individual patients (see Berrios & Markova, 1992; David, 1990). The term has at times been misused to promote a "Eurocentric" world view (Perkins & Moodley, 1993). In psychoanalytic usage, a distinction is made between emotional and intellectual insight. The latter can be used for constructive purposes or for defence (pseudo-insight).

Interpretation

In the simplest sense, "interpretation" means an explanation that the therapist gives to the patient of something that he believes he has understood that would be helpful to the patient to consider at that particular time. It may concern the latent meaning of what the patient is doing or saying, it may address the mechanisms of defence, the content, or the transference, or it may be a direct statement about the meaning of symbols given independently of the patient's associations. As a general rule, defence should be attended to before content, and premature interpretation of content or symbolic expressions is usually a mistake and sometimes a serious one. In psychotherapeutic practice, interpretation usually involves a long period of elucidating meanings in the material of dreams, symptoms, or associations that the patient brings into the therapy. Interpretation should offer information that the patient is capable of understanding and tolerating at the particular time, in the simplest possible terms. Ill-timed, misdirected, or unduly complicated interpretations may be at best ineffectual and at worst harmful. (A psychotic patient who believes he is sane may experience such an ill-conceived intervention as an attempt by the therapist to drive him mad, or as a confession by the therapist that he is afraid of the patient.) Although interpretations are potentially powerful devices, open to misuse, they are not necessarily the exclusive preserve of the experienced psychotherapist. Because the term itself may suggest that the practitioner has oracular powers, the term "intervention" may often be appropriate to describe the wide variety of verbal contributions that the therapist may make (see Sandler, Dare, & Holder, 1992). In sensitive hands, not necessarily psychotherapeutic, such interventions may prove extremely helpful.

Mourning

In its normal form, "mourning" is a response to loss of a loved object, following bereavement, accompanied by grief, and pursuing a course that ultimately leads to recovery and a renewed interest in life. This healing process may be arrested or distorted in many ways, and since the time of Freud's classic work "Mourning and Melancholia" (1917e [1915]) the subject of unresolved or pathological mourning has received much attention by psychiatrists and psychoanalysts (e.g. Bowlby, 1980, 1988; Klein, 1940; Parkes, 1975; Pedder, 1982). Freud was the first to consider melancholia (psychotic depression) as a pathological form of mourning, and Klein extended the term to embrace losses in the inner world of object relations—losses that may be independent of external reality. Whereas depression may be associated with grief, normal or abnormal, the "depressive position" refers to a related but dissimilar use of the term.

Object

In psychoanalytic usage, an "object" is usually a person, a part of a person, or a symbol representing the whole or part person, to which the subject relates in order to achieve instinctual satisfaction. In object-relations theory, priority is given to the need for persons rather than simply the wish to satisfy instinctual drives. Theoretical developments have led to the conceptualization of *internal* objects and object-relationships in the inner world of unconscious phantasy, and of *psychic* (or *psychological*) reality. These concepts concern the interplay of mental representations, usually unconscious, with external (actual) objects in the outer world.

Psychodynamic

Although several theoretical and clinical approaches deal with concepts of mental forces in dynamic interplay, the term "psychodynamic" is widely used to define the approach founded on basic analytic concepts of unconscious mental life, conflict and defence, internal reality, transference/countertransference, repetition–compulsion, acting out, and working through in the therapeutic process. The same considerations apply to the term "*psychoanalytic psychotherapy*".

Psychoneurosis

"Psychoneurosis" is essentially a psychogenic condition with a range of symptoms of which anxiety and inhibitions are prominent. It is usually differentiated from psychosis on the basis of the intactness of the sense of reality in the former. In Kleinian psychoanalytic theory, neurotic disorders may represent the belated expression of psychotic processes that have not been successfully negotiated in early life.

Psychosis, psychotic

The term "psychosis" refers to a broad category of mental disorders, which are characterized by severe abnormalities of thought processes. These are associated with disturbance of the sense of reality and often with delusions, hallucinations, and disruption of the sense of personal identity. Psychotic elements may occur in severe neuroses, psychosomatic disorders, sexual perversions, and personality disorders. Psychoses may be *organic*, if caused by demonstrable organic disease, or *functional*, if no organic pathology can be found. Functional psychoses are regarded by some as purely *psychogenic*, requiring psychological understanding and treatment. At the other extreme, some hold to the view that they are purely *biogenic*. A more integrated approach might allow for the possibility that both elements make a contribution. The concept of psychotic and non-psychotic parts of the personality in the individual, introduced by Bion, provided a new perspective to the understanding of psychosis and an emphasis in psychotherapy on making contact with the sane part of the person, presumed to be present, but often hidden, in every psychotic patient.

Predisposition: Biologically oriented psychiatry maintains that a predisposition to schizophrenic, manic–depressive, and some other psychoses exists in the form of a genetically determined biological disorder, and there is evidence for this view in a significant proportion of cases. Psychoanalytic thinking, whilst not rejecting the significance of innate biological differences, tends to view vulnerability in terms of failure of adequate formation of primitive object relations in infancy, leading to the use of mental defence mechanisms to protect the fragile core of the personality. This *defence* view contrasts with a *deficit* view held by some psychoanalytic theorists who question the Kleinian emphasis on the role of conflict in early infancy.

Precipitation: In cases of gradual onset of psychosis, there may be no obvious precipitating cause, and a gradual decompensation of mental defence mechanisms may prove to be a satisfactory explanation. Where the onset is more acute, the cause may be found in an inability to cope with stress, often in the external world and involving combinations of such factors as disappointment, frustration, object loss, or separation. Arousal of guilt and anxiety over envious, sexual, or acquisitive wishes may be involved. These anxieties sometimes take the form of threats to the sense of coherent and continuous self; they have been variously termed *traumatic anxiety, organismic panic,* and *ontological anxiety* to indicate their overwhelming nature.

Prognosis: The best prognostic outlook of all is for the young person with little or no sign of previous disturbance who breaks down acutely under major stress. About one-third of acutely psychotic patients recover in a matter of weeks or months, with or without specific treatment, and experience no further attack. A similar proportion have recurrent attacks that may lead to chronicity. These first two groups are likely to be suitable subjects for psychotherapy, with or without the help of anti-psychotic medication. A further, more chronically suffering group is held to be unlikely to respond to a psychotherapeutic approach and is best helped with medication, cognitive and behavioural methods of treatment, and long-term rehabilitation and support. Even with the most refractory and chronic patients it has been shown that the long-term outcome is better than had been thought. From a psychotherapeutic point of view, it is clear that suitability for psychotherapy and early treatment are the most important prognostic factors.

Regression

In the face of psychological stress the individual may revert to an earlier and less mature level of functioning. This "regression" can be understood as a defensive retreat to infantile stages of development, stages that are never completely outgrown and may at times have the constructive potential of a withdrawal to a safe base, where mental forces can be re-grouped. Regression occurring in the course of psychotherapy can have a beneficial effect (therapeutic regression) or a bad one (malignant regression), depending on the maturity of the patient and the skill of the therapist. Opinion is divided on the question of encouraging this process in patients with severe personality disorders (see Winnicott's concept of "false self", 1960, and Balint's "new beginning", 1952). In psychotic patients, the use of regression as a deliberate technique is generally considered as at the very least unwise and at the worst dangerous, with the possible exception of a few specially experienced practitioners. The psychotic patient is usually quite regressed enough, at least in the acute stage, and the problem is usually that of containing the regression within the therapy and the institution. Lehtinen (1993) believes that regression in an acute psychotic attack can be substantially alleviated by family therapy meetings on first contact.

Reparation

Melanie Klein's views on the ubiquity of aggressive phantasies and destructive desires in early life have sometimes been received with scepticism, even shock, by those who have not recognized or accepted the central position accorded loving and reparative feelings in her theories of development. In her analytic work with small children, she recognized the distress and guilt that accompanied destructive wishes and observed the growth of feelings of remorse and desire to repair damage done in phantasy to ambivalently loved figures who are the target of envious and jealous hatred. Such reparative desires often take the form of obsessional activity, partly understandable as an attempt to preserve the object or to repair damage by magical means. In the course of psychotherapy with adults, failed attempts at reparation may often be discerned, and manic states may sometimes be found to contain similar strivings. Such manic reparation, like other failed attempts, does not succeed, partly because the subject is unaware of the damage he believes he has done and is perhaps still doing, and partly because he also does not know how to go about repairing it (see Riviere, 1936). The emergence of depressive guilt and reparative wishes marks the higher level of maturity and integration of the *depressive position*, which is regarded by Klein as the mainspring of true creative processes (see Segal, 1981). The application of this concept to the psychotherapy of the adult adds an optimistic note to the uncovering of such unconscious, painful facts of mental life. Reparation can become a possibility, and it is the task of the psychotherapist to help the patient differentiate between where his personal responsibility lies and where it does not, and to find ways of making amends. The concept of the need to repair *internal* as well as *external* objects permits the possibility of working through feelings of regret and mourning, even if the victim of the destructive wishes is long dead.

Schizophrenia

The term "schizophrenia" was introduced to define a group of severe psychotic disorders characterized by a dissociation or splitting of the mental functions, in contrast to an earlier view of a single specific mental disease leading to dementia (dementia praecox). It has been variously considered as an illness, a syndrome, a way of living, or even as a medical fiction invented to satisfy relatives, society, and psychiatrists (cf. Szasz, 1961). It has no single agreed cause but is best considered as a syndrome or group of disorders with a range of possible contributory or causative factors—biogenic, sociogenic, and psychogenic. The development of the detailed and complex DSM 3R classification system (the revised version of the third edition of the *Diagnostic and Statistical Manual of the American Psychiatric Association*) has gone a long way towards preventing this rigid labelling: its "multi-axial" diagnostic procedure allows for diagnosis to be regularly revised in the light of changes in the clinical condition of the patient. Thus in a case where emotional feelings are prominent, a diagnosis of *schizo-affective psychosis* is usually deemed appropriate, and unless six months of continuous illness have passed, the diagnosis *schizophreniform* should be made. Much research work includes these two diagnoses in the category of "schizophrenia". Where there is a recent precipitating stress, the diagnosis *reactive psychosis* is available, and where uncertainty remains, *psychosis* (unspecified) is often used.

Self

The term "self", as used in psychoanalysis, refers to the individual as a reflective *agent*, aware of his own identity. It belongs to a different frame of reference from the term "*ego*", with which it is sometimes confused. The latter refers to a structure in the mind, parts of which are unconscious and necessitate a degree of insight to become known to the self. The various adjectival forms commonly encountered—such as *self-esteem*, *self-preservation*, *self-mutilation*, *self-observation*—are usually regarded as referring to a *whole* self.

However the concept of *part*-selves that may exist in a state of identification with other (part or whole) objects, may at times promote the question "*which* self?" or "*which* object?", particularly in the case of the psychotic person. These partial identifications may be of long standing and have complex, condensed meanings. Rey (1994), regarding mental processes as having coordinates in space and time, has provided a formula to help the psychotherapist who wishes to explore the details of such a process: "What part of the subject situated where in space and time does what, with what motivation, to what part of the object situated where in space and time, with what consequences for the object and the subject?"

Symbolic and concrete thinking

Schizophrenic thinking shows a literal, "concrete" quality in which symbol and metaphor, which normally provide a mental distance from objects and processes (a *representation*) and which facilitate abstract and conceptual thinking, are not recognized as such. Symbols and metaphors are then thought about as realities. In this respect, it resembles the thinking of dream-life, following the laws of *primary process*, in particular in the use of *condensation* and *displacement*. Different explanations have been advanced to account for this concreteness, which often appears to be the consequence of an impairment or diminished use of the capacity to differentiate and to classify items according to their similarities. For example, a thing that *resembles* another thing may be treated as if it were *identical* with the other. Concrete thinking can be partly understood as the regressive revival, or uncovering, of the "sensorimotor" mode of thinking held by some to be characteristic of infancy, which widely evolves into metaphorical and abstract thinking. In this view, the future psychotic has suffered a failure of this normal developmental process and remains vulnerable to its revival, with the loss of the weakly established capacity for recognition of metaphor and symbol. Freud described this regressive process as the original "thing-presentations" replacing the higher level of organization of mental representations, the "word-presentations". Concrete thinking involves a loss of differentiation between the thing symbolized and the symbol, which is associated with a confusion between self and object and between internal and external reality. Such confusion has been considered as the outcome of possible excessive projective identification (used as a defence against envy or separation). If the object is not sufficiently differentiated from the self, a symbol, the main function of which is to represent the object in its absence, will remain confused with the thing symbolized (see Segal on the "symbolic equation", 1981). This is one of the characteristics of concrete thinking (see Rosenfeld, 1987; Searles, 1965).

Unconscious

Mental processes are regarded as being "unconscious" when the subject is unaware of them. Some of these can be re-called to consciousness without great difficulty (*descriptively* unconscious, or *preconscious*), others, held in repression, cannot (*dynamically* unconscious). As a noun, the term refers to a functioning structure in the mind (the *system unconscious*), which constitutes the larger part of mental life and follows a logic and rules of its own. Freud called these characteristics the *primary processes* of thought, in contrast to the *secondary processes* of the conscious mind, and he demonstrated how they dominate the thinking of dreams and of neurotic and psychotic symptoms. The concept of the unconscious has recently been approached from the perspective of mathematical logic, as a differentiating and classifying system (Matte-Blanco, 1988). The *collective* unconscious is a term of Jung's, designed to describe the realm of archetypes, universal innate ideas, or the tendency to organize experience in innately determined patterns. This usage has a conceptual connection with Klein's use of the term *"unconscious phantasy"* as the psychic expression of innate libidinal and destructive instincts that are held to underlie mental processes and to accompany all mental activity.

NOTES

Introduction

1. The "need-adapted" approach to the treatment of psychotic patients, developed in Finland, provides a sophisticated model which we describe in some detail in chapter eight. This model assesses from the outset the needs of the patient for the next five years.

2. In the United Kingdom, this ward was unique in its application of a psychoanalytic perspective to the treatment of severely disturbed patients within a general psychiatric setting. A good deal of psychodynamic work has been pursued at a high level, with substantial resources, in privately funded centres in the United States, the most famous of which are the Menninger Clinic, Chestnut Lodge, and the Maclean Hospitals. Some centres in Switzerland, Norway, and Finland have a tradition of psychodynamic work with psychotic patients within the State Welfare Services. Britain has historically been less well served: of note is the work done by the Arbours Association in London and by Napsbury and Shenley hospitals.

3. Hobson (1985) has pointed out that psychotherapy is a form of conversation, albeit one of a unique nature, in which patient and clinician are "equal but asymmetrical" (see also Coltart, 1992).

4. "It is my conviction that the psychotic patient's speech and behaviour (particularly in sessions) invariably make a statement about his relationships to the therapist . . . it is important to pay minute attention to the patient' communications, and to seek to conceptualize and understand what these communications mean in the transference relationship". (Rosenfeld, 1987).

5. "Team" has become a fashionable term, which can, at times, be used to conceal work of questionable quality behind a facade of collaboration. True teamwork involves the cooperative deployment of different skills in order to reach the best possible decisions and most appropriate treatment. At best, it is a sophisticated and psychodynamically complex activity, which is more difficult to achieve than is usually recognized. (Similar considerations apply to the use of the term "group".)

Chapter one

1. First names were usually used by staff members who had been working together for some time.

Chapter three

1. A recent review (Higgitt & Fonagy, 1992) has illuminated the complexity of the concepts of borderline and narcissistic personality disorder, outlined the contributions of the most significant workers in the field, and described the difficulties, diagnostic and therapeutic, that these patients present.

2. Terry Thomas was a popular British actor who portrayed an eccentric but likeable upper-class crook and philanderer.

Chapter four

1. Reference to the work of Dr Henri Rey, to whom I am deeply indebted, has been simplified by the publication of his most important writings. It is to this volume, *Universals of Psychoanalysis in the Treatment of Borderline and Psychotic States*

(1994) that reference is made, rather than to less accessible, original publications, although these are also given in the reference section.

2. A horror of imprisonment in states of mind or situations which are feared to go on forever can occur in schizoid thinking, reflecting, in temporal and spatial terms, the dread of total abandonment and annihilation, and the despair of ever finding a "containing" good object.

Chapter six

1. This case has been reported elsewhere in detail (Jackson, 1993b).

2. Many patients mistake the objectivity and technical consistency of the therapist as a mechanical and impersonal professionalism. Although psychotherapeutic care that is not authentic for the therapist is not good psychotherapy, the deliberate use of personal feelings in the interests of "being human" is usually a breach of technique. However, such spontaneous eruptions may sometimes have positive consequences (cf. Coltart, 1992).

Chapter eight

1. Matte-Blanco (1988), points out that we live in two worlds at once but usually only notice one of them in dreams or psychosis and that they each have their own distinct systems of logic (see also "Unconscious" in glossary).

2. Grotstein (1977a, 1977b) has shown how these views can be reconciled and has suggested the possibility that it is only psychoanalysis that can alleviate this, ultimately psychogenic, or psychosomatic, deficiency.

3. "The schizophrenic unconsciously attacks his thoughts, feelings and perceptions, which are felt to be an endless source of unmanageable pain" (Ogden, 1986, 1989, 1990).

4. A comprehensive review of contemporary psychoanalytic theories of psychosis has been provided by Freeman (1988). Key psychoanalytic texts on psychosis are those of Searles (1965); Arieti (1974); Kernberg (1975); Rosenfeld (1975, 1987); Grotstein (1977a, 1977b, 1981b); Feinsilver (1986);

Pao (1979); Frosch (1983); Rey (1994). For more popular accounts, see Crowcroft (1957) and Arieti (1979).

5. See Birchwood, Hallett, and Preston (1988) for discussion of a biological approach to primary prevention, and the hope for biological markers which would allow early detection of vulnerability to schizophrenia.

6. Cullberg has reformulated these groups as acute breakdown, sealed crisis, and malignant isolation syndrome, and also proposed a three-dimensional classification according to the likely relative contributions of psychodynamic, organic, and genetic factors. He has outlined the different strategies required for appropriate treatment (Cullberg, 1993a, 1993b). Lehtinen (1993) has reported on comparable work.

7. However, with appropriate development, psychiatry could look forward to a robust and attractive future (see Cawley, 1990, 1993; Cox, 1991).

8. Impatience with demands to produce evidence of results is easily generated in psychotherapists who have done successful work. "If one has had the good fortune to observe the raising of Lazarus from the dead, it is foolish to demand a control sample" (Cancro, 1986).

9. Certain influential studies of the outcome of individual psychotherapy of schizophrenic patients (May, 1986; McGlashan, 1984) have been erroneously used as evidence of the unsuitability of this form of treatment (see Alanen et al., 1994, p. 18).

10. Although such countries have the advantage of small populations and prosperity, their admirable attitude of concern towards psychotic and other vulnerable people is not simply a consequence of relative affluence.

11. The work of Leff and his colleagues has been largely responsible for this advance. Such psychoeducational orientation can have drawbacks if applied within a purely biomedical view of the nature of schizophrenia. See Alanen et al. (1994, p. 20) for a critical comment.

REFERENCES AND BIBLIOGRAPHY

Abraham, K. (1911). Notes on the Psycho-Analytical Investigation and Treatment of Manic–Depressive Insanity. In: *Selected Papers on Psycho-Analysis*. London: Hogarth. [Reprinted London: Karnac Books, 1979.]

Abraham, K. (1924). A Short Study of the Development of the Libido, Viewed in the Light of Mental Disorders. In: *Selected Papers on Psycho-Analysis*. London: Hogarth. [Reprinted London: Karnac Books, 1979.]

Alanen, Y. O. (1992). Psychotherapy of Schizophrenia in Community Psychiatry. In: *Psychotherapy of Schizophrenia, Facilitating and Obstructive Factors*. Oslo: Scandinavian University Press.

Alanen, Y. O., Anttinen, E. E., Kokkola, A., et al. (1990). Treatment and Rehabilitation of Schizophrenic Psychoses. The Finnish Treatment Model. *Nordic Journal of Psychiatry* (Supplement No. 22), 44.

Alanen, Y. O., Laakso, L., et al. (1986). *Towards Need-specific Treatment of Schizophrenic Psychoses*. London: Springer-Verlag.

Alanen, Y. O., Lehtinen, K., Räkköläinen, V., & Aaltonen, J.

(1991). Need-Adapted Treatment of New Schizophrenic Patients: Experiences and Results of the Turku Project. *Acta Psychiatrica Scandinavica, 83*: 363–372.

Alanen, Y. O., Ugelstad, E., Armelius, B., et al. (1994). *Early Treatment for Schizophrenic Patients. Scandinavian Psychotherapeutic Approaches*. Oslo: Scandinavian University Press.

Anderson, R. (Ed.) (1992). *Clinical Lectures on Klein and Bion*. London: Tavistock/Routledge.

Anonymous (1992). First Person Account: Portrait of a Schizophrenic. *Schizophrenia Bulletin, 18*: 333–335.

Arieti, S. (1974). *Interpretation of Schizophrenia*. London: Crosby, Lockwood, Staples.

Arieti, S. (1979). *Understanding and Helping the Schizophrenic: A Guide for Family and Friends*. New York: Basic Books. [Reprinted London: Karnac Books, 1993.]

Auchincloss, E. L., & Weiss, R. W. (1992). Paranoid Character and the Intolerance of Indifference. *Journal of the American Psychoanalytical Association, 40* (4): 1013–1038.

Balint, M. (1952). *Primary Love and Psycho-Analytic Technique*. London: Hogarth. [Second edition, London: Tavistock, 1965. Reprinted London: Karnac Books, 1985.]

Balint, M. (1957). *The Doctor, His Patient and the Illness*. London: Pitman Medical.

Balint, M. (1968). *The Basic Fault*. London: Tavistock Publications.

Barnes-Gutteridge, W. (1993). Imagination and the Psychotherapeutic Process. *British Journal of Psychotherapy, 9* (3): 267–279.

Bateson, G., Jackson, D. D., Haley, J., & Weakland, J. (1956). Toward a Theory of Schizophrenia. *Behavioural Science, 1*: 251–264.

Benedetti, G. (1987). *The Psychotherapy of Schizophrenia*. New York: New York University Press.

Benedetti, G. & Furlan, P. M. (1993). *The Psychotherapy of Schizophrenia*. Berne: Hofgreber & Huber.

Berrios, G. E., & Markova, I. S. (1992). The Meaning of Insight in Clinical Psychiatry. *British Journal of Psychiatry, 160*: 850–860.

Bion, W. R. (1957). Differentiation of the Psychotic from the Non-psychotic Personalities. *International Journal of Psycho-Analy-*

sis, 38: 266–275. [Also in: *Second Thoughts*. London: Heinemann, 1967. Reprinted London: Karnac Books, 1984.]

Bion, W. R. (1959). Attacks on Linking. In: *Second Thoughts*. London: Heinemann, 1967. [Reprinted London: Karnac Books, 1984.]

Bion, W. R. (1970). Container and Contained Transformed. In: *Attention and Interpretation* (pp. 106–124). London: Tavistock Publications. [Reprinted London: Karnac Books, 1984.]

Birchwood, M., Hallett, S., & Preston, M. (1988). *Schizophrenia: An Integrated Approach to Research and Treatment*. London/ New York. Longman.

Bleuler, E. (1950). *Dementia Praecox*. New York: International Universities Press.

Bowen, M. (1961). The Family as the Unit of Study and Treatment. *American Journal of Orthopsychiatry, 31*: 40–60.

Bowlby, J. (1980). *Loss*. London: Penguin Books.

Bowlby, J. (1988). *A Secure Base: Clinical Implications of Attachment Theory*. London: Routledge.

Cancro, R. (1986). General Considerations Relating to Theory in the Schizophrenic Disorders. In: D. Feinsilver (Ed.), *Towards a Comprehensive Model for Schizophrenic Disorders: Psychoanalytic Essays in Memory of Ping-Nie Pao*. New York: Analytic Press.

Cawley, R. H. (1983a). The Principles of Treatment and Therapeutic Evaluation. In: M. Shepherd (Ed.), *Handbook of Psychiatry. Vol. 1: General Psychopathology*. Cambridge: Cambridge University Press.

Cawley, R. H. (1983b). Psychiatric Diagnosis: What We Need. *Psychiatric Annals, 13* (10): 777–782.

Cawley, R. H. (1990). Educating the Psychiatrist of the 21st Century. *British Journal of Psychiatry, 157*: 174–181.

Cawley, R. H. (1993). Psychiatry Is More Than a Science. *British Journal of Psychiatry, 162*: 154–160.

Clare, A. (1986). The Disease Concept in Psychiatry. In: R. Hill, R. Murray, & A. Thorley (Eds.), *The Essentials of Post-graduate Psychiatry*. London: Grune & Stratton.

Coltart, N. E. C. (1992). *Slouching towards Bethlehem*. London: Free Association Books.

Coltart, N. E. C. (1993). *How to Survive as a Psychotherapist*. London: Sheldon Press.

Cox, J. L. (1991). A Psychiatrist with Beds: Evolution and Evaluation of Socio-Therapy on an Acute Admission Ward. *Psychiatric Bulletin, No. 15*: 684–686.

Crowcroft, A. (1957). *The Psychotic*. London: Penguin Books.

Cullberg, J. (1991). Recovered versus Non-Recovered Schizophrenic Patients among Those Who Have Had Intensive Psychotherapy. *Acta Psychiatrica Scandinavica, 84*:242–245.

Cullberg, J. (1993a). A Proposal for a 3-Dimensional Aetiological View of the Schizophrenias (I). *Nordic Journal of Psychiatry, 47*: 355–359.

Cullberg, J. (1993b). A 3-Dimensional View of the Schizophrenias (II): Hypothetical Clinical Consequences. *Nordic Journal of Psychiatry, 47*:421–424.

Cullberg, J., & Levander, S. (1991). Fully Recovered Schizophrenic Patients Who Received Intensive Psychotherapy. *Nordic Journal of Psychiatry, 45*: 253–262.

David, A. S. (1990). Insight and Psychosis. *British Journal of Psychiatry, 156*: 798–808.

Engel, G. L. (1962). *Psychological Development in Health and Disease*. Philadelphia: Saunders.

Fairbairn, W. R. D. (1952). *Psychoanalytic Studies of the Personality*. London. Tavistock.

Falloon, I. R. H., Boyd, J. L., & McGill, C. (1984). *Family Care of Schizophrenia*. New York: Guildford Press.

Feinsilver, D. (Ed.) (1986). *Towards a Comprehensive Model for Schizophrenic Disorders: Psychoanalytic Essays in Memory of Ping-Nie Pao*. New York: Analytic Press.

Fenton, W. S., & McGlashan, T. H. (1987). Sustained Remission in Drug-Free Schizophrenic Patients. *American Journal of Psychiatry, 144*: 1306–1309.

Freeman, T. I. (1981). On the Nature of Persecutory Delusions. *British Journal of Psychiatry. 139*: 529–532.

Freeman, T. I. (1985). Psychotherapy and General Psychiatry—Integral or Separable. *Psychoanalytic Psychotherapy, 1* (1): 19–29.

Freeman, T. I. (1988). *The Psychoanalyst in Psychiatry*. London: Karnac Books.

Freeman, T. I. (1989). Psychotherapy within General Psychiatry. *British Journal of Psychiatry, Bulletin No. 13*: 593–596.

Freud, S. (1900a). *The Interpretation of Dreams. Standard Edition,* Vols. *4* & 5.

Freud, S. (1911c [1910]). Psycho-Analytical Notes on a Case of Paranoia (Dementia Paranoides). *Standard Edition, Vol. 12*: 1–80.

Freud, S. (1914c). On Narcissism: An Introduction. *Standard Edition, Vol. 14*: 69–102.

Freud, S. (1915e). The Unconscious. *Standard Edition, Vol. 14*: 161–215.

Freud, S. (1917e [1915]). Mourning and Melancholia. *Standard Edition, Vol. 14*: 237–259.

Freud, S. (1923b). *The Ego and the Id. Standard Edition, Vol. 19*: 13–59.

Freud, S. (1925d). *An Autobiographical Study. Standard Edition, Vol. 20*: 7–70.

Frosch, J. (1983). *The Psychotic Process.* New York: International Universities Press.

Gabbard, G. (1992). The Decade of the Brain. *American Journal of Psychiatry, 149* (8): 991–998.

Greenberg, J. R., & Mitchell, S. A. (1983). *Object Relations in Psychoanalytic Theory.* London: Harvard University Press.

Grotstein, J. S. (1977a). The Psychoanalytic Concept of Schizophrenia I: The Dilemma. *International Journal of Psycho-Analysis, 58*: 403–425.

Grotstein, J. S. (1977b). The Psychoanalytic Concept of Schizophrenia II: Reconciliation. *International Journal of Psycho-Analysis, 58*: 403–425.

Grotstein, J. S. (1981a). Attacks Against Linking: The Phenomenon of Blocking of Thoughts. In: *Splitting and Projective Identification.* Northvale, NJ & London: Jason Aronson.

Grotstein, J. S. (1981b). *Splitting and Projective Identification.* Northvale, NJ & London: Jason Aronson.

Grotstein, J. S. (1981c). Who Is the Dreamer Who Dreams the Dream and Who Is the Dreamer Who Understands It? In: *Do I Dare Disturb the Universe?: A Memorial to W. R. Bion.* Beverly Hills: Caesura Press. [Reprinted London: Karnac Books, 1988.]

Gunderson, J. G., Frank, A. F., Katz, H. M., et al. (1984). Effects of Psychotherapy of Schizophrenia: Comparative Outcome of Two Forms of Treatment. *Schizophrenia Bulletin, 10*: 564–598.

212   REFERENCES AND BIBLIOGRAPHY

Hale, R., & Campbell, D. (1991). Suicidal Acts. In: J. Holmes (Ed.), *Textbook of Psychotherapy in Psychiatric Practice*. London: Churchill Livingston

Hansen, J. B. (1993). Psychotherapy of Schizophrenia: In Public. In: J. B. Hansen (Ed.), *Crossing the Borders*. Ludvika, Sweden: Dualis Forlag.

Higgitt, A., & Fonagy, P. (1992). Psychotherapy in Borderline and Narcissistic disorders. *British Journal of Psychiatry*, *161*: 23–43.

Hill, D. (1970). On the Contribution of Psychoanalysis to Psychiatry: Mechanism and Meaning. *British Journal of Psychiatry*, *117*: 609–615.

Hill, D. (1978). The Qualities of a Good Psychiatrist. *British Journal of Psychiatry*, *133*: 97–105.

Hingley, S. M. (1992). Psychological Theories of Delusional Thinking: In Search of Integration. *British Journal of Medical Psychology*, *65* (4):347–356.

Hinshelwood, R. D. (1989). *A Dictionary of Kleinian Thought*. London: Free Association Books.

Hinshelwood, R. D. (1994). *Clinical Klein*. London: Free Association Books.

Hobbs, M. (1990). The Role of the Psychotherapist as Consultant to In-Patient Psychiatric Units. *Psychiatric Bulletin*, *14*: 8–11.

Hobson, R. F. (1985). *Forms of Feeling*. London & New York: Tavistock.

Jackson, M. (1991). Psychotherapy in Psychotic Disorders. In: J. Holmes (Ed.), *Textbook of Psychotherapy in Clinical Practice*. London: Churchill Livingstone.

Jackson, M. (1992). Learning to Think about Schizoid Thinking. *Psychoanalytic Psychotherapy*, *6* (3): 191–203.

Jackson, M. (1993a). Manic–Depressive Psychosis: Psychopathology and Individual Psychotherapy Within a Psychodynamic Milieu. *Psychoanalytic Psychotherapy*, *7* (2): 103–133.

Jackson, M. (1993b). Psychoanalysis, Psychiatry, Psychodynamics: Training for Integration. *Psychoanalytic Psychotherapy*, *7* (1): 1–14.

Jackson, M., & Cawley, R. (1992). Psychodynamics and Psychotherapy on an Acute Psychiatric Ward: The Story of an Experimental Unit. *British Journal of Psychiatry*, *160*: 41–50.

Jackson, M., & Jacobson, R. (1983). In: P. Pichot, P. Berner, R. Wolf, et al. (Eds)., *Psychoanalytic Hospital Treatment in Psychiatry: The State of the Art, Vol 4* (pp. 209–216). New York: Plenum Press.

Jackson, M., & Pines, M. (1986). The Borderline Personality: Concepts and Criteria. *Neurologica Psychiatrica, 9*: 54–67.

Jackson, M., Pines, M., & Stevens, B. (1986). The Borderline Personality: Psychodynamics and Treatment. *Neurologia et Psychiatrica, 9*: 66–68.

Jackson, M., & Tarnopolsky, A. (1990). The Borderline Personality. In: R. Bluglass & P. Bowden (Eds.), *The Principles and Practices of Forensic Psychiatry*. London: Churchill Livingstone.

Jacobson, R., Jackson, M., & Berelowitz, M. (1986). Self-Incineration: A Controlled Comparison of Inpatient Suicide Attempts. *Psychological Medicine, 16*: 107–116.

Johnson, J. (1993). Catatonia: The Tension Insanity. *British Journal of Psychiatry, 162*: 733–738.

Joseph, B. (1986). Envy in Everyday Life. *Psychoanalytic Psychotherapy, 2*: 13–22. [Also in: *Psychic Equilibrium and Psychic Change.* London: Routledge]

Karon, B. P., & VandenBos, G. R. (1980). *Psychotherapy of Schizophrenia: The Treatment of Choice.* New York: Jason Aronson.

Kernberg, O. F. (1975). *Borderline Conditions and Pathological Narcissism.* New York: Jason Aronson.

Kernberg, O. F. (1984). *Severe Personality Disorders: Psychotherapeutic Strategies.* New Haven, CT: Yale University Press.

Killingmo, B. (1989). Conflict and Deficit: Implications for Technique. *International Journal of Psycho-Analysis, 70* (1): 65–79.

Klein, M. (1935). A Contribution to the Psychogenesis of Manic–Depressive States. In: *Contributions to Psycho-analysis.* London: Hogarth Press.

Klein, M. (1940). Mourning in Its Relation to Manic–Depressive States. In: *Love, Guilt and Reparation and Other Works, 1921–1945: The Writings of Melanie Klein, Vol.1* (pp. 344–389). London: Hogarth Press & The Institute of Psychoanalysis. [Reprinted London: Karnac Books, 1992.]

Klein, M. (1955). On Identification. In: M. Klein, P. Heimann, R. E. & Money-Kyrle, *New Directions in Psycho-Analysis: The Signifi-*

cance of Infant Conflict in the Pattern of Adult Behaviour (pp. 309–345). London: Tavistock. [Reprinted London: Karnac Books, 1985.]

Klein, M. (1957). *Envy and Gratitude.* In: M. Klein, *Envy & Gratitude: and Other Works 1946-1963.* London: Hogarth Press & The Institute of Psychoanalysis, 1975. [Reprinted London: Karnac Books, 1993.]

Laplanche, J., & Pontalis, J.-B. (1973). *The Language of Psychoanalysis.* London: Hogarth Press. [Reprinted London: Karnac Books & The Institute of Psychoanalysis, 1988.]

Leff, J., Kuipers, L., Berkowitz, R., et al. (1982). A Controlled Trial of Social Intervention in the Families of Schizophrenic Patients. *British Journal of Psychiatry, 141*: 121–134.

Lehtinen, K. (1993). Family Therapy and Schizophrenia in Public Mental Health Care. *Annals of the University of Turku, Ser. D, 106.*

Levander, S., & Cullberg, J. (1993). Sandra: Successful Psychotherapeutic Work with a Schizophrenic Woman. *Psychiatry, 6*: 284–293.

Lewis, A. J. (1967). *The State of Psychiatry.* London: Routledge & Kegan Paul.

Lewontin, R. C. (1993). *The Doctrine of DNA: Biology an Ideology.* London: Penguin Books.

Lidz, R. W. & Lidz, T. (1949). The Family Environment of Schizophrenic Patients. *American Journal of Psychiatry, 106*: 332–345.

Matte-Blanco, I. (1988). *Thinking, Feeling and Being.* London: Routledge.

May, P. R. A. (1986). *Treatment of Schizophrenia.* New York: Science House.

McGlashan, T. H. (1984). The Chestnut Lodge Follow-Up Study, II. *Arch.Gen. Psychiatry, 41*: 587–601.

McNeil, T. F, Cantor-Grace, E., Nordstrom, L. G, & Rosenlund, T. (1993). Head Circumference in "Preschizophrenic" and Control Neonates. *British Journal of Psychiatry, 162*: 517–523.

Milton, J. (1992). Presenting the Case for NHS Psychotherapy Services. *Psychoanalytic Psychotherapy, 6* (2): 151–167.

Moore, B. E., & Fine, M. D. (1968). *A Glossary of Psychoanalytic Terms and Concepts.* New York: The American Psychoanalytic Association.

Mosher, L., & Burti, L. (1989). *Community Mental Health: Principles and Practice*. New York: W. W. Norton.

Mueser, K. T, & Barenbaum, H. (1990). Psychodynamic Treatment of Schizophrenia: Is There a Future? *Psychological Medicine, 20*: 253–262.

Mullen, P. (1986). The Mental State and States of Mind. In: R. Hill, R. Murray, & A. Thorley (Eds.), *The Essentials of Post-graduate Psychiatry*. London: Grune & Stratton.

Ogden, T. H. (1986). *The Matrix of the Mind*. London: Jason Aronson. [Reprinted London: Karnac Books, 1992.]

Ogden, T. H. (1989). *The Primitive Edge of Experience*. London: Jason Aronson. [Reprinted London: Karnac Books, 1992.]

Ogden, T. H. (1990). On the Structure of Experience. In: Boyer & Giovacchini (Eds.), *Master Clinicians on Treating the Regressed Patient*. London: Jason Aronson.

O'Shaughnessy, E. (1992). Not Thinking in a Bizarre World. In: R. Anderson (Ed.), *Clinical Lectures on Klein and Bion*. London: Routledge.

Pao, Ping-Nie (1968). On Manic–Depressive Psychosis: A Study of Transition States. *Journal of the American Psychoanalytic Association, 16*: 809–832.

Pao, Ping-Nie (1979). *Schizophrenic Disorders*. New York: International Universities Press.

Pao, Ping-Nie (1983). Therapeutic Empathy and the Treatment of Schizophrenics. *Psychoanalytic Inquiry*: 145–167.

Parkes, C. M. (1975). *Bereavement: Studies of Grief in Adult Life*. London: Tavistock.

Pedder, J. (1982). Failure to Mourn and Melancholia. *British Journal of Psychiatry, 141*: 329–337.

Perkins, R., & Moodley, P. (1993). The Arrogance of Insight. *Psychiatric Bulletin, 17*: 233–234.

Petot, J. M. (1991). *Melanie Klein: the Ego and the Good Object*. Madison: International Universities Press.

Pylkkanen, K. (1989). A Quality Assurance Programme for Psychotherapy. *Psychoanalytic Psychotherapy, 4*: 13–22.

Räkköläinen, V., Lehtinen, K., & Alanen, Y. O. (1991). Need-Adapted Treatment of Schizophrenic Processes: The Essential Role of Family-Centred Therapy Meetings. *Contemporary Family Therapy 13* (6).

Rey, J. H. (1979). Schizoid Phenomena in the Borderline. In: J. le Boit & A. Capponi (Eds.), *Advances in the Psychotherapy of the Borderline Patient*. London: Jason Aronson. [Also in: E. Spillius (Ed.), *Melanie Klein Today*. London: Routledge, 1988.]

Rey, J. H. (1986). Reparation. *Journal of the Melanie Klein Society*, 4: 5–35.

Rey, J. H. (1992). Awake, Going to Sleep, Asleep, Dreaming, Awakening, Awake. *Free Associations*, 3 (27). 439–454.

Rey, J. H. (1994). *Universals of Psychoanalysis in the Treatment of Borderline and Psychotic States: Space–Time and Language Factors*. London: Free Association Books.

Ricoeur, P. (1970). *Freud and Philosophy: An Essay on Interpretation*. New Haven & London: Yale University Press.

Ritter, S. (1989). *The Bethlem Royal and Maudsley Hospital Manual of Nursing Procedures*. London: Harper and Row.

Riviere, J. (1936). A Contribution to the Analysis of the Negative Therapeutic Reaction. *International Journal of Psycho-Analysis*, 17: 304–320. [Reprinted in: A. Hughes (Ed.), *The Inner World and Joan Riviere: Collected Papers 1920–1958* (pp. 134–153). London: Karnac Books, 1991.]

Robbins, M. (1992). Psychological and Biological Approaches to Mental Illness: Schizophrenia. *Journal of the American Psychoanalytical Association 40* (2): 425–454.

Roberts, G. (1992). The Origins of Delusion. *British Journal of Psychiatry*, 161: 298–308.

Rosen, J. N. (1953). *Direct Analysis: Selected Papers*. New York: Grune & Stratton.

Rosenfeld, H. A. (1963). Notes on the Psychopathology and Psychoanalytic Treatment of Depression and Manic–Depressive Patients. *Research Reports of the American Psychiatric Association*, 73–83.

Rosenfeld, H. A. (1971). A Clinical Approach to the Psychoanalytic Theory of the Life and Death Instincts: An Investigation into the Aggressive Aspects of Narcissism. *International Journal of Psycho-Analysis*, 52: 169–178.

Rosenfeld, H. A. (1975). *Psychotic States: A Psychoanalytic Approach*. London: Hogarth Press. [Reprinted London: Karnac Books, 1982.]

Rosenfeld, H. A. (1987). *Impasse and Interpretation*. London: Tavistock.

Rubin, P., Karle, A., Moller-Madsen, S., et al. (1993). Computer-ised Tomography in Newly Diagnosed Schizophrenic and Schizophreniform Disorder: A Controlled Blind Study. *British Journal of Psychiatry, 163*: 604–612.

Rycroft, C. (1968). *Imagination and Reality*. London: Hogarth Press. [Reprinted London: Karnac Books, 1987.]

Sandler, J., Dare, C., & Holder, A. (1992). *The Patient and the Analyst*. London: Karnac Books.

Schultz, C. G. (1975). An Individualised Psychotherapeutic Approach with the Schizophrenic Patient. *Schizophrenia Bulletin No. 13*.

Scott, R. D., & Ashworth, P. L. (1967). Closure at the First Schizophrenic Breakdown: A Family Study. *British Journal of Medical Psychology, 40*: 109–145.

Searles, H. A. (1965). *Collected Papers on Schizophrenia and Related Subjects*. London: Hogarth Press. [Reprinted London: Karnac Books, 1986.]

Segal, H. (1964). *Introduction to the Work of Melanie Klein*. London: Heinemann. [second ed., London: Hogarth, 1975. Reprinted London: Karnac Books & The Institute of Psychoanalysis, 1988.]

Segal, H. (1981). *The Work of Hanna Segal: Delusion and Artistic Creativity and Other Psychoanalytic Essays*. London: Jason Aronson. [Reprinted London: Karnac Books, 1986.]

Segal, H. (1991). *Dream, Phantasy & Art*. London : Routledge.

Sjöström, R. (1985). Effects of Psychotherapy in Schizophrenia. A retrospective study. *Acta Psychiatrica Scandinavica, 71*: 513–22.

Spillius, E. (Ed.) (1988). *Melanie Klein Today*. London: Routledge.

Stanton, A. H., Gunderson, J. G., Knapp, P. H., et al. (1984). Effects of Psychotherapy in Schizophrenia: 1. Design and Implementation of a Controlled Study. *Schizophrenia Bulletin, 10*: 520–563.

Steiner, J. (1982). Perverse Relationships Between Parts of the Self: A Clinical Illustration. *International Journal of Psycho-Analysis, 63*: 241–251.

Steiner, J. (1987). The Interplay Between Pathological Organisations and the Paranoid–Schizoid and Depressive Positions. *International Journal of Psycho-Analysis, 68*: 69–80.

Steiner, J. (1993). The Recovery of Parts of the Self Lost Through

Projective Identification: The Role of Mourning. In: *Psychic Retreats*. London: Routledge.

Stern, D. (1985). *The Interpersonal World of the Infant*. New York. Basic Books.

Szasz, T. (1961). *The Myth of Mental Illness*. New York: Hoeber.

Tienari, P. (1992a). Implications of Adoption Studies on Schizophrenia. *British Journal of Psychiatry, Supplement 18*: 52–58.

Tienari, P. (1992b). Interaction Between Genetic Vulnerability and Family Environment. In: *Psychotherapy of Schizophrenia: Facilitating and Obstructive Factors*. Oslo: Scandinavian University Press.

Ugelstad, E. (1979). Possibilities of Organising Psychotherapeutically Oriented Treatment Programmes for Schizophrenia Within Sectorised Psychiatric Service. In: C. Muller (Ed.), *Psychotherapy of Schizophrenia*. Amsterdam: Excerpta Medica.

Ugelstad, E. (1985). Success and Failure with Individual Psychotherapy with Psychotic Patients. *Nordic Journal of Psychiatry, 39* (4): 279–284.

Werbart, A. (1992a). Exploration and Support in Psychotherapeutic Environments for Psychotic Patients. *Acta Psychiatrica Scandinavica, 86*: 12–22.

Werbart, A. (1992b). How to Use Therapeutic Environments in the Treatment of Schizophrenia. In: *The Psychotherapy of Schizophrenia: Facilitating and Obstructive Factors*. Oslo: Scandinavian University Press.

Williams, W. P. (1993). Aspects of a Therapeutic Milieu (unpublished PhD thesis).

Winnicott, D. W. (1958). The Depressive Position in Normal Emotional Development. In: *Through Paediatrics to Psycho-Analysis*. London: Hogarth, 1975. [Reprinted London: Karnac Books, 1992.]

Winnicott, D. W. (1959). Classification: Is There a Psychoanalytic Contribution to Psychiatric Classification? In: *The Maturational Process and the Facilitating Environment*. London: Hogarth Press, 1965. [Reprinted London: Karnac Books, 1990.]

Winnicott, D. W. (1960). Ego Distortion in Terms of True and False Self. In: *The Maturational Process and the Facilitating Environment*. London: Hogarth Press, 1965. [Reprinted London: Karnac Books, 1990.]

Wynne, L. C., & Singer, M. T. (1965). Thought Disorder and Family Relations of Schizophrenics. *Arch. Gen. Psychiat., 9*: 191–198.

Yeats, W. B. (1906). *The Collected Poems*. London: Papermac, 1982.

Yorke, C., Wiseberg, S., & Freeman, T. (1989). *Development and Psychopathology*. New Haven & London: Yale University Press.

INDEX

community care, deficiencies in, 3
concrete thinking, 33, 66, 156
    definition, 200–201
condensation, 200
"conflict" theorists, 169
container:
    –contained theory [Bion], 188
    therapist as, 149
"containing" good object, 205
containment, 37, 101, 170
    [Bion], 169
    definition, 188
    in hospital, xiii, 175
    and lasting change, xiv
    maternal [Bion], 137
    through projection, 42
countertransference, 6, 36, 44,
        157, 195
    and identification, 191
    vs. personal responses, 149
    understanding, 186
couple therapy, 181
Cox, J. L., 206
Crowcroft, A., 205
Cullberg, J., 112, 166, 173, 182,
    206

Dare, C., 194
David, A. S., 193
David: catatonia [diagnostic
        interview], 117–133
Davison, S., 162
death:
    desire for, 48
    instinct [Freud, Klein], 169
    preoccupation with, 100
defences, 6
delusion:
    definition, 189
    erotic, 189
    grandiose, 189
    persecutory, 189
delusional object, 39
delusional thinking, 40
    in psychosis, 1
dementia praecox, 199
denial, and identification, 191
depression, 132, 133

definition, 150
manic–, 135–153
and mourning, 194
and personality disorder, 71
psychotic, 136, 150, 194
    (melancholia), 48
    and delusions, 189
severe, and inhibition of eating,
    98
"true", 150
depressive anxiety, 189
depressive guilt, 189, 198
depressive position, 92, 137, 194,
    198
    [Klein], 169, 189
destructive narcissism [Rosenfeld],
    151, 169
diagnostic–therapeutic interview,
    8–10
    aims of, 38
    examples:
        Anthony [schizophrenic self-
            destructiveness], 47–69
        Carmen [psychotic anorexia],
            91, 98–112, 169
        David [catatonia], 117–133
        Nicola [manic-depressive
            psychosis], 6, 135–153, 169
        Rick [psychotic character], 71–
            95
        Sally [paranoid schizophre-
            nia], 15–46
        Susanna [psychotic anorexia],
            110, 112–115
diffusion of identity, 192
disintegration [Kohut], 172
displacement, 200
doctrine of DNA [Lewontin], 5
dream:
    life, 171
    -like thinking, 167

early superego [Klein], 169
ECT, see electro-shock treatment
ego:
    boundaries, weak, 41
    function, deficit in, 22, 24, 45,
        101, 169

mourning, 35, 148
  capacity for, xiv
  definition, 194
  healthy, for loss, 44
  melancholia as, 136
  pathological, 67, 194
  working through, and repara-
    tion, 198
Mueser, K. T., 4
Mullen, P., 179
mutism, 97, 98

"nameless dread" [Bion], 172
Napsbury Hospital, 203
narcissism, destructive [Rosenfeld],
    169
narcissistic object relation, xiv
National Schizophrenia Project
    [Finland], 173
"need-adapted" treatment model,
    173, 180
negative therapeutic reaction,
    150
  [Freud], 169
neurobiological therapy, 165
neurobiology, 176, 178
neurosis, vs. psychosis, 42
"new beginning" [Balint], 197
Nicola: manic-depressive psychosis
    [diagnostic interview], 6,
    135–153, 169
non-symbolic thinking, 156
Nordstrom, L. G., 2
"nursing process" procedures, 161

obedience, automatic, 117
object:
  containing:
    good, 205
    internalization of [Bion], xiv
  definition, 194–195
  delusional, 39
  internal, 47, 195
  relations, 48, 131, 194, 195
    and development of ego, 170
    capacity for, and sense of
      identity, 192
    early disturbed, 169

fragmentation of, 170
inner, losses in, and mourn-
    ing, 194
internal, and self-destructive-
    ness, 48
mature, and depressive
    position, 189
narcissistic, xiv
part-, and obsessionality, 91
primitive, and psychosis, 196
replaced by identifications,
    22, 35
-relations theory, 48, 194
transitional, 40
observation room, use of, 17
obsessionality, 73, 75, 76, 79, 80,
    82, 88, 89, 91, 198
obsessive–compulsive disorder, 71,
    72, 94
oedipal anxieties, 90
oedipal conflict, 89, 93
oedipal desires, 130
oedipal phantasies, 75
oedipal rivalry, 131
Ogden, T. H., 190, 205
omnipotent psychotic mechanisms,
    xiv
omnipotent self, 150
omnipotent thinking, 22, 34, 40,
    64, 75, 90, 101, 132, 171
  and identification, 191
  regressive revival of, 131
ontological anxiety, 196
organismic panic, 196
O'Shaughnessy, E., 169

panic:
  anxiety, 171
  organismic, 196
Pao, Ping-Nie, 167, 172, 205
paranoid delusion, 42, 171
paranoid–schizoid position, 189
paranoid schizophrenia: Sally
    [diagnostic interview], 15–
    46
parent, good-enough, 36
Parkes, C. M., 194
parricidal wish, 131

psychotic conditions *(continued)*
  and delusions, 189
  (melancholia), psychodynamics
    of, 48
psychotic identification, 132
"psychotic part of the personality"
  [Bion], 151
psychotic patients, psychothera-
    peutic attitude towards, 9
psychotropic drugs, 3
Pylkkanen, K., 3, 173

radio, as friend, 26
Räkköläinen, V., 162, 175
"Rat Man", 109
reactive psychosis, 199
reality, 31, 34, 38, 39, 40, 43, 63,
    64, 72, 89, 90, 91, 115,
    131, 167, 194
  -adaptive supportive (RAS)
    psychotherapy, 182
  emotional, patient's, 165
  lack of contact with, in psycho-
    sis, 1, 171
  psychic (or psychological), 6,
    195
    and external, 201
  sense of, disturbed, 195
  testing:
    and insight, 193
    failure of, 41, 42, 101
regression, 22, 35
  and containment, 188
  definition, 197–198
  as deliberate technique, 197
  malignant, 197
  therapeutic, 197
reparation:
  definition, 198
  manic, 198
  wish for, 11
repetition compulsion, 6, 157, 195
repressed memory, 68
repression, and pathological
    splitting, 192
Rey, J. H., xii, xix, 109, 110, 200,
    204
  on catatonia, 110

Rick: psychotic character [diagnos-
    tic interview], 71–95
Ritter, S., 161, 164
rituals, 74
Riviere, J., 198
Robbins, M., 176
Roberts, G., 189
Rosen, J. N., 97
Rosenfeld, H. A., xii, xiv, 9, 136,
    169, 201, 204, 205
  on destructive narcissism, 151,
    169
Rosenlund, T., 2
Rubin, P., 2
Rycroft, C., 171, 187

Sally: paranoid schizophrenia
    [diagnostic interview], 15–
    46
Sandler, J., 194
S.A.N.E., xix
SANETALK, 3
schizo-affective psychosis, 199
"schizoid" character,
    psychodynamic attitude
    towards, 156
schizoid states, 71
schizophrenia, 1, 2, 3, 4, 49, 98,
    117, 131, 161, 199
  aetiology of, family conflict in,
    174
  biological markers for, 206
  biomedical view of, 206
  catatonic, 97
  chronic, 66
    iatrogenic nature of, 173
  definition, 1, 2, 4, 199
  diagnosis of, 7, 199
  genetic studies of, 4
  hebephrenic, 49
  individual psychotherapy in,
    studies of outcome, 206
  need-adapted treatment for, 173
  and neurobiological deficit, 3,
    172–173
  paranoid: *Sally* [diagnostic
    interview], 15–46
  pathogenesis of, 168–170